Diarmuid Griffin

Killing Time

Life Imprisonment and Parole in Ireland

palgrave
macmillan

Diarmuid Griffin
National University of Ireland
Galway, Ireland

ISBN 978-3-030-10246-3 ISBN 978-3-319-72667-0 (eBook)
https://doi.org/10.1007/978-3-319-72667-0

Softcover re-print of the Hardcover 1st edition 2018

Cover credit: Pinghung Chen / EyeEm

Printed on acid-free paper

This Palgrave Macmillan imprint is published by Springer Nature
The registered company is Springer International Publishing AG
The registered company address is: Gewerbestrasse 11, 6330 Cham, Switzerland

For my parents.

Preface

The parole of life sentence prisoners had not been subject to empirical research in Ireland prior to this study. In fact, little was publicly known about the parole process and its operations. Addressing that information void, this book examines the legal and policy framework surrounding life imprisonment and provides an insight into the practice of releasing life sentence prisoners. Focusing on the ultimate penalty and the method of administering the release of life sentence prisoners can contribute to an understanding of the operation of a small-scale penal system such as Ireland. In addition, the parole process was identified as sufficiently unique and distinct from other jurisdictions, with a poorly articulated position on the factors influencing decision-making within that process, providing an interesting counterpoint to broader penal trends. An examination of the parole of life sentence prisoners may also contribute to an exploration of the sociology of punishment in Ireland more generally. There is certainly cause for closer scrutiny. Recent years have witnessed significant increases both in terms of the life sentence prisoner population and the length of time a life sentence prisoner can expect to serve in prison.

In Western jurisdictions, the decision-making processes of criminal justice institutions have come in for intense scrutiny during the latter decades of the twentieth century and parole, in particular, has attracted much debate. The resulting reforms to parole processes often focused on constraining the discretion afforded to decision-makers through the adoption of a formal approach to decision-making. In the context of life imprisonment, many jurisdictions have witnessed an increase in the life sentence prisoner population but there is a considerable lack of consistency in terms of its use as a sanction. Furthermore, there is little consensus as to the length of time a life sentence prisoner should be required to serve in prison prior to release. Nonetheless, commonalities can be identified across various release processes with parole in many countries being transformed from a political, discretionary and informal process to an increasingly formalised and judicial one. Within this formal framework decisions are often taken by an independent body, a minimum term set by the courts or in statute must be served prior to becoming eligible for release and decision-makers are constrained by criteria and guidelines when deliberating on individual cases.

The level of scrutiny and analysis witnessed in other jurisdictions has not materialised in Ireland. Criminal justice sometimes appears to be insulated from the broader pressures of penal transformation, with the country showing a reluctance to look beyond its own horizons. This Hibernian exceptionalism can be identified in many aspects of the country's criminal justice system such as its approach to policing, probation, prosecution and the trial process, sentencing, capital punishment, prisoner enfranchisement and coercive confinement. In the context of life imprisonment, a parole authority exists but the process of release is avowedly political and informal with decision-makers acting with wide discretion when deliberating on individual cases. A non-statutory, advisory Parole Board makes recommendations to the Minister for Justice and Equality who ultimately decides at what point a life sentence prisoner is released. An offender becomes eligible for release having served seven years in prison, however this has ceased to act as a meaningful threshold with the average life sentence prisoner now serving more than three times this amount prior to release. While it may be clear that life sentence prisoners are now required to serve significantly longer in prison than what might have been expected a decade or a number of decades previously, it is not clear *why* this is happening.

This monograph provides a rationale for the upward trend in time served by life sentence prisoners as expressed by parole decision-makers.

In addition to examining the publicly available materials on parole, the analysis of the process is informed by qualitative research conducted with Parole Board members, Ministers for Justice and former members of the Sentence Review Group. The participants in this research were decision-makers during a period that coincided with a sharp rise in time served and, in the absence of any significant legislative or policy reforms, there must be some correlation between their approach to decision-making and time served. The data analysis reveals that parole decision-makers view public protection as central to the process and decision-makers engage in their own version of risk assessment when deliberating on individual cases. However, the risk of reoffending features amidst an array of other factors that also influence parole outcomes. Personal interpretations of the purposes of punishment, including retribution, deterrence and rehabilitation, feature strongly. Public opinion was also deemed to be important, while participants were acutely aware of the political landscape in which parole operates when deliberating on individual cases. The incorporation of such a broad range of factors into the process is permissible due to the wide discretion available to parole decision-makers. It is difficult to reconcile the findings in this research with the narrow legal interpretation given to the mandatory life sentence and the dissonance between law and practice will be explored as well as the potential impact of reforming the process on parole outcomes. The book highlights the level of influence that individuals can exert on criminal justice decision-making when discretion is wide and safeguards are not robust. For the life sentence prisoner, the discretion that once permitted leniency now operates in the service of severity.

Galway, Ireland Diarmuid Griffin

Acknowledgements

This book started out as a doctoral thesis at the Institute of Criminology, University College Dublin. I would like to express my sincerest gratitude to my supervisor Professor Ian O'Donnell for his support, guidance and encouragement throughout the research process. The project faced many challenges from the beginning, and it would not have been possible to bring this research to completion were it not for his input, insight and ability to find a way forward when the barriers to progress appeared insuperable. Professor Dirk van Zyl Smit and Professor Nicky Padfield examined the thesis, and I appreciate their feedback and recommendations in relation to publication. Professor van Zyl Smit, alongside Professor Jonathan Simon and Professor Shane Kilcommins, reviewed the book, and I am obliged to them for their feedback and kind words of support. I am particularly grateful to Professor Kilcommins for his advice and guidance over the course of my career. As a postgraduate student at University College Cork, he encouraged me to pursue a career in research and had confidence in me, which I did not have in myself. This had a big impact on me at the time and changed the direction of my career. Thanks must also go to the editorial team of the criminology series at Palgrave, particularly Josie Taylor, Steph Carey and Jules Willan.

I am grateful to the Department of Justice and Parole Board for their support in advancing the research, and I would also like to thank the participants that agreed to be interviewed for this study. The insight provided into the operation of the parole process would not have been possible without their honesty. I appreciate the assistance provided by Josephine Lawless, formerly of the office of the Parole Board, in facilitating my many queries as well as Éamon Ó'Cuív TD and Máire Aine Ní Fhlatharta for agreeing to table so many parliamentary questions on life sentence prisoners on my behalf. This research was supported by my employer, NUI Galway, and I am fortunate to have been able to draw from the resources of the university to advance the project. My colleagues and friends, Carmel Flynn, Des McSharry, Tom O'Malley, Ursula Connolly, Eoin Daly, Eilionóir Flynn, Anna Louise Hinds and Nicola Murphy, provided great support and advice. I would also like to thank the staff at the National Library of Ireland for their assistance throughout the completion of this book.

Many friends provided help along the way, and a number of them deserve special mention. David Doyle encouraged me to write this book and hassled me continuously until I submitted a book proposal. I would not have started or completed the project were it not for him. He gave up so much of his time to review and provide feedback on the book that I think he knows more about parole than I do! I am grateful to him for his friendship and support. I was lucky to have friends offer to review parts of this work or provide support in a variety of different ways. I would particularly like to thank Roberta Guiry, Louise Kennefick, Deirdre Healy, Aoife O'Donoghue, Sinead Ring, Derek O'Brien, Catherine-Ellen O'Keeffe, Joe McGrath, Muiris Griffin and Lughaidh Kerin. Tony Swaine, Grace 'Hoffy' Hosford and Liam Thornton provided lots of welcome distractions along the way. David Corcoran and Eoin Stapleton were there for 'debriefing and cocktails' at all stages! Thanks for the encouragement and the adventures.

I would not have been able to complete this book without the kindness and support of Fionn, Sinead, Rían and Caoila. Thank you for putting up with me and putting me up over the years. Finally, I would like to thank my parents, Maurice and Lorraine, for teaching me the value of education and for their love and encouragement in the writing of this book, as with all things. This book is dedicated to them.

Contents

List of Figures

1

Same Crime, Different Time

I immediately discovered she wasn't breathing – I was terrified. I started to shake her and was crying and telling her I loved her. I still love her.
Robert Brophy
People (DPP) v Brophy 1970.

Introduction

In 1969, Robert Brophy, a 23-year-old man, was found guilty of the murder of his fiancé, Anna Porter. Brophy had been in a relationship with Porter for approximately four years, although it was somewhat tumultuous. Porter had been in receipt of psychiatric treatment. The on-going nature of this and its effect on the arrangement of their wedding was causing conflict in the relationship. Prior to the murder, Porter had told Brophy that she had met 'another fellow' and she had organised a date with him. In a diary entry the day before the murder, Brophy documented suicidal feelings as well as thoughts in relation to killing Porter. This diary entry also detailed his desire to continue the relationship. The following evening, Brophy and Porter had an argument regarding their engagement and Porter's mental health treatment. Brophy grabbed her

D. Griffin, *Killing Time*, https://doi.org/10.1007/978-3-319-72667-0_1

by the arm, she pulled away and fell to the floor. Brophy knelt down and strangled her. After realising he had killed her, Brophy called the police, gave a full statement to the *Gardaí* (Irish police) and was remanded in custody. Although Brophy pleaded guilty to manslaughter, the prosecution did not accept this plea and a murder charge was pursued at trial.

After six hours of deliberation, the jury sought clarification on the legal distinction between murder and manslaughter. Mr. Justice Pringle directed the jury: 'If you are satisfied, beyond reasonable doubt, that the accused intended to kill or to cause serious injury to Anna Porter, then you must convict him of murder; if you are not so satisfied then you convict him of manslaughter' (*People (DPP) v Brophy* 1970). Two hours later the jury returned a verdict of guilty of murder. They took the unusual step of adding a note to their verdict stating that they 'strongly' and 'unanimously' recommended mercy in sentencing. Directly after the verdict was delivered in court, Mr. Justice Pringle stated: 'Robert Brophy, you have been found guilty of murder. I have no option but to sentence you to penal servitude for life' (the equivalent of life imprisonment at that time). He added that the recommendation of the jury would be conveyed to 'the proper authorities'. The proper authority in this instance was the Minister for Justice (Minister), who had the discretion to release a person serving such a sentence. In 1975, the then Minister, Patrick Cooney, exercised this discretion releasing Brophy back into the community, having served just six years in prison. The average time served by offenders subject to this sentence during the 1970s was 7.5 years (Prison Service 2010, p. 17). Following his release, Brophy set up a small shop dealing in stamps, had a relationship with another woman and fathered a child (*People (DPP) v Brophy* 1992). In 1990, Brophy was convicted of indecent assault and was sentenced to five years' imprisonment. The severity of the penalty imposed by the trial judge was not too far off the actual time served by Brophy for the murder of Porter. The Court of Criminal Appeal subsequently quashed the conviction for indecent assault due to the infirmity of the evidence against Brophy, finding it to be 'unsafe and unsatisfactory' (*People (DPP) v Brophy* 1992, p. 721).

In 1997, Steven Davis was found guilty of the murder of Mary Doogue, his girlfriend of two years. Davis was 17 when he started seeing Doogue, ten years his senior. He was father to one of her six children. On 19

October 1995, Doogue went drinking at midday and continued to drink alcohol in various locations for the rest of the day. Davis returned from work at 7 p.m. and when he discovered Doogue was not at home, he went out to find her. He began drinking himself. At midnight, witnesses saw Davis and Doogue have an argument on the street, with Davis assaulting Doogue. The *Gardaí* intervened and told the couple they should go home. At 3 a.m. Davis and Doogue returned home. Davis had slung Doogue over his shoulder and brought her upstairs to bed, according to the babysitter. The following day, at approximately 4 p.m., Davis sent one of the children to find a doctor. On arrival, the doctor discovered Doogue to be in 'an appalling condition'. She was taken to the hospital in an ambulance and suffered a cardiac arrest in transit, dying shortly thereafter. According to the pathologist giving evidence at the trial, Doogue died from delayed shock due to injuries sustained from being violently assaulted (*Irish Times* 1995, 1997a, b, c, d, e).

At the trial, the jury returned a majority verdict (eleven to one) of guilty of murder, following seven hours of deliberation. Mr. Justice Budd stated that he had no discretion in the imposition of a mandatory life sentence for murder. The trial judge expressed his concern regarding the intrusive media coverage of the trial, particularly the publication of photographs by a number of newspapers of Davis handcuffed and chained to a prison officer during the trial (*Irish Times* 1997d). The Court of Criminal Appeal subsequently held that the publication of such images was prejudicial to an accused person standing trial but, given the weight of the evidence against Davis, it was not appropriate to quash the conviction (*People (DPP) v Davis* 2001). Davis was released in 2012 by the then Minister, Alan Shatter, having served 16 years in prison, a decade longer than Brophy. Davis served significantly less time than other life sentence prisoners released that year, with the average time served reaching 22 years in 2012 (*Dáil Question* No. 403: Alan Shatter, 22 October 2013). Following his release from prison, Davis successfully reintegrated back into society and took up employment in the construction industry (Donald 2014).

There are parallels between the cases of Brophy and Davis. In fact, Brophy and Davis are representative of many of those serving life sentences: a young male that has killed a partner or family member in a domestic context. Neither had a history of violence or criminality prior to the incident and both had shown remorse for their offending behaviour. On conviction, they were subject to the mandatory sentence for murder and were released back into the community at the discretion of the Minister. But, given the similarities in their profiles, why did they serve such different periods of time for the same crime? The disparity in time served by Brophy and Davis is not an anomaly. A life sentence prisoner committed in recent times can expect to serve significantly longer in prison than his counterparts committed in the preceding decades. But what is driving this trend? This monograph explores the factors influencing the increase in time served by life sentence prisoners.

From Leniency to Severity

There has been a transition from leniency to severity in Ireland over the last forty years, if time served by life sentence prisoners is taken as a measure. There has also been a significant increase in the life sentence prisoner population. Life sentence prisoners constitute 11.4 per cent of sentenced prisoners in custody, a ratio of one in every nine sentenced prisoners (Prison Service 2016, p. 24). The life sentence prisoner population has increased by 153 per cent from 2001 to 2016 (from 139 to 352) (see Table 1.1). The overall prison population increased by 19.5 per cent during the same period (Prison Service 2001–2016). Ireland's life sentence prisoner population is high when compared with other European countries (Council of Europe 2017, pp. 92–93). In 2014 there were approximately 27,000 life sentence prisoners in custody in Europe (a sample of 22 countries), an increase of 66 per cent from 2004 (European Committee for the Prevention of Torture (CPT) 2015, pp. 34–35). Ireland outstripped this rate with the life sentence prisoner population increasing by 78 per cent over the same period. Although, many countries have witnessed an increase in life sentence prisoners as a percentage of the overall prison population in recent decades, a considerable level of cross-jurisdictional variety exists in terms of its use as a sanction (Griffin and O'Donnell 2012). Life does not ordinarily mean life in prison and there must be a process in place whereby life sentence prisoners can be released back into the community having served a period of time in

Table 1.1 Life imprisonment in Ireland (2001–2016)

Year	Prisoners in custody	Lifers in custody	Lifers committed	Lifers released	Lifers recalled	Avg. years
2001	3112	139	14	5	1	15
2002	3165	n/a	13	3	1	11
2003	3176	166	11	1	0	14
2004	3199	193	29	1	1	19.5
2005	3151	221	17	2	1	14.5
2006	3191	234	18	n/a	1	n/a
2007	3321	239	23	6	0	15.5
2008	3544	264	20	2	3	15.5
2009	3881	276	22	5	1	17.5
2010	4290	286	18	6	1	18.25
2011	4390	291	22	5	1	20
2012	4318	305	22	4	1	22
2013	4158	319	22	4	1	17.5
2014	3915	344	25	4	1	20
2015	3722	345	19	6	0	17.5
2016	3718	352	16	7	4	22
Total:			311	61	18	

Sources:

Figures for 'prisoners in custody' (the annual average daily population including prisoners on remand) 'lifers committed' (number of new life sentence prisoners received into custody), and 'lifers in custody' are from annual reports and strategy statements of Irish Prison Service

Figures for 'lifers released', and 'avg. years' for 2001 to 2009 are from Brandon, R. (2010). Figures for 'lifers recalled' for 2001 to 2016 and figures for 'lifers released', and 'avg. years' for 2010 to 2016 are from: *Dáil Question* No. 335: Alan Shatter, 12 November 2013; *Dáil Question* No. 513: Alan Shatter, 26 November 2013; *Dáil Question* No. 403: Alan Shatter, 22 October 2013; *Dáil Question* No. 643: Frances Fitzgerald, 08 July 2014; *Dáil Question*: Frances Fitzgerald 17 December 2014; *Dáil Question* No. 111: Frances Fitzgerald, 24 January 2017; *Dáil Question* No. 112: Frances Fitzgerald, 24 January 2017. n/a indicates that data were not available

prison (van Zyl Smit et al. 2014). Yet, there is little consensus as to the meaning of the life sentence particularly with regard to the length of time a life sentence prisoner should serve in prison and the appropriate process of release.

In Ireland, an examination of committal and release provides an insight into the increase in this category of prisoners. In short, since 2001, the number of life sentence prisoners committed to prison has not been met with a similar number of releases. There has been an average (mean) of 19

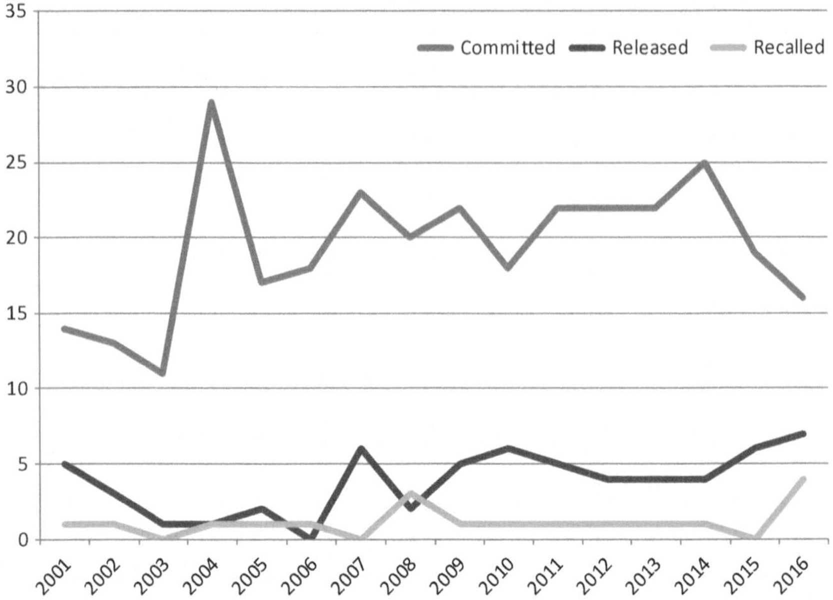

Fig. 1.1 Life sentence prisoners committed, released and recalled (2001–2016)

life sentence prisoners committed annually over the last 16 years with an average (mean) of 4 life sentence prisoners being released (see Fig. 1.1). The lack of parity between committal and release has had a cumulative effect on the life sentence prisoner population resulting in an increase in the population, year-on-year. In turn, the low number of releases is due to an increase in the average time a life sentence prisoner serves in prison prior to being released back into the community over the last number of decades. It averaged: 7.5 years from 1975 to 1984; 12 years from 1985 to 1994; 14 years from 1995 to 2004; 18 years from 2005 to 2014; and 19.75 years for 2015 and 2016. In 2012 and 2016 the average time served peaked at 22 years. These figures only provide an insight into the average time served of those released. Many life sentence prisoners continue to serve time in prison far beyond this average. The current longest-serving life sentence prisoner has been in prison since 1964 (Lally 2015). By way of contrast, in the 1970s, one life sentence prisoner was released after just three years in prison (Wilson 2004, p. 89). The earlier decades of the twentieth century show even greater variety. Those subject to the death penalty often had their sentence commuted to penal servitude for life (or life imprisonment) (O'Malley 2016, p. 623). These sentences were further remitted by the executive, meaning that the prisoners serving them were released back into the community. The range of time served is considerable, with those subject to penal servitude for life having served anything from 5 months to 17 years during the period 1925–1955 (205 *Dáil Debates* Cols. 323–4: Charles Haughey, 24 October 1963). The average (mean) time served of those serving penal servitude for life was 5.75 years. This indicates that, although there were occasional examples of severity, for much of the twentieth century the average time served remained in single digits. It was during the 1980s when time served began its upward trajectory, a trend that has yet to show any signs of stabilising.

It is instructive to take the average time served by life sentence prisoners in 2016 and employ it to hypothesise about life imprisonment and release (see Fig. 1.2). Life sentence prisoners released in 2016 had served an average of 22 years in prison. They would almost certainly have been convicted of murder and sentenced to a mandatory life sentence in 1994 (Courts Service 2001–2015). It is highly probable that these offenders would be male (97 per cent of the life sentence prisoners are male: *Dáil Question* No. 82: Frances Fitzgerald, 08 November 2016), approximately 30 years of age on committal (and 52 on release) (Dooley 2001, p. 11) and that the victim would have been a family member, spouse, friend or acquaintance (O'Donnell 2005, p. 105). On committal, life sentence prisoners might have had an expectation of being released in 2006, given that the average length of time served in 1994 was 12 years. However, by the time this cohort of prisoners reached 2006, the average time served had increased to 18 years. In fact, it would have been necessary for life sentence prisoners to continue to adjust expectations upwards throughout the process as the average time served increased by ten years from 1994 to 2016.

Ireland is not the only country to experience an increase in time served by life sentence prisoners. In eight states in the United States, where data are available, the average time served by life sentence prisoners increased

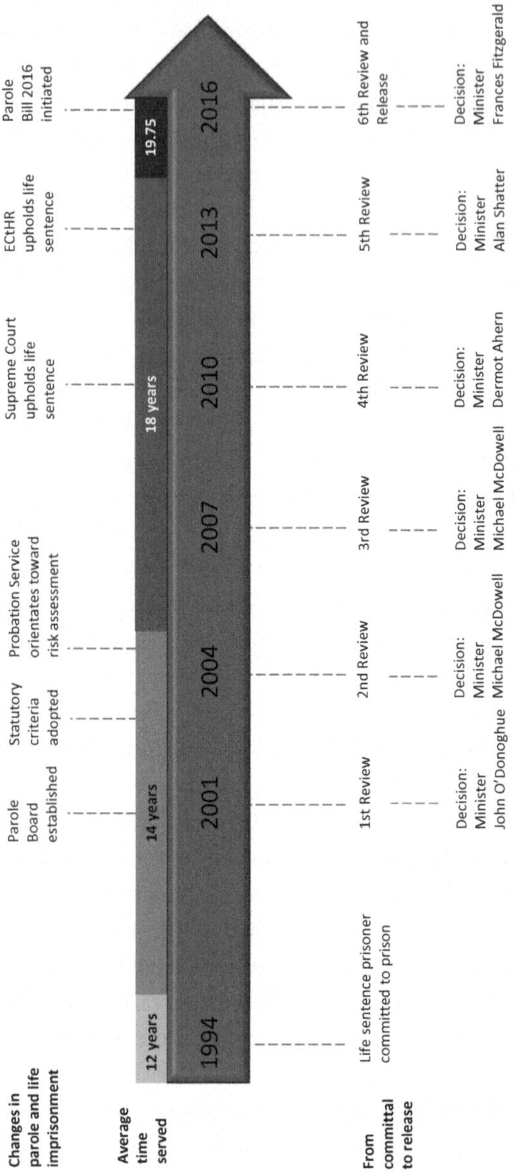

Fig. 1.2 Timeline of a life sentence prisoner committed in 1990 and released in 2016 serving average of 22 years

from 11.6 years in the 1980s to 23.2 years from 2000 to 2013 (Ghandnoosh 2017, p. 3). Perhaps this is not surprising given that the United States is known for its broader drive towards punitiveness (Cavadino and Dignan 2006; Zimring and Johnson 2006). Civil law European countries tend to be more heavily influenced by human rights norms, which can operate to constrain punitive inclinations but this is mediated through the legal, cultural and political factors of each jurisdiction (Griffin and O'Donnell 2012). Nordic countries are often notable for their exceptionalism in relation to broader punitive trends and this is credited to inclusive social, economic and welfare policies as well as a commitment to human rights protections (Lahti 2000; Lappi-Seppälä 2016a; Snacken 2010). Yet these countries have also witnessed increases in time served, though the trend is less pronounced than in Ireland. The average time served in Denmark increased from 13 years in the 1970s and 1980s to 17 years currently (Lappi-Seppälä 2016b, p. 476). In Sweden, a country that converts life sentences to determinate sentences, the average time served has increased from 7.5 years in the 1980s to 16.5 years in the last ten years (Lappi-Seppälä 2016b, p. 477). Finland has a more varied trajectory, with time served ranging from 16.5 years in the 1970s, 11 years in the 1980s and 1990s and 15 years in the 2010s (Lappi-Seppälä 2016b, p. 476).

An increase in time served by life sentence prisoners may appear consistent with a more punitive approach but such an analysis would be overly simplistic. The complexity of release processes in individual countries makes it challenging to identify the 'true purpose' of such systems (Dünkel et al. 2010, p. 404). Release is influenced by a multitude of factors, the impact of which is often shaped by local contingencies. In the United States, the growth in time served can be linked to the politicisation of the parole process. This has resulted in the adoption of legislation delaying when a life sentence prisoner becomes eligible for parole, state governors appointing members to parole authorities in an attempt to reduce the granting of parole and the narrowing of rights afforded to life sentence prisoners (Ghandnoosh 2017, pp. 4–8). In Sweden an analysis of the trends in life sentences necessitates an examination of legislative reforms, judicial decisions and psychiatric practice. Life imprisonment is a maximum rather than a mandatory term for murder. In the 1970s, 65 to 70 per cent of homicide offenders were subject to psychiatric treatment rather than being sentenced to prison but by the late 2000s 80 per cent of offenders were receiving prison sentences (Lappi-Seppälä 2016b, p. 479). A sharp increase in the use of the life sentence in the 2000s resulted in an intervention by the Supreme Court stating that life imprisonment should only be imposed in the most serious cases of murder (Lappi-Seppälä 2016b, p. 479). The government responded to this decision by implementing reforms that raised the penalties for murder (Lappi-Seppälä 2016b, p. 479). The courts and the government have since been engaged in a cat-and-mouse situation whereby the punitive tendencies of the legislature are being resisted or overturned by the Supreme Court.

In Ireland, time served may have changed significantly but there have been few structural changes to the life sentence or the release process over the last number of decades. Capital punishment for murder was replaced with penal servitude for life (Criminal Justice Act 1964), which was subsequently abolished and replaced with life imprisonment (Criminal Justice Act 1990). Life imprisonment is mandatorily imposed on conviction for murder, and it may be, but rarely is imposed as the maximum penalty for other serious offences. The decision as to whether a life sentence prisoner is released, and at what point, rests with the Minister. A non-statutory, advisory Parole Board was established in 2001 to make recommendations to the Minister on the release of long-term and life sentence prisoners. Prior to this, the Sentence Review Group, which replaced the 'prison review' system in 1989, advised the Minister on the release of life sentence prisoners. Common to all three iterations is the informal and discretionary nature of their role in the decision-making process. The recommendations of the Parole Board are based on reports provided by various criminal justice agencies and an interview with the prisoner. These recommendations by the Parole Board to the Minister are almost always accepted in full (85 per cent from 2002 to 2015) (Parole Board 2002–2015). The Parole Board is not constrained by any set of legal criteria or formal guidelines. The Minister, when deliberating on release, is to have regard to a number of factors set out in statute including: the threat to the safety and security of the public; the seriousness of the offence; previous convictions; and the length of time served (Criminal Justice Act 1960 (s. 2) as amended by the Criminal Justice (Temporary Release of Prisoners) Act 2003).

Since 1989, a life sentence prisoner is required to serve seven years in prison before becoming eligible for release. But this is not reflective of time served with the average life sentence prisoner now serving over three times this amount of time. It is more accurate to state that a life sentence prisoner becomes eligible for review at seven years but will not become eligible for release until much later in the process. If release is not recommended, the life sentence prisoner must be reviewed no more than three years after the last review. It is useful to return to the life sentence prisoner who served the 22-year average prior to release in 2016 (see Fig. 1.2). On the basis that reviews are conducted every three years, six reviews would have been conducted prior to release, from the first review at the seven-year point in 2001 until the eventual release in 2016. Five different ministers would have deliberated on the recommendations of the Parole Board. It is likely that the first five reviews related to sentence management and at the final and sixth review the life sentence prisoner was recommended for release, 15 years after first engaging with the parole process. Throughout this process, a life sentence prisoner is not entitled to an oral hearing or legal representation and the decision to release is a privilege entirely at the discretion of the Minister (*Ryan v Governor of Limerick Prison* 1988).

The rationale for the increase in time served has yet to be clearly articulated by those responsible for parole in Ireland. Perhaps the key to uncovering the cause of the increase in time served is rooted in the release process and, more particularly, the factors influencing parole decision-makers when deliberating on the release or further detention of a life sentence prisoner. The requirement that life sentence prisoners serve lengthier periods in prison may be representative of a commitment to broader penal trends or may be due to changing social and legal processes that are impacting on penal outcomes (Garland 2013, p. 484). Perhaps the increase in time served is reflective of the global shift towards punitivism in criminal justice systems. Punitivism is ordinarily associated with being supportive of retributivist and exclusionary theories of punishment while being unsupportive of punishment with rehabilitative goals (Maruna and King 2009, p. 9). Are the recent trends in parole outcomes the result of a deliberate pursuit of a more punitive and expressive approach to decision-making, with the life sentence acting as a means of satisfying a form of populist punitiveness? A corollary to the rise of punitivism is the growing dominance of risk in criminal justice systems and a shift towards more risk-averse decision-making (Garland 2001; Pratt 2007; Feeley and Simon 1992). Is it possible to correlate the increase in time served with a greater understanding by policy makers and decision-makers of this penal trend? Are parole outcomes reflective of an orientation towards a more risk-averse approach to decision-making?

Caution is required when examining the impact of punitivism and risk as, historically, Ireland tended to resist many of the influences that led to change in criminal justice arrangements across other Western jurisdictions. This apparent exceptionalism to broader trends is not unique to Ireland as there is a growing understanding of the diversity of penal landscapes such that speaking in terms of commonalities and cross-national trends has become difficult (see: Baumer et al. (2002) on Iceland; and McAra (2008) on Scotland; Nelken 2009; Garland 2013). The Irish criminal justice system has often shown a reluctance to look beyond its own cultural, political and historical realities (O'Donnell 2011). But there is evidence of a punitive turn and an orientation towards risk in some aspects of the criminal justice system, although it appears to be more of a sampling exercise (O'Donnell 2005; Healy 2012). Of course, the increase in time served may simply be a product of local factors related to the idiosyncrasies of Irish criminal justice, particularly the *ad hoc* and discretionary approach that often influences policy development and decision-making. Criminal justice policies in Ireland are frequently based on short-term goals, are unusually responsive to local demands and clientelism and are often adaptable and reversible (Healy 2012). Although there has been little by way of legal reform, there have been some policy modifications to parole that have had impact. Nonetheless, the process has remained political, discretionary and informal. In order to elucidate the impact of penal trends and local contingencies on life imprisonment, data analysis from a qualitative study on parole decision-making during a period that coincided with a sharp rise in time served (from 15.5 years in 2007 to 22 years in 2012) will be employed. The methodological approach adopted is set out below, followed by an examination of the key factors identified in the research that appear to influence parole decision-makers.

A Note on Methodology

Prior to this study, little was known about the administration of the life sentence and the process of releasing these life sentence prisoners back into the community. The annual reports of the Parole Board and Prison Service shed little light on the workings of parole generally or on the release of life sentence prisoners. This information void appears to reflect a broader approach adopted by agents of the criminal process to the generation of reliable and comprehensive data (O'Donnell 2008) but contrasts with other jurisdictions where information provision on decision-making has formed a key part of on-going reforms in parole (Padfield et al. 2010). In Ireland, there is little information on the mechanics of the decision-making process, the criteria used to assess offenders eligible for release and the sentence management for life sentence prisoners. This study aimed to go beyond the legal rules governing release and examine how these rules and procedures operate in practice. The findings are employed to provide a rationale for the upward trend in time served by life sentence prisoners prior to release.

The analysis in this monograph is informed by qualitative research conducted with parole decision-makers, namely Parole Board members (members), Ministers, and former members of the Sentence Review Group. A relatively contained group of individuals have been members of the Parole Board since its establishment and these individuals were identified as the focus of the qualitative aspect of the research. The qualitative method was deemed suitable given the absence of high quality and rich information on decision-making in this context. Interviews were conducted with individuals who were members of the Parole Board between 2007 and 2012. In total, interviews were held with 14 out of a potential 17 members (one additional member died during this period). Given the focus on decision-making it was important to obtain the political perspective. To that end, requests were made to interview all Ministers since the establishment of the Parole Board. Three former Ministers consented to be interviewed. Limitations specific to the qualitative aspects of this research project were evident from the outset, particularly the limited number of participants due to the small number of members of the Parole Board. In particular, the data analysis is reflective of decision-makers' perspectives on their decision-making process rather than being representative of the rationale for decisions in individual cases. To secure anonymity, statements of participants are referenced using an assigned number for each participant (Parole Board member 01 = PB01; Minister for Justice 1 = MJ1; Sentence Review Group member 1 = SRG1). The former Chairman of the Sentence Review Group waived anonymity and is identified in the text. A detailed account of the methodological approach adopted for the qualitative aspect of the research is provided in the Appendix. The qualitative research is primarily employed across Chaps. 3, 4, and 5.

In addition to the qualitative research, a quantitative component was also initiated. The quantitative research was focused on the review dossier compiled on behalf of the Parole Board for the purpose of decision-making. The review dossier contains a wealth of information on the decision-making process including the recommendations of the Parole Board and the decision of the Minister. This aspect of the research project was pursued to the fullest extent possible but, regrettably, the Department of Justice and Equality (Department) and Parole Board did not collect the data and this resulted in the termination of the research agreement. The initiation, implementation and completion of this research was continually resisted by the Department and the Parole Board. Resistance was never explicit, rather it was implicit and passive. Allowing for time to unfold was the principal method of resistance. Meetings and correspondence were always positive in nature with assurances given that progress would be made. Despite the continuum of enthusiasm, both the Department and the Parole Board did not follow-through on their undertakings both in terms of making a determination on access as well as the implementation of the project. When negotiating access, the Department never officially said 'no' but it took 37 months of persistence for them to say 'yes'. During this time, the decision was to not make a decision. Once the research was sanctioned and an agreement to collect the data was in place, there was another lapse into silence. At the point of termination, almost four years had passed since the original application to the Parole Board, two years and five months since the application to the Department and ten months since the research agreement came into operation. A total of 13 (out of an estimated 280) questionnaires were completed during this time. In addition, a request made to the Parole Board to conduct further interviews with members appointed post-2012 was refused and a request to observe Parole Board decision-making was denied (correspondence with Parole Board, April 2009–July 2015).

An important aim of this research was to move beyond an analysis of legal form or nomenclature to examine the practice of releasing life sentence prisoners through the parole process. Essentially, it was an attempt to examine law in action. Ironically, the research process was characterised by inaction. It is important to situate this within the broader context of criminal justice research in Ireland. Unlike many other Western jurisdictions, criminology and criminal justice research in Ireland is still in a 'fledgling state', with little by way of infrastructure or institutional support (O'Donnell 2011, pp. 488–90). Resistance to the publication of information held by the Department and a suspicion of 'outsiders' interested in examining aspects of the criminal process has existed for many decades. There exists a 'closed, secretive and silo driven culture' within the Department that has proved difficult to displace (Department of Justice and Equality 2014). Further, criminal justice research does not necessarily fit neatly with the work of policy-makers and differing views are taken in relation to the role of criminologists in public life (O'Donnell 2011; Loader and Sparks 2011). Given the lack of research conducted on life imprisonment and release, the project presented the Parole Board and the Department with an opportunity to open the process up to external evaluation. The findings might have proven useful in shaping policy and practice. But this was not enough to progress the matter. Heylin (2001, p. 86) documented the resistance he experienced in this regard as a senior staffer working within the Department. He noted that 'a political reluctance to do anything, including evaluating, to disturb an unsatisfactory situation may be due to fear of extreme reactions or consequences, the scale of the response required to tackle the underlying problem, or an inability to see a workable proposal for improvement'.

The concerns expressed by the Department related to the potential political issues that might arise from the research. This may be reflective of the politicisation of crime control over the last number of decades, with issues of crime and disorder increasingly being viewed as a means to gain (or lose) political capital (Garland 2001; O'Donnell and O'Sullivan 2003). Given that the Minister holds individual responsibility for release, the matter was undoubtedly more politically sensitive in nature than most research projects. At a practical level, administrators and policy-makers may be consistently responding to events at 'crisis pitch' such that they do not have the time necessary to facilitate evaluation nor the capacity to absorb the lessons arising from the evaluation (Heylin 2001, p. 83). The termination of the quantitative research placed a limitation on the research findings. Nonetheless, the qualitative research generated high quality and rich information that is illuminative of individual decision-making and the nature of the decision-making process more generally.

In addition to the challenges in progressing the quantitative research, the bureaucratic resistance to general information provision when formally engaging with the institutional structures of the Department often proved frustrating. For example, a request by the author for data on time served by life sentence prisoners in recent years was made to the Prison Service, the Parole Board and the Department, as this information was not publicly available. The Prison Service and the Department did not respond to these requests while the Parole Board's response was that they did not have access to this data (correspondence with Parole Board, 02 May 2013). This experience was not replicated when attempting to access information through an alternative (and political) route. Following the lack of success through seeking information from the bodies responsible, the data was requested through contacting a local politician. The politician responded positively and immediately tabled a parliamentary question (*Dáil Question* Nos. 403 & 411: Alan Shatter, 22 October 2013). Months had passed waiting for a response from the official agencies with responsibility for this area of criminal justice. By contrast, a request made on a Monday to a politician resulted in the generation of the information seven working days later. Much of the data on life sentence prisoners contained in this monograph is as a result of numerous parliamentary questions asked between 2013 and 2017 by a politician (who does not have any particular policy interest in life sentence prisoners) at the request of the author (who happens to live in his constituency). The data generated from these parliamentary questions include: figures on the annual average time served by life sentence prisoners; the number of life sentence prisoners released and recalled; gender and offence breakdown of the life sentence prisoner population; number of life sentence prisoners living in the community; the reasons for the recall of life sentence prisoners; age on committal and release; and figures on the release of politically-motivated prisoners.

In Ireland, political arrangements are such that those elected to parliament can become preoccupied with satisfying their constituents (often described as 'parish pump politics') rather than their role as legislators or policy-makers (O'Donnell 2011). This culture may have proved frustrating when engaging formally with the agents of the criminal justice system, yet it was employed to positive effect when the author engaged politically, rather than bureaucratically. This is not simply an oddity specific to this research project but part of a culture that impacts on the release of prisoners and criminal justice decision-making generally. There has been a long history of politicians lobbying on behalf of constituents in an attempt to secure early release and better conditions for those offenders. This ordinarily occurs through writing to the Minister on behalf of the constituent or through tabling a parliamentary question in the *Oireachtas* (Irish parliament). The practice has included lobbying on behalf of those convicted of murder and sex offences (O'Brien 2008; Hennessy 2006). This culture of localism and clientelism, which pervades Irish politics, has implications for the development of strategic thinking, decision-making and the implementation of same (O'Donnell 2011, pp. 496–7). These themes were brought to the surface throughout the research process in terms of the implementation of the research project and circumventing bureaucracy through 'parish pump politics' in order to generate data on life imprisonment. But there is also relevance in the context of the data analysis when exploring parole decision-making. After all, the data controllers (politicians, the Department and the Parole Board) are also the agents responsible for policy and practice in parole. More significantly, they are the key players in determining the length of time a life sentence prisoner will serve in prison.

The Role of Risk

It would be reasonable to suppose that risk has played an increasingly important role in parole decision-making and is an obvious starting point when examining potential factors influencing the release of life sentence prisoners. Over the last three decades of the twentieth century, a global shift away from the traditional objectives of rehabilitation has been documented with a focus on risk and the tightening of controls on selected groups through a more efficient managerial process. In the context of parole, many jurisdictions now make use of a range of practices designed to quantify, classify and control risk (Harcourt 2007; Kemshall 2003; Bonta 1996) with risk assessment tools being employed in assisting parole decision-makers in determining the likelihood of reoffending or rule violation upon release (Padfield et al. 2010; Andrews and Bonta 2000). Risk assessments are regularly utilised by parole decision-makers in other jurisdictions in an attempt to produce more reliable and accurate decisions (Bonta 1996). Ireland has yet to fully embrace the effects of the 'risk society' (Beck 1992). Nonetheless, there is evidence of a shift towards risk in criminal justice, particularly in relation to agencies connected with the parole process. For example, the Probation Service and Prison Psychology Service provide a risk assessment report to the Parole Board to assist with their decision-making. These reports provide decision-makers with a clinical assessment (a judgement by a professional on the risk of reoffending) and actuarial assessment (a statistical prediction of the likelihood of reoffending/rule violation) on the life sentence prisoner under review. This is a comparatively recent development with the Probation Service changing its terminology from 'welfare' to 'risk' in 2004 to better reflect the goals of the service (Prendergast 2012; Probation Service 2008). Furthermore, public protection has consistently been cited as the key factor taken into consideration by both the Parole Board and various Ministers when reviewing life sentence prisoners (Parole Board 2004, p. 7; 2015, p. 5). The Criminal Justice (Temporary Release of Prisoners) Act 2003 may also have had an impact, as a number of criteria to which the Minister must have regard focus on the risk of future harm, albeit in a vague manner.

Parole Board members frequently referenced the importance of risk assessment reports from the Probation Service and the Prison Psychology Service on their decision-making: 'If a psychologist flags to you that a person is either a high risk or a risk of some nature, well you'd be very, very foolish to ignore it, and I would not ignore that' (PB14). Notwithstanding this, members demonstrated a limited understanding of the rudiments of risk and its technologies. They do not receive training and are not comfortable with the language of risk and actuarialism: 'I think some of the reports actually were very detailed and probably would have been difficult to come to grips with if you didn't maybe have a background in psychology. So you'd be trying to cut to the conclusion' (PB10). An indication by the Probation Service or Prison Psychology Service that a life sentence prisoner is categorised as anything other than low risk will not be ignored and will most likely result in a recommendation not to release, irrespective of time served.

A positive risk assessment from the Probation Service specifying that a life sentence prisoner is at a low risk of reoffending is not the only risk-based hurdle that must be overcome. In addition, the offender must satisfy the Parole Board's own version of risk assessment. Members adopted a unique approach to risk assessment. At times members expressed scepticism towards formal risk assessments and placed significant weight on their 'common sense' approach: 'I think [the risk assessment is] useful but it doesn't take a genius to figure out if somebody presents a risk or not' (PB03). Members identified risk factors that they deemed relevant in their own deliberations in individual cases, although the extent to which this practice articulated by members can be described as 'risk assessment' in the objective, knowable and probabilistic form ascribed to risk-based approaches is questionable. The risk factors impacting on members own assessment of risk when deliberating on individual cases included: criminal history; the nature of the offence; treatment participation; offender re-entry; anti-social attitudes; substance use; family and community influences; educational attainment; age; institutional conduct; learning disability; and mental illness. Establishing whether the risk factors identified by members are of predictive value for this category of offenders is beyond the scope of the research (Padfield et al. 2000, p. 140). Nonetheless, it is clear that members *believe* that these factors are of predictive value and that they are engaged in a form of risk assessment. Thus, a life sentence prisoner must address these factors to the satisfaction of the Parole Board with little clarity as to what factors are of significance. The bar is set high as members are avowedly risk averse: '[The Parole Board is] only recommending release for prisoners that are a very, very low risk of reoffending' (PB05). A number of members stated that where a life sentence prisoner continued to present a significant risk to the public they could potentially serve a sentence of life imprisonment in the real sense: 'I think there are a small group of people who probably will remain in prison for the rest of their lives' (PB06). Despite the conservative approach adopted, a number of life sentence prisoners on release have reoffended during the lifetime of the Parole Board (including for theft, burglary, drug and firearm offences).

In addition to a heightened awareness of risk and its technologies, the increase in time served may be reflective of a change in the risk profile of those convicted of life sentences. But, the homogeneity of the offence type (primarily murder), the relationship to the victim (a family member, spouse, friend or acquaintance) (O'Donnell 2005, p. 105) and age range (an average of 30 years of age on committal in the 1990s and in 2016) (Dooley 2001, p. 11; *Dáil Question* No. 827: Frances Fitzgerald, 20 June 2017) has remained relatively stable over the last number of decades. There is evidence of an increased use of the discretionary life sentence for other violent offences (sexual offences, attempted murder, manslaughter) yet this is a recent development and remains at a low level (5 per cent of life sentence prisoners in custody in 2015) (*Dáil Question* No. 81: Frances Fitzgerald, 08 November 2016). Sex offenders were often viewed as a cause for concern amongst parole decision-makers due to the level of risk presented: 'And we have debated at Board level whether we would grant early release to sex offenders and we can see from all the material that they're going to reoffend and there's nothing we can do, and there's no point in us in even considering them for early release' (PB05). A significant change witnessed in this jurisdiction is the increase in murders associated with 'gangland' activity since the late 1990s (O'Donnell and O'Sullivan 2001; Campbell 2010). Those convicted may present a higher risk profile depending on the relevance of factors such as criminal history, antisocial and procriminal attitudes in individual cases: 'One high risk example was an individual who was belonging to a gang, seemed to be doing okay inside, but I would say very high risk of offending. We knew that no matter what happened, no matter what was said, no matter what he did, he'd be going back to join the group' (PB10). Members consistently emphasised the problem that this particular population presented when deliberating on the issue of release. By way of contrast, decision-makers emphasised that low-risk life sentence prisoners regularly appeared before the Parole Board and low risk was often associated with a lack of previous criminal history and the 'once off' nature of the offence: 'Another sort of one-off situation could be a family situation where a son murders a father, a father murders a son, a father murders a mother, these are one-off, they're not criminals in the true sense of the word' (PB09).

Irrespective of how risk is incorporated into the practice of the Parole Board, it is likely that members have become increasingly aware of the importance of risk and this has contributed to a more conservative approach that has developed over the years: 'The Parole Board are [either] doing a very good job or they're not taking any chances whatsoever' (PB01). The Parole Board's version of risk assessment is difficult to identify, define and order. Risk assessment, the aim of which is to reduce uncertainty in an attempt to produce more reliable and accurate decisions may not be the dominant framework. With risk assessments being subsumed into a decision-making process that is unusually flexible, where 'common sense' assessments are deemed to be of significant importance, determining the impact of risk and risk assessments on decision-making is problematic. What can be concluded is that a life sentence prisoner who is perceived by the Parole Board to be at a medium or high risk of reoffending will not be recommended for release. The inverse, a perception of a low risk of reoffending, will not necessarily translate into a recommendation to release. In such a case, there are additional factors that might prevent such an outcome.

A Punitive Turn?

Since the establishment of the Parole Board, decision-making appears to have moved primarily in a punitive direction. The average length of time served in the first five years of the Parole Board was 15 years (2001–2005) compared with 20 years over the last five (2012–2016). Criminologists note that if you peer past the veneer of risk, the incapacitation of serious and violent offenders for lengthy periods in prison is often closely related to satisfying populist punitiveness irrespective of the ability to objectively demonstrate dangerousness (Garland 2001; Simon 1998). Similar to the ambivalence towards risk in criminal justice up until recently, Ireland is notable for its resistance of punitivism (Kilcommins et al. 2004). Yet, there is some evidence of a punitive turn in aspects of the criminal justice system (O'Donnell and Jewkes 2011; O'Donnell 2013). Although Ireland started from a low base, the imprisonment rate accelerated at a pace out of step with other European and common law jurisdictions in the 2000s (O'Donnell 2013; Walmsley 1999, 2011, 2016; Prison Service 2001–2016). O'Donnell (2013, p. 316) notes that the increase in the prison population from 2005 to 2009 reflected a political commitment to penal expansionism and the embrace of punitivism. But, there is evidence of a decline in the general prison population in recent years (O'Donnell 2017). It is fair to say that issues of law and order are more prominent in the public's consciousness since the 1990s, when concern about crime, particularly of the 'gangland' variety, reached levels not witnessed previously (or since) (Hamilton 2014, pp. 35–39). But it would be presumptive to categorise the public's views as aligned with punitivism given the long history of restraint in this regard. Further, the punitive impulse amongst politicians can be relatively uneven in the Irish context.

A punitive streak is certainly evident in the approach of parole-decision makers. The murder rate (Parole Board 2006, p. 4), the prevalence of knife and gun-related crimes (Parole Board 2009, p. 5), the public abhorrence of the crime (Parole Board 2007, p. 4), and the importance of retribution and general deterrence (Parole Board 2005, p. 4) have all been cited by the Parole Board as relevant to its recommendations. Punitive sentiments have been consistently emphasised by the Parole Board: 'Persons concerned in acts of lawlessness on the streets must realise that retribution lies in wait' (Parole Board 2003, p. 5). Decision-makers were acutely aware of trends external to the process, such as the increase in lethal violence, and there appears to be a view that an appropriate method of responding to this is through increasing time served in individual cases under review: 'I indicated that so common had murder become that human life had been cheapened and that the Board must react to that' (Parole Board 2006, p. 4). Members and Ministers were particularly keen to secure public support: 'I think you have to consider the public interest and the public confidence in the criminal justice system, and you do need to be sending messages that particular offences are taken with the highest seriousness' (PB12). Decision-makers also perceived public opinion to be punitive in nature and believed that the public view the parole process as lenient: 'Public opinion was against a shorter period of time' (PB09). As one former Minister remarked: 'People had got to the notion thinking that a life sentence was seven years and I mean that was often said on radio and television that people were getting out after seven years and they didn't believe that after I was finished' (MJ1). The foundations of these views are probably more reflective of individual perception rather than empirical reality. It is more accurate to describe public attitudes to crime as 'ambivalent' where punitive sentiments co-exist alongside rehabilitative instincts (O'Donnell 2013, p. 323). Similarly, punitive attitudes operated alongside a strong commitment expressed by decision-makers as to the rehabilitative potential of the parole process.

Analysing the increase in time served can have the paradoxical effect of appearing to indicate increased punitiveness while a deeper analysis of the process might reveal elements of tolerance in individual decision-making. In 2012 the average time served hit a peak of 22 years for the first time in Irish history. This figure is based on the release of four life sentence prisoners. One of the four individuals released that year was Malcolm Macarthur, an offender that had attracted considerable public and political attention since the commission of his offence in the 1980s. Macarthur had served 30 years in prison, a term far in excess of his contemporaries from that era. Macarthur's release in 2012 pushed the average time served upwards for 2012. In the eight years prior to his release various Ministers had refused to accept the Parole Board's recommendation to permit him periods of release. In some respects, the average time served for 2012 and the lengthy detention of Macarthur fit with a populist and punitive interpretation of decision-making. An alternative analysis could view the eventual release of Macarthur as a decision taken by the then Minister, irrespective of negative public perception or the potential political consequences. As such, this decision can be interpreted as an act of leniency rather than severity irrespective of its impact on increasing time served for the annual average in 2012. This also highlights the danger of interpreting penal trends where data is limited and figures remain relatively small, as is the case with life sentence prisoners. Outliers can easily distort the mean.

If credence is to be given to the public statements of the Parole Board and individual expressions by parole decision-makers, it is undoubted that external and changeable factors such as the crime rate and perceptions of public opinion are being incorporated into the decisions on the release of life sentence prisoners and that this has contributed to a shift upwards in time served. These considerations are external to those contained in the legislation and extraneous to the offender's status and circumstances. The approach of continuing the detention of an offender based on external factors serves to undermine the centrality of risk in decision-making and could prove counterproductive in securing an offender's commitment to engaging in the process. What real incentive is there for a life sentence prisoner to participate meaningfully when, despite being informed of the importance of engaging with the available services to reduce risk levels, there are additional insuperable barriers preventing a recommendation or decision to release? Further, the logic of bringing external factors to bear on individual decision-making can be called into question. Will parole decision-makers take a more lenient approach to release if the homicide rate decreases significantly? If it is not appropriate to reduce time served in individual cases on the basis of an overall decrease in annual homicides it should not be acceptable to increase time served when there is a spike.

Accounting for Politics

Life sentence prisoners are subject to the vagaries of politics. The release of life sentence prisoners is a decision made at the discretion of a politician, the Minister, following the advice of the Parole Board, a group of individuals appointed by the Minister. Parole decision-makers were open about the influence that politics had on their recommendations and outcomes. The discretion afforded the Parole Board permits it to adapt its recommendations to account for politics and the perception as to the political approach, thus raising concerns regarding the meaning of the high rates of acceptance by the Minster of Parole Board recommendations. These high rates can be interpreted in two ways: either the Board exerts considerable influence on parole outcomes, or it is effective at anticipating ministerial preferences. Members noted that in circumstances where there was a belief that the Minister would not accept a recommendation then that recommendation would not be made: 'Inevitably the Board is going to tailor its recommendations to what it views as the Ministers likely-to-accept recommendations'. (PB02). Incorporating political preference is possible due to the lack of constraint placed on decision-makers. O'Donnell (2011) argues that bureaucratic arrangements in Ireland contain substantial imperfections with few developed structures thus permitting greater room for subjective decision-making. In such an environment, individuals can play a significant role in outcomes ranging from 'cipher to author' (O'Donnell 2011, p. 492; Rogan 2010).

The relatively small number of individuals released undoubtedly helped keep life sentence prisoners at the periphery of public and political concern for many decades. They did not occupy much space in the public arena, with little information in the public domain on life imprisonment or release for much of the twentieth century. This has changed more recently with the growth in media interest in criminal justice matters (O'Donnell 2005; Campbell 2010; O'Connell 1999). Members and Ministers cited offenders with high media profiles as causing particular problems due to the potential political fallout arising from a recommendation and/or decision to release. This effects the recommendation to release negatively in such cases: 'If you have a high-profile media case and you recommend X, Y and Z, but you know the Minister is not going to sanction that, well then, you take a more conservative view' (PB01). Parole Board members were explicit about accounting for the different approach of Ministers: 'One has to be honest that, depending on the Minister of the day and the kind of perspective they have on these issues, it can move [time served] (PB12). Since the establishment of the Parole Board, Ministers have taken a keen interest in exercising their discretion of release. Although statutory criteria exist which the Minister must have regard, it appears that these may have little impact on constraining deliberations: 'I decide based on my own intuition and experience as a public representative' (MJ2). Former Ministers were explicit that a decision to release a life sentence prisoner presented a political risk. The potential for adverse publicity, political criticism and personal electoral consequences were cited as negatives that could impact on release decisions: 'I mean obviously if you let a rapist out and the next thing he does is rape another person, whoever does it… whoever is responsible for it, will be visited with the responsibility for that act, so you do have to protect people' (MJ1). Yet, to date, it is a risk that politicians have been reluctant to divest themselves of.

Law as a Counterpoint

Judicial oversight could provide a counterpoint to a system where a politician determines the length of time served, the process is characterised by informality and those subject to it are not afforded much by way of procedural rights. Indeed, the Irish judiciary have a tradition of acting as a counterpoint to the adoption of punitive legislation and policies (Kilcommins et al. 2004, pp. 183–94). They continue to enjoy considerable discretion in sentencing (although not for the offence of murder) and unlike many other jurisdictions have not experienced the erosion of this discretion through legislative measures, sentencing grids and guidelines in the pursuit of punitivism (O'Malley 2016, pp. 6–19). Inroads by the legislature on judicial discretion have been attempted through mandatory and presumptive sentencing for firearms and drug offences but the judiciary have acted to resist this punitive approach through judicial interpretation. For example, a ten-year mandatory minimum sentence must be imposed for possession of drugs with an estimated street value of €12,500 unless 'exceptional circumstances' arise (s. 15A, Misuse of Drugs Act 1977, as amended by s. 4 of the Criminal Justice Act 1999). This sentence has been effectively circumvented by the judiciary with only 3 per cent of cases resulting in a ten-year sentence over a five-year period with the remainder (97 per cent) presumably deemed to be of an 'exceptional' nature (34 per cent of cases resulted in a suspended sentence) (Lally 2016). This evidences the 'continued potential of the judiciary to resist the controlling, retaliatory tendencies of contemporary criminal justice' (Kilcommins et al. 2004, p. 193).

While this individuated justice may act as a barrier to the punitive tendencies of the legislature, it is not always operationalised in favour of the offender. Despite a number of legal challenges, there has been little progress in securing procedural rights for those subject to the parole process (*Barry v. Sentence Review Group* 2001; *Grogan v. Parole Board* 2008). The Minister enjoys 'considerable discretion' when deciding on the release of an offender, including life sentence prisoners (O'Malley 2006, p. 435) and the only means of challenging the decision is through the narrow scope of judicial review, which is concerned with fairness of procedure rather than examining the merits of the decision itself. The Supreme Court and the European Court of Human Rights (ECtHR) have determined that the mandatory life sentence is compatible with the provisions of the Irish Constitution and the European Convention on Human Rights (ECHR) (*Lynch and Whelan v Minister for Justice* 2012; *Lynch and Whelan v Ireland* 2013, 2014). The Supreme Court concluded that the life sentence was 'wholly punitive' in nature, that the executive was not involved in the sentencing process and that individuals subject to the process had recourse to the courts to review the legality of the sentence imposed or the exercise of the executive discretion of temporary release. The mandatory nature of the life sentence for murder was justified on the basis that murder is 'the ultimate crime against society as a whole' (*Lynch and Whelan v Minister for Justice* 2012). At the ECtHR the applicants argued that, in practice, the Minister had regard to the risk of reoffending in deliberating on release and that further detention based on risk was a form of preventive detention. An assessment that the life sentence is in some manner preventive is more significant in Ireland than elsewhere as the incorporation of preventive detention or an incapacitative measure into any aspect of criminal justice decision-making creates issues of compatibility with the Constitution (*People (Attorney General) v O'Callaghan* 1966). This argument was not accepted by the ECtHR, which largely endorsed the interpretation of the life sentence by the Supreme Court. Given the statements of parole decision-makers, it appears that, in practice, the length of time served is considerably influenced by considerations of public protection. Further, the Supreme Court and the ECtHR did not find that the executive was exercising a sentencing power when determining the date at which a life sentence prisoner was released. Yet the reality is that the Minister determines length of time served by life sentence prisoners and all stakeholders in the process are aware of this. It is difficult to reconcile the interpretation of the courts with the practice of parole decision-making. The courts have not proven to be an effective avenue for life sentence prisoners in challenging the legality of their detention or in securing greater procedural rights while attempting to navigate the process.

Conclusion

Returning to the cases of Brophy and Davis, what can be offered by way of explanation in terms of the difference in time served? Although Brophy was sentenced to penal servitude for life and Davis life imprisonment, there is little to distinguish these sentences other than the title itself. Further, the legal structure surrounding the life sentence and the release process has not changed in any significant manner since Brophy was sentenced. There is some evidence of policy change, absent during Brophy's era but relevant to Davis' release. A minimum term of seven years, adopted in 1989, to be served prior to review and release by all life sentence prisoners is relevant. Brophy's release predated this as is evident from the six years he served in prison. Further, the method of review has changed somewhat. Davis will have been subject to the review and recommendation process of the Parole Board while Brophy's release was mediated through an internal 'prison review'. Although the parole process has remained informal, with the Parole Board merely acting in an advisory capacity to the Minister, a more complex process is now in place whereby a life sentence prisoner will be assessed and reported on by various agencies and reviewed periodically by the Parole Board until it is determined that the offender is suitable for a recommendation to release. A key factor of significance must be the orientation towards risk and risk assessment since the establishment of the Parole Board. Risk assessments would not have featured in decision-making for Brophy as such tools did not form part of the process and agencies such as the Probation Service were focused on issues of welfare rather than risk. With a shift towards risk evident in the operations of the Probation Service and the expressions of parole decision-makers as to the centrality of risk to the decision-making process, it is clear that risk assessment would have been a central feature of Davis' review and release.

It is also important to account for the changed landscape within which the decision to release Brophy and Davis was taken. Brophy's conviction and release coincided with low homicide and crime rates and followed an era in Irish history notable for its lack of concern about issues of crime and criminal justice (Adler 1983). O'Donnell (2005, p. 101) observes that there were so few killings during the mid-century '…the population was almost on first name terms with every victim and perpetrator'. By the mid-90s, lethal violence had increased substantially with issues of crime and disorder taking great prominence in public and political discourse. A spate of gangland killings led to a perception amongst the public that human life was being devalued (O'Donnell and O'Sullivan 2003). During the 1960s there was approximately one homicide per month whereas from 2004 to 2013 there was one per week (O'Donnell 2005, p. 103; Doyle 2018). The lack of social, cultural and economic change in Ireland for much of the twentieth century was rapidly transformed in the 1990s *via* a buoyant economy, changes to the structure of families and the workforce, population demographics and the spread of technology and mass media (Campbell 2008; Kilcommins et al. 2004). The United Kingdom, where social and economic change of this nature occurred through the latter decades of the twentieth century, also experienced a growth in populist punitiveness with law-and-order approaches becoming increasingly embedded. These sentiments were largely absent from the politico-media landscape in Ireland until the 1990s and themes of redemption, until recently, echoed across the criminal justice system (O'Donnell and Jewkes 2011). But it seems that the release of life sentence prisoners has not been immune to populist punitiveness with Parole Board decision-makers consistently referencing concern in relation to the rise in lethal violence, the need to address public concern about crime and the ability of the parole process to exact retributive sentiments while sending out a message of general deterrence. The method chosen to communicate this message appears to have been through the increase in time served by life sentence prisoners. This means that individual life sentence prisoners like Davis, convicted during or since the 1990s, may be required to serve additional periods in prison due to an increased homicide rate or a general concern about 'gangland' crime. Of course, the murder committed by Davis, similar to the majority of murders, was unrelated to any form of 'gangland' activity.

Ultimately, the decision to release both Brophy and Davis was a political one made at the discretion of the Minister of the day. But, those decisions were made in different political eras with media and public opinion exerting greater influence on decision-makers in the twenty-first century than in the 1970s. For example, the release of Brophy was not reported on and there are no newspaper articles on his release. While most homicides in the state tend to be reported on at trial stage, interest in release is a more recent development. The trial of Davis had attracted so much attention that the Court of Criminal Appeal found the nature of some of the reporting to be prejudicial (*People (DPP) v Davis* 2001). When Davis was released back into the community he was subject to an *exposé* in the tabloid press: '*Slaughter meter man: Thug who kicked lover to death now works in housing estates*' (Donald 2014). Given that release at some point is on the horizon for life sentence prisoners, time served might be a matter of determining what is palatable, both publicly and politically. This is evidenced by the concern expressed by parole decision-makers about the political risk of releasing life sentence prisoners, particularly those with some level of notoriety.

Principal amongst the contingencies that have shaped the parole process is its discretionary and informal nature. These attributes once operated to the benefit of life sentence prisoners subject to the process in the 1970s, such as Brophy. The increase in time served indicates that this is no longer the case, with life sentence prisoners now expected to serve a period of imprisonment that would have been unconscionable a number of decades previously. Nonetheless, this acts as a reminder that the individual and discretionary approach does not always serve punitive ends. It can also operate in the opposite direction. Although Brophy and Davis served varying lengths of time in prison they are no different to other life sentence prisoners across the decades. They are all subject to a process whereby individual decision-makers operate with little constraint and can greatly influence outcomes. These outcomes are reliant on the factors that they themselves permit to influence their deliberations at any given time.

Life sentences are rarely imposed and are exceptional as a punishment in a sentencing system characterised by determinacy (life sentences accounted for 16 out of 12,163 committals to prison in 2016: Prison Service 2016, p. 32). Yet, the ultimate penalty available in a state has a social, political and cultural significance that goes beyond its use as a sanction, both within and outside the criminal justice system. It also acts as the 'benchmark of severity' by which other penalties for less serious offences are established (Ghandnoosh 2017, p. 11). Examining the potential factors influencing parole outcomes for life sentence prisoners provides an opportunity to focus on a process, the subjects of which have committed the most serious offences in the state and are serving the lengthiest penalties. The themes identified in this chapter are explored throughout this book and the following chapters examine: the rise of life imprisonment; the process of release in practice; the influence of risk and external factors on decision-makers; the disjoint between the legal interpretation and the practice of life imprisonment and; the potential impact of reforming the parole process.

References

Adler, F. (1983). *Nations not obsessed with crime*. Littleton: Rothman.

Andrews, D. A., & Bonta, J. (2000). *The level of service inventory-revised*. Toronto: Multi-Health Systems.

Baumer, E. P., Wright, R., Kristinsdottir, K., & Gunnlaugsson, H. (2002). Crime, shame, and recidivism. The case of Iceland. *British Journal of Criminology, 42*(1), 40–59.

Beck, U. (1992). *Risk society: Towards a new modernity*. London: Sage.

Bonta, J. (1996). Risk-needs assessment and treatment. In A. T. Hartland (Ed.), *Choosing correctional options that work: Defining the demand and evaluating the supply* (pp. 18–32). Thousand Oaks: Sage.

Campbell, L. (2008). The culture of control in Ireland: Theorising recent developments in criminal justice. *Web Journal of Current Legal Issues*, 1. Retrieved from http://webjcli.ncl.ac. uk/2008/issue1/pdf/campbell1.pdf.

Campbell, L. (2010). Responding to gun crime in Ireland. *British Journal of Criminology, 50*(3), 414–434.

Cavadino, M., & Dignan, J. (2006). Penal policy and political economy. *Criminology & Criminal Justice, 6*(4), 435–456.

Council of Europe. (2017). *Annual penal statistics: SPACE 1-Prison populations, survey 2015*. Strasbourg: Council of Europe.

Courts Service. (2001–2015). *Annual reports*. Dublin: Courts Service.

Department of Justice and Equality. (2014). *Report of the independent review group on the Department of Justice and Equality*. Dublin: Department of Justice and Equality.

Donald, N. (2014, October 7). Slaughter meter man: Thug who kicked lover to death now works in housing estates. *Sunday World*. Retrieved from http://www.sundayworld.com

Dooley, E. (2001). *Homicide in Ireland 1992–1996*. Dublin: Stationery Office.

Doyle, D. M. (2018, forthcoming). Crime in Ireland, 1922–2012. In R. MacMahon (Ed.), *Crime in Ireland since 1800*. London: Routledge.

Dünkel, F., van Zyl Smit, D., & Padfield, N. (2010). Concluding thoughts. In N. Padfield, D. van Zyl Smit, & F. Dünkel (Eds.), *Release from prison: European policy and practice* (pp. 395–444). Devon: Willan.

European Committee for the Prevention of Torture and Inhuman or Degrading Treatment or Punishment (CPT). (2015). *25th general report of the CPT*. Strasbourg: ECPT.

Feeley, M., & Simon, J. (1992). The new penology: Notes on the emerging strategy of corrections and its implications. *Criminology, 30*(4), 449–474.
Garland, D. (2001). *The culture of control: Crime and social order in contemporary society*. Oxford: Oxford University Press.
Garland, D. (2013). Penality and the penal state. *Criminology, 51*(3), 475–517.
Ghandnoosh, N. (2017). *Delaying a second chance: The declining prospects for parole on life sentences*. Washington, DC: Sentencing Project.
Griffin, D., & O'Donnell, I. (2012). The life sentence and parole. *British Journal of Criminology, 52*(3), 611–629.
Hamilton, C. (2014). *Reconceptualising penality: A comparative perspective on punitiveness in Ireland, Scotland and New Zealand*. Oxon: Routledge.
Harcourt, B. E. (2007). *Against prediction: Profiling, policing and punishing in an actuarial age*. Chicago: University of Chicago Press.
Healy, D. (2012). Advise, assist and befriend: Can probation supervision support desistance? *Social Policy & Administration, 46*(4), 377–394.
Heylin, G. (2001). Evaluating prisons, prisoners and others. *Studies in Public Policy*. Retrieved from http://www.tara.tcd.ie/handle/2262/60511
Hennessy, M. (2006, October 24). FG deputy criticised for query about sex offender. *Irish Times*, p. 7.
Irish Times. (1995, October 23). Man charged with murder of woman. *Irish Times*, p. 6.
Irish Times. (1997a, March 4). Counsel tells court of 'great violence' and multiple injuries done to mother of six. *Irish Times*, p. 3.
Irish Times. (1997b, March 5). Murder trial is told of extensive abdomen injuries to mother of six. *Irish Times*, p. 6.
Irish Times. (1997c, March 7). Murder trial hears of couple's 'fight. *Irish Times*, p. 4.
Irish Times. (1997d, March 19). Verdict expected in Athy murder trial. *Irish Times*, p. 6.
Irish Times. (1997e, March 22). Kildare man gets life sentence for brutal murder of his girlfriend. *Irish Times*, p. 4.
Kemshall, H. (2003). *Understanding risk in criminal justice*. Berkshire: Open University Press.
Kilcommins, S., O'Donnell, I., O'Sullivan, E., & Vaughan, B. (2004). *Crime, punishment and the search for order in Ireland*. Dublin: Institute of Public Administration.
Loader, I., & Sparks, R. (2011). *Public criminology*. New York: Routledge.

Lahti, R. (2000). Towards a rational and humane criminal policy? Trends in Scandinavian penal thinking. *Journal of Scandinavian Studies in Criminology and Crime Prevention, 1*(2), 141–155.
Lally, C. (2015, March 29). Dwyer likely to be "new Malcolm Macarthur" and serve decades in jail. *Irish Times*. Retrieved from https://www.irishtimes.com/news/crime-and-law/dwyer-likely-to-be-new-malcolm-macarthur-and-serve-decades-in-jail-1.2157355
Lally, C. (2016, November 28). Judges' sentencing reflects nature of organised crime gangs. *Irish Times*. Retrieved from https://www.irishtimes.com/news/crime-and-law/judges-sentencing-reflects-nature-of-organised-crime-gangs-1.2884195
Lappi-Seppälä, T. (2016a). Nordic sentencing. *Crime and Justice, 45*(1), 17–82.
Lappi-Seppälä, T. (2016b). Life imprisonment and related institutions in the Nordic countries. In D. van Zyl Smit & C. Appleton (Eds.), *Life imprisonment and human rights* (pp. 461–505). Hart: Oxford.
Maruna, S., & King, A. (2009). Once a criminal, always a criminal? Redeemability and the psychology of punitive public attitudes. *European Journal on Criminal Policy and Research, 15*(1–2), 7–24.
McAra, L. (2008). Crime, criminology and criminal justice in Scotland. *European Journal of Criminology, 5*(4), 481–504.
Nelken, D. (2009). Comparative criminal justice: Beyond ethnocentricism and relativism. *European Journal of Criminology, 6*(4), 291–311.
O'Brien, P. (2008, July 8). Revealed: Political lobbying of prisoners. *Irish Examiner*. Retrieved from http://www.irishexaminer.com
O'Connell, M. (1999). Is Irish public opinion towards crime distorted by media bias? *European Journal of Communication, 14*(2), 191–212.
O'Donnell, I. (2005). Crime and justice in the Republic of Ireland. *European Journal of Criminology, 2*(1), 99–131.
O'Donnell, I. (2008). Stagnation and change in Irish penal policy. *Howard Journal of Crime and Justice, 47*(2), 121–133.
O'Donnell, I. (2011). Criminology, bureaucracy and unfinished business. In M. Bosworth & C. Hoyle (Eds.), *What is criminology?* (pp. 488–501). Oxford: Oxford University Press.
O'Donnell, I. (2013). Penal policy in Ireland: The malign effect of sustained neglect. *Studies: An Irish Quarterly Review, 102*(407), 315–323.
O'Donnell, I. (2017). Ireland's shrinking prison population. *Irish Criminal Law Journal, 27*(3), 70–77.

O'Donnell, I., & Jewkes, Y. (2011). Going home for Christmas: Prisoners, a taste of freedom and the press. *Howard Journal of Crime and Justice, 50*(1), 75–91.
O'Donnell, I., & O'Sullivan, E. (2001). *Crime control in Ireland: The politics of intolerance*. Cork: Cork University Press.
O'Donnell, I., & O'Sullivan, E. (2003). The politics of intolerance—Irish style. *British Journal of Criminology, 43*(1), 41–62.
O'Malley, T. (2006). *Sentencing law and practice*. Dublin: Thomson Round Hall.
O'Malley, T. (2016). *Sentencing law and practice*. Dublin: Thomson Round Hall.
Padfield, N., Liebling, A., & Arnold, H. (2000). *An exploration of decision-making at discretionary lifer panels*. London: Home Office.
Padfield, N., Smit, D. V. Z., & Dünkel, F. (Eds.). (2010). *Release from prison: European policy and practice*. Devon: Willan.
Parole Board. (2002–2015). *Annual reports*. Dublin: Parole Board.
Pratt, J. (2007). *Penal populism*. New York: Routledge.
Prendergast, M. (2012). Practitioner perceptions on the merits, challenges and ethical dilemmas of LSI-R in practice. *Irish Probation Journal, 9*(1), 111–131.
Prison Service. (2001–2016). *Annual report*. Dublin/Longford: Irish Prison Service.
Probation Service. (2008). *Strategy statement 2008–2010*. Dublin: The Stationery Office.
Rogan, M. (2010). Charles Haughey, the Department of Justice and Irish prison policy during the 1960s. *Administration, 57*(3), 65–86.
Simon, J. (1998). Managing the monstrous: Sex offenders and the new penology. *Psychology, Public Policy and Law, 4*(1–2), 452–467.
Snacken, S. (2010). Resisting punitiveness in Europe? *Theoretical Criminology, 14*(3), 273–292.
van Zyl Smit, D., Weatherby, P., & Creighton, S. (2014). Whole life sentences and the tide of European human rights jurisprudence: What is to be done? *Human Rights Law Review, 14*(1), 59–84.
Walmsley, R. (1999). *World prison population list*. Essex: International Centre for Prison Studies.
Walmsley, R. (2011). *World prison population list*. Essex: International Centre for Prison Studies.
Walmsley, R. (2016). *World prison population list*. Essex: International Centre for Prison Studies.

Wilson, M. (2004). On an imaginary lead: Defensibility and post-release supervision of life-sentenced prisoners by the Probation and Welfare Service. *Irish Probation Journal, 1*(1), 86–96.
Zimring, F. E., & Johnson, D. T. (2006). Public opinion and the governance of punishment in democratic political systems. *The Annals of the American Academy of Political and Social Science, 605*(1), 265–280.

Table of Legal Instruments

Criminal Justice Act 1960.
Criminal Justice Act 1964.
Criminal Justice Act 1990.
Criminal Justice Act 1999.
Criminal Justice (Temporary Release of Prisoners) Act 2003.
Misuse of Drugs Act 1977.

Table of Cases

European Court of Human Rights

Lynch and Whelan v Ireland Application nos 70495/10 and 74565/10, 18 June 2013.
Lynch and Whelan v Ireland Application nos 70495/10 and 74565/10, 8 July 2014.

Ireland

Barry v Sentence Review Group [2001] 4 IR 167.
Grogan v Parole Board [2008] IEHC 204.
Lynch and Whelan v Minister for Justice [2012] 1 IR 1.
People (Attorney General) v O'Callaghan [1966] IR 501.
People (DPP) v Brophy, [1970] Court of Criminal Appeal NAI 49/69, October 23.
People (DPP) v Brophy [1992] ILRM 709.
People (DPP) v Davis [2001] 2 ILRM 65.
Ryan v Governor of Limerick Prison [1988] IR 198.

Table of Parliamentary Debates

205 *Dáil Debates* Cols. 323–4: Charles Haughey, 24 October 1963.
Dáil Question No. 81: Frances Fitzgerald, 8 November 2016.
Dáil Question No. 82: Frances Fitzgerald, 8 November 2016.
Dáil Question No. 827: Frances Fitzgerald, 20 June 2017.
Dáil Question Nos. 403 & 411: Alan Shatter, 22 October 2013.

2

The Rise of Life Imprisonment

The most important penological issue on the European agenda today is life imprisonment.
Judge Paulo Pinto de Albuquerque
European Court of Human Rights (2015).

Introduction

The life sentence, which existed in many jurisdictions prior to the decline in use and eventual abolition of capital punishment, has become the new 'ultimate penalty' across most of the Western world (Sheleff 1987). A small number of countries opt for the imposition of lengthy determinate sentences for the most serious offences,[1] while in the United States life imprisonment coexists with the death penalty. The increase across Western countries in the number of offenders serving the new 'ultimate penalty', a phenomenon of the last number of decades (Coyle 2004, pp. 96–8; Penal Reform International 2007, pp. 2–4; Council of Europe 2017; van Zyl Smit and Appleton 2017), has begun to attract critical attention from international institutions, human rights organisations and academic commentators (United Nations (UN) 1994; Council of Europe 2003; European

D. Griffin, *Killing Time*, https://doi.org/10.1007/978-3-319-72667-0_2

Committee for the Prevention of Torture (CPT) 2007; Amnesty International and Human Rights Watch 2005; van Zyl Smit and Appleton 2016; van Zyl Smit 2001; Appleton and Grøver 2007). The adoption of the life sentence as the 'ultimate penalty' was to be reserved for the most 'drastic crime' (Sheleff 1987). The UN (1994, p. 16) states that the life sentence should only be imposed on 'offenders who have committed the most serious crimes'. Despite the assumption by death penalty supporters and opponents alike that the natural alternative to execution is a life sentence (Appleton and Grøver 2007, p. 507), the adoption of the life sentence may also be viewed as the selection of a hard line penalty that governments believe will 'placate a public hostile to abolition' (Hodgkinson et al. 2008, p. 266). Any alternative sentence necessitates consideration of the demands of justice including retribution, deterrence, rehabilitation and incapacitation, as well as remaining proportionate to the gravity of the offence (Hood and Hoyle 2015). However, if the rationale for the abolition of the death penalty is based on a human rights argument, then it is also important to ensure that its replacement is consistent with that perspective and does not amount to a cruel and degrading punishment in a different form (Hood 2001, p. 346). This chapter examines the rise of life imprisonment as the ultimate penalty and the legal framework and procedures in place for the imposition of the life sentence.

The New Ultimate Penalty

Academic discourse on the life sentence has observed that such was the focus on the abolition of capital punishment that little consideration went into the examination of the alternative sanction put in its place (Bedau 1989, p. 482; Newcomen 2005, p. 1). While the entrenchment of life imprisonment as the alternative to the death penalty in most jurisdictions is clearly evident, there is little consensus as to the meaning of life imprisonment resulting in diverse practices in terms of its use. For example, in the United States, it appears that an appropriate alternative to execution is that murderers should be sentenced to life without parole (Appleton and Grøver 2007, p. 507; American Civil Liberties Union 2013). By way of contrast, Norway abolished the use of life sentences in

1981 on the basis that life imprisonment was incompatible with its conception of humanity (Lappi-Seppälä 2016, p. 472). Instead, the legislature increased the maximum determinate sentence available from 15 to 21 years. Most countries provide for the imposition of a life sentence for homicide offences (often murder) and may provide for the imposition of a life sentence for other serious offences. It is common practice for a life sentence prisoner to be released from prison at some point although the length of time a life sentence prisoner is required to serve and the process of release may vary from country to country and from case to case.

With the decline in use of capital punishment and the insertion of the life sentence as the ultimate penalty, it was somewhat inevitable that concern would focus on the apparent growth of the life sentence prisoner population. It is estimated that in 2000, there were 274,432 life sentence prisoners across the world and this has increased to 536,185 in 2014 (van Zyl Smit and Appleton 2017). An increase in the use of life sentences appears to fit neatly with the thesis that there exists a global shift towards more punitive criminal justice systems (Garland 2001; Feeley and Simon 1992; Allen 1981; Pratt et al. 2005). Yet, the cross-jurisdictional data presents a complex picture that is somewhat difficult to order. In the Western world, common law countries contrast starkly with many civil law European countries in terms of the actual percentage of prisoners serving life sentences. In Europe, Scotland currently takes poll position with 16.8 per cent of the overall prison population constituting life sentence prisoners, with Northern Ireland (13.7) and Greece (13.1) following (Council of Europe 2017, p. 92). At one point, England and Wales had more life sentence prisoners than the aggregate population in the rest of Europe, although this is no longer the case (van Zyl Smit and Appleton 2016, p. 226). In the United States, the number of life sentence prisoners has risen dramatically over the last number of decades, from 34,000 in 1984 to 159,520 in 2012 with one out of every nine prisoners now serving life sentences (Mauer and Nellis 2016, p. 24). In Australia, 5 per cent of sentenced prisoners are serving a life sentence or an indeterminate sentence (Australian Bureau of Statistics 2013). Many European states maintain significantly lower levels of life sentence prisoners as a percentage of their overall prison population although the range is quite significant. Countries such as Romania (0.6 per cent), Czech Republic (0.3 per cent) and Lithuania (1.7 per cent) have comparatively low levels of life sentence prisoners as a percentage of the overall prison population when put in contrast with Cyprus (4.8 per cent) Italy (4.7 per cent) and Germany (3.7 per cent) (Council of Europe 2017, p. 92).

Data on the life sentence prisoner population cannot be taken uncritically as indicative of a particular penal trend. Factors such as fluctuations in the general population, deaths in custody and the cumulative nature of the data require careful consideration (Nelken 2010; O'Donnell 2004; Tonry 2007). There are particular difficulties that arise in the context of an examination of life sentences. Countries may have included persons subject to sentences of preventive detention (for example, mentally ill offenders and persons considered as dangerous) under the category 'life imprisonment' because in such cases the length of detention or imprisonment is not fixed (Harcourt 2011; Council of Europe 2017). Additionally, the point at which capital punishment ceased as a practice and was legally abolished across different countries impacts upon the number of life sentence prisoners. Many common law and western European countries became *de facto* abolitionist during the 1950s, 1960s and 1970s albeit legal abolition of the use of death penalty for all crimes often occurred at a later date during the 1980s and 1990s (see for example: Denmark (*de facto*: 1950; *de jure*: 1978); France (*de facto*: 1977; *de jure*: 1981); Italy (*de facto*: 1947; *de jure*: 1994). Eastern European countries tend to have a later timeline in terms of the transition to abolition *de facto* and *de jure* (see for example: Lithuania (*de facto*: 1995; *de jure*: 1998); Poland (*de facto*: 1988; *de jure*: 1998); Slovakia (*de facto*: 1989; *de jure*: 1990) (Hood and Hoyle 2015). The movement towards abolition in these countries was influenced significantly by the requirements of membership to the European Union and the Council of Europe (Snacken 2010). As a result, they have a significantly lower life sentence prisoner population as the historic and cumulative effect of such long-term offenders has yet to fully impact the prison population in a similar manner to western European countries.

The frequency of the use of life imprisonment as a sanction in practice and not just the length of time it has been on the statute books requires examination. For example, life sentence prisoners in the Netherlands constitute 0.6 per cent of the overall prison population despite the country having replaced the death penalty with life imprisonment as early as 1870

(Van Hattum and Meijer 2016, pp. 147–148). In practice, life sentences were rarely imposed during the twentieth century although the number of life sentences has increased substantially since the turn of the century as the process has become susceptible to a 'prevailing punitive climate' (Van Hattum and Meijer 2016, p. 158). The discretion available at the sentencing stage when imposing a life sentence is particularly important when considering the number of life sentence prisoners in each jurisdiction. Stokes (2008, p. 282) highlights that cross-jurisdictional variations 'occur in the types of crimes carrying the sanction of life imprisonment [and] whether sentences are mandatory or discretionary'. A mandatory life sentence for murder is imposed in a small number of European countries (Ireland, England and Wales, Germany and Cyprus) whereas most adopt a discretionary approach for murder and homicide offences (Appleton and van Zyl Smit 2016, p. 219). Similarly, the number of offences for which a life sentence can be imposed is also of significance. In England and Wales, there are over 50 offences that attract a maximum penalty of life imprisonment (Appleton and van Zyl Smit 2016, p. 220) whereas life imprisonment can only be imposed for murder in many European countries (van Zyl Smit and Appleton 2016; Lappi-Seppälä 2016, p. 480). The fluctuation in the number of convictions for crimes that attract a life sentence will also impact on the percentage of life sentence prisoners. Examining the Nordic countries of Finland, Denmark and Sweden it is clear that Finland has almost double the number of life sentence prisoners than Sweden while Denmark has almost ten times less (Lappi-Seppälä 2016, pp. 481–2). The number of those convicted of homicide in Finland is almost twice that of Sweden, thus explaining the difference. The lower rate in Denmark cannot be explained through the homicide rate rather it is the difference in sentencing policy that has had the effect of limiting the number of life sentences imposed (Lappi-Seppälä 2016, p. 482). As is evident, the percentage of life sentence prisoners is as a result of the influence of a range of country-specific factors.

In Ireland, there has been a significant increase in the number of life sentence prisoners in custody (from 139 in 2001 to 352 in 2016) as well as a percentage of the annual average prison population (from 4.5 per cent in 2001 to 9.5 per cent in 2016) (Prison Service 2001–2016). There are a total of 435 life sentence prisoners in Ireland, with 352 (81 per cent) in custody and 83 (19 per cent) on release in the community (*Dáil Question* No. 112: Frances Fitzgerald, 24 January 2017). The number of life sentence prisoners committed to prison has shown some growth from 2001 to 2016 although this has been inconsistent (ranging from 11 to 29 committals per annum) (see Table 1.1). Data before 2001 are not available. The vast majority of life sentence prisoners are male (97 per cent) with only 11 females (3 per cent) serving a life sentence (*Dáil Question* No. 82: Frances Fitzgerald, 08 November 2016). Similar, to other jurisdictions, the increase in the number of life sentence prisoners has been influenced by a range of factors and the following explores the use of the life sentence as a sanction in Ireland.

From Capital Punishment to Life Imprisonment

In Ireland, the transition towards the abolition of capital punishment and the subsequent adoption of a life sentence followed along the trajectory of other western European countries. The use of capital punishment gradually diminished in the nineteenth century with murder becoming the only common offence to carry the death penalty following the enactment of the Offences Against the Person Act 1861. After the Irish Free State came into existence in 1922, it might have been expected that capital punishment, often associated with colonial rule and English tyranny, would have been abolished altogether but its retention was justified as a safeguard against subversion, the risk posed by the Irish Republican Army (IRA) and the reluctance of the state to appear weak during the descent into civil war (Doyle and O'Donnell 2012). Many of those convicted of murder and subject to the death penalty had their sentences commuted to a term of imprisonment throughout the twentieth century with very few executions taking place on an annual basis (205 *Dáil Debates* Cols. 323–4: Charles Haughey, 24 October 1963). The Constitution of 1937 vested in the President the power to commute or remit any punishment imposed by the court, on the advice of the government (Article 13.6), thus suggesting that it was envisaged that capital punishment was to be retained (O'Malley 1995, p. 3). This power of commutation was conferred upon the government *via* the Criminal Justice Act 1951 (O'Malley 2010, pp. 212–4). Some, albeit limited debate surrounded the use of capital punishment in the intervening decades with the last execution in the state carried out in 1954 (O'Malley 1995, pp. 2–3). Section 1 of the Criminal Justice Act 1964 abolished the death penalty for all offences except treason, offences under military law and 'capital murder' (which includes the murder of a member of *An Garda Síochána* (Irish police), prison officer, head of state etc.). Those convicted of 'capital murder' now serve a life sentence with a minimum term of 40 years prior to becoming eligible for release (less remission of 25 per cent (Rule 59(2), Prison Rules 2007; *Callan v Ireland* 2013)). Although it was no longer possible to impose the death penalty in any circumstance, a referendum was held in 2002 amending the Constitution preventing the *Oireachtas* (Irish parliament) from enacting legislation to re-introduce the death penalty and removing all references to it from the text. Capital punishment for murder was replaced with a mandatory sentence of penal servitude for life (Criminal Justice Act 1964, s. 2), which was subsequently abolished and replaced with life imprisonment (Criminal Justice Act 1990, s. 2).

Life Imprisonment for Murder

A mandatory sentence of life imprisonment is imposed for murder (Criminal Justice Act 1990, s. 2).[2] For a significant period of the twentieth century, penal servitude for life and capital punishment operated alongside each other and when the death penalty was imposed it was often commuted to penal servitude for life (Department of Justice 1962). As capital punishment fell into decline, penal servitude for life transitioned into the most significant penal sanction available in this country, as in many others. Little distinction existed between penal servitude for life and life imprisonment in practice (*Application of McLoughlin* 1970). Section 4 of the Criminal Justice Act 1964 states that for an accused to be convicted of murder, it must be proved that 'the accused person intended to kill, or cause serious injury'. While liability is construed on these grounds, there exists a considerable variety in terms of the commission of the offence that might distinguish one offender from another within this category. A person who intended to kill could and possibly should be treated differently from a person who intended to cause serious injury. A person who engages in a 'mercy killing' might have intended to kill but is different from a murderer motivated by anger or a person responsible for a terrorist bombing (O'Malley 2016, pp. 307–8; Morris and Blom-Cooper 2011). The mandatory nature of the life sentence does not afford the trial judge discretion to incorporate any such distinctions at sentencing. Aggravating and mitigating factors are not explored when sentencing a person convicted of murder and no distinctions are made in terms of the gravity of the offence or the circumstances of the offender. In effect, the penalty is determined the moment the verdict of guilty is delivered in court.

Mandatory sentences are relatively rare in Ireland with sentencing based primarily on judicially developed principles affording the trial judge considerable discretion. The principle of proportionality, namely that the sentence must be proportionate to the gravity of the offence and the personal circumstances of the offender, forms the cornerstone of sentencing in Ireland (*People (Attorney General) v Poyning* 1972; *State (Healy) v Donoghue* 1976; O'Malley 2016). The Supreme Court has upheld the constitutionality of the mandatory life sentence, noting that murder as an offence is 'unique in nature' thus validating the uniform penalty for all murders (*Lynch and Whelan v Minister for Justice* (2012, p. 10; Law Reform Commission 2013, p. 17). Outside of the legal interpretation of the mandatory life sentence, concerns have been raised. In a review of mandatory sentences, a minority of Law Reform Commissioners (2013, pp. 121–122) were of the view that it should be repealed on the basis that not all murders are equally heinous and the mandatory nature of the sentence cannot reflect the 'variations of culpability' within the offence of murder. As O'Malley (2016, p. 307) notes, mandatory life imprisonment for murder is not constitutionally required and there are strong policy reasons for revisiting the regime.

In addition, it appears the lack of discretion at sentencing may also be having an impact on the rate of contestation through trial by jury for murder offences. In 2014, 19 life sentences were imposed for murder, 16 of those were as a result of a conviction following trial by jury with only three defendants pleading guilty. A further three were acquitted through jury trial and three were found not guilty by reason of insanity (Courts Service 2015, p. 66). This is the inverse of the situation across all other offences.

The vast majority of defendants enter a plea of guilty at the early stages of the criminal process. During the same year, 92 per cent of convictions on indictment followed a plea of guilty, while only 3 per cent of cases were as a result of conviction by jury (Director of Public Prosecutions 2015, p. 37). There are many reasons as to why a person might plead guilty early on in the process but the system also incentivises such pleas (O'Malley 2016, p. 162). A person who pleads guilty can expect a reduction in his or her sentence as a result. The rationale for taking this into consideration at sentencing can be related to the elimination of the need for a trial and the uncertainty of conviction that might result. It also saves the victim the hardship of giving evidence against the accused. Due to the mandatory nature of the life sentence, there is no incentive for a person charged with murder to plead guilty. If an offender pleads guilty to murder he will be subject to the same penalty, a life sentence. Those charged with murder can also enter a plea of 'not guilty to murder but guilty of manslaughter' or 'not guilty to murder but guilty of manslaughter on the grounds of diminished responsibility' and the Director of Public Prosecutions (DPP) may accept these pleas (Courts Service 2014, p. 58). In the absence of a plea for the lesser offence of manslaughter being accepted, perhaps it is unsurprising that there is a significantly higher rate of those opting for trial by jury in the hope of an acquittal or conviction of manslaughter (which attracts a maximum rather than a mandatory life sentence).

A further factor that may influence the life sentence prisoner population is the murder rate, the resultant number of those convicted of the offence and therefore subject to the mandatory penalty. At a general level, there has been a significant increase in the number of homicides from an annual average of 10.1 in the 1950s to 61.6 in the 2000s (O'Donnell 2005, p. 103; Central Statistics Office 2013). Since the turn of the century, the number of those convicted for murder and therefore subject to the life sentence has ranged from 13 to 30 annually meaning there have been a relatively consistent number of life sentence prisoners being committed to prison over the last fifteen years (Courts Service 2001–2015). Given the principle of proportionality upon which sentencing in Ireland is based, it is highly likely that if the sentence was discretionary rather than mandatory it would be imposed far less frequently given that the trial judge would have to take into consideration any mitigating factors in the individual case when determining the quantum of punishment. It is also probable that those charged with murder would plead guilty on a more frequent basis in the knowledge that a guilty plea will reduce the penalty from the maximum sentence in all but the exceptional of circumstances (*People (DPP) v O'Neill* 2015). This would not necessarily mean that there would be a reduction in time served in prison. Lengthy determinate sentences have been imposed for offences outside of homicide. In *People (DPP) v Piotrowski* (2014) the Court of Criminal Appeal imposed an 18-year sentence in lieu of five concurrent life sentences for serious sexual offences. However, it would mean that sentence length would be determinate for most murders and that determination would be made at a sentencing hearing rather than through the parole process. As the situation currently stands, with 94.7 per cent of the life sentence prisoner population serving a life sentence for murder, a key factor in the increase of the life sentence prisoner population is simply down to the mandatory nature of the sentence.

Discretionary Life Sentences

A life sentence can be imposed as a maximum penalty for a range of different offences, including: manslaughter[3]; attempted murder[4]; rape and sexual offences[5]; sexual act or attempted sexual act with a child[6]; incest[7]; arson[8]; false imprisonment[9]; robbery[10]; syringe offences[11]; possession of a firearm with intent to endanger life[12]; and drug trafficking.[13] The discretionary imposition of a life sentence is rare with the judiciary consistently indicating a reluctance to use the top range of the penalty available (*People (DPP) v Conroy (No.2)* 1989). Out of a total number of 342 life sentence prisoners in custody in 2015, 12 (3.5 per cent) were for sexual offences, 3 were for manslaughter (0.9 per cent), and 3 for attempted murder (0.9 per cent) (*Dáil Question* No. 81: Frances Fitzgerald 08 November 2016). The discretionary imposition of a life sentence should only be imposed for the 'worst imaginable variation of the offence' (*People (DPP) v McC* 2008, p. 106). The Supreme Court has indicated that where a life sentence is being considered due to the exceptional nature of the offending, there is a strong incentive to impose a determinate sentence as it is unsatisfactory for a court to impose a life sentence without knowing the 'tariff' period that will be served by the offender (*People (DPP) v McC* 2008, p. 106; *People (DPP) v S.(P.)* 2009). Thus, it is preferable to devise a determinate sentence where possible:

> The distinctive feature of the sentence of life imprisonment is that it is indeterminate. Unlike a prisoner serving a fixed term, the life sentence prisoner does not know when, if ever, he or she will be released. It is for this reason that even in very bad cases, the court will think first of a lengthy determinate sentence. (*People (DPP) v O'Neill* 2015)

Based on this approach, a series of decisions of the Court of Criminal Appeal have replaced sentences of life imprisonment imposing lengthy determinate sentences instead. In *People (DPP) v S.(P.)* (2009) the trial judge imposed four consecutive life sentences for a number of serious offences including rape under section 4 and attempted rape of two young males aged 11 and 13. The Court of Criminal Appeal noted that the exceptional depravity of the offences and the breach of trust were aggravating factors. The court considered that the defendant's previous record of offending made him a danger to the public. However, it noted that his early guilty plea and expression of remorse needed to be accounted for in mitigation. The court ordered a 15-year sentence with the last two and a half years suspended on condition the offender comply with a 10-year post-release supervision order. This approach of imposing a significant determinate sentence with a post-release supervision order instead of a life sentence is evident in a number of cases in the area of sexual offences. In *People (DPP) v K.(G.)* (2008) the Court of Criminal Appeal reduced a life sentence for aggravated sexual assault to 16 years imprisonment with the last 3 years suspended and a 10-year post-release supervision order. The imposition of post-release supervision orders for sex offenders is reflective of the need to supervise those perceived to represent a risk of reoffending upon release. In *People (DPP) v Griffin* (2011) a life sentence imposed by the trial judge for child sexual abuse offences was reduced to 15 years. In *People (DPP) v Ward* (2012) the Court of Criminal Appeal imposed a 20-year sentence in lieu of two concurrent life sentences.

In the 1990s, a number of serious sexual offence cases came before the courts for sentencing where the offender had entered a guilty plea

(O'Malley 2013, p. 551). In these cases, there was a concern regarding the imposition of a maximum sentence of life imprisonment as the guilty plea is considered a mitigating factor ordinarily resulting in a reduction in sentence (O'Malley 2013, p. 551; *People (DPP) v Jackson* 1993). This issue was addressed by the legislature through section 29(2) of the Criminal Justice Act 1999 which permits the court to impose the maximum sentence notwithstanding a guilty plea where the court is satisfied that there are such exceptional circumstances relating to the offence to warrant such a penalty. While judicial resistance to the imposition of life sentences where discretion is permitted still exists, life sentences have been upheld in cases of attempted murder, manslaughter, sexual offences and offences of child sexual abuse. A sentence of life imprisonment is more likely to be imposed in serious cases of child sexual abuse than other sexual offence cases. O'Malley (2013, p. 672) found, in a sample of 110 cases of child sexual abuse from 1999 to 2004, 5 per cent of cases resulted in a life sentence being imposed. In relation to sexual offences generally, the Court of Criminal Appeal (*People (DPP) v McC* (2003, p. 618) stated that '…the kind of circumstances that might justify [life imprisonment] would be if the rape had been accompanied by extreme violence or if, say there had been a gang rape and in addition there were previous rape convictions'. Life sentences have been upheld despite the accused entering a guilty plea although this is only permitted in 'extremely rare' cases as it may prove to be a disincentive to those who have committed serious offences when considering a guilty plea (*People (DPP) v O'Neill* 2015). Furthermore, a life sentence cannot be imposed for the purposes of preventive detention alone (*People (Attorney General) v O'Callaghan* 1966) meaning the rationale for the imposition of a discretionary life sentence must be primarily connected to the gravity of the offence and the circumstances of the offender and not solely based on factors relating to the risk of reoffending (*People (DPP) v Daniels* 2014). The offence for which a life sentence is imposed is still primarily murder, yet there is certainly evidence to suggest that there have been incremental changes both in the legislative and judicial approach rendering it possible to impose a discretionary sentence of life imprisonment for offences of violence against the person, even where mitigating factors exist.

Life Meaning Life

There are a number of countries that maintain systems of parole for life sentence prisoners but make provision for certain offences or offenders for which parole is not available (United States, Australia, Bulgaria, England and Wales, France, Hungary, Slovakia, Switzerland and Turkey) (Ghandnoosh 2017; Fitzgibbon 2016; *Vinter and Others v United Kingdom* 2013, para. 68). In addition to this, there is evidence of a trend towards the introduction of incapacitative measures across a range of jurisdictions for those categorised as dangerous (Malsch and Duker 2012). In Europe, in order 'for a life sentence to remain compatible with Article 3 of the ECHR, there must be both the prospect of release and a possibility of review' (*Vinter and Others v United Kingdom* 2013, para. 110). But continued detention of a life sentence prisoner may be justifiable on 'legitimate penological grounds' (para. 131). Outside of Europe, the United States is notable for its increasing use of 'life without parole' sentences, the imposition of lengthy minimum terms that go beyond the lifespan of the prisoner, and the reluctance of releasing authorities to grant parole to eligible life sentence prisoners (Mauer et al. 2004; Mauer and Nellis 2016; Ghandnoosh 2017). Life without parole or irreducible life sentences have resulted in difficulties in dealing with an ageing prison population and the concomitant health problems that arise (Advisory Committee on Geriatric and Seriously Ill Inmates 2005; European Ministers of Justice 2002).

Neither statute nor common law makes provision for life without parole in Ireland. Yet it is not outside the realm of possibilities that an individual may be incarcerated for the remainder of their natural lives as release is contingent on the discretion of the Minister for Justice (Minister), who is not obliged to exercise the power to release at any point. There are a number of life sentence prisoners that have served or are serving lengthy periods in prison that have the prospect of review but where the prospect of release is remote (Lally 2015b). In 2012, a life sentence prisoner died in hospital having served 36 years of a life sentence. Initially, he remained under 24-hour guard by two prison officers while receiving medical treatment for a stroke. He was only granted temporary release after he was medically declared to be in a vegetative state. Despite his medical condition, the Prison Service decided to electronically tag him during this period (Naughton 2013). His counterpart, convicted for the same crimes, remains in prison. There are others within the prison system that have served periods far in excess of the average time served by life sentence prisoners (Lally 2015b). Those serving a sentence for capital murder or murder under section 3 of the Criminal Justice Act 1990 with a minimum term of 40 years of imprisonment (less remission of 25 per cent (Rule 59(2), Prison Rules 2007: S.I. No. 252 of 2007; *Callan v Ireland* 2013) may well serve a life sentence in prison in the real sense.

Consecutive and Concurrent Sentences

A further matter arises in relation to the length of sentence where a person may be convicted of a number of murders or a number of offences including a murder. The issue in the sentencing context is whether a life sentence can or should run concurrently or consecutively with another sentence. Consecutive life sentences, by virtue of their indeterminate nature create difficulties both from a legal and administrative perspective. The matter is ordinarily left to the discretion of the court; however it is a general principle to impose concurrent sentences for offences arising out of the same incident (O'Malley 2016, pp. 110–118). Ultimately, whether the sentence is concurrent or consecutive, it must reflect the totality of the offending (*People (DPP) v McC* 2003). The matter can become complicated due to the indefinite nature of the life sentence. In *People (DPP) v Whelan* (2003) the defendant pleaded guilty to the murder of one woman and the attempted murder of another. Whelan was sentenced to a mandatory life sentence for murder and a consecutive sentence of 15 years for the attempted murder. The sentences were to run in this order. The defendant argued on appeal that the trial judge had erred in imposing an indeterminate sentence without specifying when and at what point the determinate sentence would begin. The Court of Criminal Appeal refused the appeal but reversed the order of the sentences requiring Whelan to serve the 15 years first and at the end of this term of imprisonment to begin serving the life sentence. The Court noted that it was undesirable to have a determinate sentence follow a life sentence but that there was no rule of law whereby the sentence for the primary offence must run first before the sentence of the secondary offence.

By virtue of the indeterminate nature of the life sentence it is difficult to envision how consecutive life sentences would operate at a practical level. It appears that while the courts can impose a number of life sentences, they must run concurrently rather than consecutively (*People (DPP) v Hennessy* 2010). The issue may be further complicated as a result of convictions for murders arising from incidents that are not connected. In *People (DPP) v Nash* (2015) the defendant was convicted of two murders arising from one incident in Roscommon in 1997. Nash was sentenced to two concurrent terms of life imprisonment. In 2015 Nash was convicted of an additional two murders committed in Dublin four months prior to the Roscommon murders. Nash had admitted to the Dublin murders when arrested for the Roscommon murders but withdrew his statement subsequently. At sentencing the trial judge refused to backdate the sentence to 1999 meaning that Nash, who had remained in prison since he was convicted of the Roscommon murders, began to serve two additional concurrent life sentences in 2015 (Lally 2015a). This will mean that his eligibility for release will be dictated by the start date of the 2015 life sentences, rather than those imposed in 1999. Ironically, if Nash had been convicted of all four murders in 1999 he would be serving four concurrent life sentences rather than two sets of consecutive life sentences with staggered start dates.

Children and Life Imprisonment

The availability and increased use of the life sentence for child offenders has been subject to criticism, particularly in the United States where the practice of imposing life without parole sentences on offenders under the age of 18 has been subject to a number of Supreme Court decisions (Amnesty International 2009; Nellis 2013; *Miller v Alabama* and *Jackson v Hobbs* (2012). In Ireland, the Children Act 2001 does not make specific provision for children convicted of murder meaning that it must be inferred from the general legislative provisions contained therein, particularly s. 156 which states that a child shall not be sentenced to imprisonment but may be sent to a children detention school (O'Malley 2016, pp. 279–280). On reaching the age of 18, a child convicted of an indictable offence may be transferred to a prison for the remainder of the detention period (s. 155 Children Act 2001 (as amended by s. 142 Criminal Justice Act 2006)). There are no mandatory sentences in the Children Act 2001, meaning a child convicted of murder may be sentenced to a period of detention up to and including life imprisonment (*People (DPP) v VW (a minor)* 1998; *People (DPP) v S.(A.)* 1998; O'Malley 2016, p. 280). In the *People (DPP) v G* (2005) a 15-year-old boy was convicted of the murder of a 14-year-old boy. The Central Criminal Court imposed a life sentence with the *proviso* that the Court review the sentence again ten years after it had begun. In exercising discretion the sentencing judge noted the lack of mitigating factors other than age and highlighted the danger posed by the offender. On appeal, both the appellant and the DPP agreed that while the imposition of a life sentence was permissible, the imposition of a determinate sentence was more appropriate in this case. The DPP argued that the imposition of a review period by the courts was not good sentencing policy (*People (DPP) v Finn* 2001). Despite this consensus, the Court of Criminal Appeal rejected the argument that a life sentence with the sentencing court retaining *seisin* of the case was inappropriate in this particular instance and upheld the life sentence. The matter returned to the Central Criminal Court in September 2014 for consideration and the original sentencing judge, White J., set a release date for July 2016 (O'Malley 2016, p. 281; Reid 2014).

Conclusion

The rise of the life sentence prisoner population in Irish criminal justice is undeniable. It is evident that such an increase can be attributed to a number of factors. Capital punishment effectively ceased as the *de facto* ultimate penalty by the middle of the twentieth century meaning that life imprisonment has been Ireland's ultimate penalty for some time and the only sanction for the offence of murder. A further factor has been the rise in lethal violence witnessed in the last number of decades in Ireland and its effect on the conviction rate. There are a number of offences in Ireland where the maximum penalty is life imprisonment yet in practice it is sparingly employed as a sanction where discretion exists. Nonetheless, there is evidence of a change in this position, with life sentences being imposed and upheld, particularly since the turn of the century. Ireland has not pursued the punitive policies in the United States and elsewhere in relation to the use of life without parole sentences and is reluctant to impose life imprisonment as a sanction against young offenders. These are all factors that operate to constrain the discretionary life sentence prisoner population. The mandatory nature of the life sentence for murder is the most significant influence on the life sentence prisoner population as the vast majority of life sentence prisoners have been convicted of murder. With no alternative but to impose a life sentence, the judiciary have no influence on time served in any real sense. It is highly likely that were the life sentence for murder discretionary rather than mandatory, the picture would look very different. The percentage of life sentence prisoners might reflect those of other civil law European countries that maintain significantly lower levels of life sentence prisoners as part of the overall prison population.

Notes

1. Andorra, Bosnia and Herzegovina, Croatia, Montenegro, Norway, Portugal, San Marino, Serbia and Spain are exceptions opting for the imposition of lengthy determinate sentences for the most serious offences (ranging from 21 years (Norway) to 45 years (Bosnia and Herzegovina): *Vinter and Others v United Kingdom* 2013.
2. Treason also carries a mandatory penalty of life imprisonment.
3. O'Malley, T. (2016) at 311.
4. Criminal Justice Act 1990, ss. 2 and 3.
5. Criminal Law (Rape) Act 1981, s. 2; rape under section 4, Criminal Law (Rape) (Amendment) Act 1990, s. 4; and aggravated sexual assault, Criminal Law (Rape) (Amendment) Act 1990, s. 3.
6. Criminal Law (Sexual Offences) Act 2006, s. 2, amended by Criminal Law (Sexual Offences) Amendment Act 2007.
7. Punishment of Incest Act 1908, ss. 1 and 2, amended by Criminal Law Amendment Act 1935; Criminal Law (Incest Proceedings) Act 1995; Criminal Law (Sexual Offences) Act 2017.

8. Criminal Damage Act 1991, s. 2.
9. Non-Fatal Offences Against the Person Act 1997, s. 15.
10. Criminal Justice (Theft and Fraud Offences) Act 2001, s. 14.
11. Non-Fatal Offences Against the Person Act 1997, ss. 6 and 8.
12. Criminal Justice Act 1984, s. 14; Offences Against the State (Amendment) Act 1998, s. 15; Criminal Justice Act 2006, s. 15.
13. Misuse of Drugs Act 1977, s. 15 as amended by Misuse of Drugs Act 1984, s. 6(3)(b).

References

Advisory Committee on Geriatric and Seriously Ill Inmates. (2005). *Report*. Harrisburg: Joint State Government Commission of the General Assembly of the Commonwealth of Pennsylvania.

Allen, F. (1981). *The decline of the rehabilitative ideal*. New Haven: Yale University Press.

American Civil Liberties Union. (2013). *A living death: Life without parole for non-violent offences*. New York: American Civil Liberties Union Foundation.

Amnesty International. (2009). *Death sentences and executions*. London: Amnesty International Publications.

Amnesty International and Human Rights Watch. (2005). *The rest of their lives: Life without parole for child offenders in the United States*. New York: Human Rights Watch.

Appleton, C., & Grøver, B. (2007). The pros and cons of life without parole. *British Journal of Criminology, 47*(4), 597–615.

Appleton, C., & van Zyl Smit, D. (2016). The paradox of reform: Life imprisonment in England and Wales. In D. van Zyl Smit & C. Appleton (Eds.), *Life imprisonment and human rights* (pp. 217–240). Oxford: Hart.

Australian Bureau of Statistics. (2013). *Prisoners in Australia*. Canberra: Australian Bureau of Statistics.

Bedau, H. A. (1989). Imprisonment vs. death: Does avoiding Schwarzchild's paradox lead to Sheleff's dilemma? *Albany Law Review, 54*(3/4), 481–495.

Central Statistics Office. (2013). *Homicide offences*. Central Statistics Office. Retrieved from http://www.cso.ie/Quicktables/GetQuickTables.aspx?FileName=cja01c1.asp&TableName=Homicide+Offences&StatisticalProduct=DB_CJ

Council of Europe. (2003). *Recommendation 22 on conditional release (parole)*. Strasbourg: Council of Europe.

Council of Europe. (2017). *Annual penal statistics: SPACE 1-Prison populations, survey 2015*. Strasbourg: Council of Europe.
Courts Service. (2001–2015). *Annual reports*. Dublin: Courts Service.
Coyle, A. (2004). Replacing the death penalty: The vexed issue of alternative sanctions. In P. Hodgkinson & W. A. Schabas (Eds.), *Capital punishment: Strategies for abolition*. Cambridge: Cambridge University Press.
Department of Justice. (1962). *Memo from government – Proposed abolition of death penalty in certain cases*. National Archives/D/Justice 21/nlg/1962.
Director of Public Prosecutions. (2015). *Annual reports*. Dublin: Office of the Director of Public Prosecutions.
Doyle, D., & O'Donnell, I. (2012). The death penalty in post-independence Ireland. *Journal of Legal History, 33*(1), 65–91.
European Committee for the Prevention of Torture and Inhuman or Degrading Treatment or Punishment (CPT). (2007). *Actual/real life sentences*. Strasbourg: CPT.
European Ministers of Justice. (2002). *Resolution no. 2 on the implementation of long-term sentences*. Moscow: 24th Conference of European Ministers of Justice, Penological Information Bulletin Nos. 23 and 24, December.
Feeley, M., & Simon, J. (1992). The new penology: Notes on the emerging strategy of corrections and its implications. *Criminology, 30*(4), 449–474.
Fitzgibbon, K. (2016). Minimum sentencing for murder in England and Wales: A critical examination 10 years after the Criminal Justice Act 2003. *British Journal of Criminology, 18*(1), 47–67.
Garland, D. (2001). *The culture of control: Crime and social order in contemporary society*. Oxford: Oxford University Press.
Ghandnoosh, N. (2017). *Delaying a second chance: The declining prospects for parole on life sentences*. Washington, DC: Sentencing Project.
Harcourt, B. E. (2011). An institutionalization effect: The impact of mental hospitalization and imprisonment on homicide in the United States, 1934–2001. *The Journal of Legal Studies, 40*(1), 39–83.
Hodgkinson, P., Kandelia, S., & Gyllensten, L. (2008). Capital punishment: A review and critique of abolition strategies. In J. Yorke (Ed.), *Against the death penalty: International initiatives and implications* (pp. 249–280). Farnham: Ashgate.
Hood, R. (2001). Capital punishment: A global perspective. *Punishment and Society, 3*(3), 331–354.
Hood, R., & Hoyle, C. (2015). *The death penalty: A worldwide perspective*. Oxford: Oxford University Press.

Lally, C. (2015a, April 21). Mark Nash: Killer murdered four people in just four months. *Irish Times*, p. 6.

Lally, C. (2015b, March 29). Dwyer likely to be "new Malcolm Macarthur" and serve decades in jail. *Irish Times*. Retrieved from https://www.irishtimes.com/news/crime-and-law/dwyer-likely-to-be-new-malcolm-macarthur-and-serve-decades-in-jail-1.2157355

Lappi-Seppälä, T. (2016). Life imprisonment and related institutions in the Nordic countries. In D. van Zyl Smit & C. Appleton (Eds.), *Life imprisonment and human rights* (pp. 461–505). Oxford: Hart.

Law Reform Commission. (2013). *Report on mandatory sentences*. Dublin: Law Reform Commission.

Malsch, M., & Duker, M. (2012). *Incapacitation: Trends and new perspectives*. Farnham: Ashgate.

Mauer, M., & Nellis, A. (2016). The impact of life imprisonment on criminal justice reform in the United States. In D. van Zyl Smit & C. Appleton (Eds.), *Life imprisonment and human rights* (pp. 23–42). Oxford: Hart.

Mauer, M., King, R. S., & Young, M. C. (2004). *The meaning of 'life': Long prison sentences in context*. Washington, DC: The Sentencing Project.

Morris, T., & Blom-Cooper, L. (2011). *Fine lines and distinctions: Murder, manslaughter and the unlawful taking of human life*. Hook: Waterside Press.

Naughton, G. (2013, July 5). Killer died from hospital infection: Coroner's Court told Geoffrey Evans died because of sepsis due to pneumonia. *Irish Times*, p. 7.

Nelken, D. (2010). *Comparative criminal justice*. London: Sage.

Nellis, A. (2013). *Life goes on: The historic rise in life sentences in America*. Washington, DC: The Sentencing Project.

Newcomen, N. (2005). Managing the penal consequences of replacing the death penalty in Europe. In N. Browne & S. Kandelia (Eds.), *Managing effective alternatives to capital punishment, Centre for capital punishment studies occasional paper series volume three – Special edition*. London: Centre for Capital Punishment Studies.

O'Donnell, I. (2004). Interpreting penal change: A research note. *International Journal of Policy and Practice, 4*(2), 199–206.

O'Donnell, I. (2005). Crime and justice in the Republic of Ireland. *European Journal of Criminology, 2*(1), 99–131.

O'Malley, T. (1995). Sentencing murderers: The case for relocating discretion. *Irish Criminal Law Journal, 5*(1), 31–66.

O'Malley, T. (2010). Ireland. In N. Padfield, D. van Zyl Smit, & F. Dünkel (Eds.), *Release from prison: European policy and practice* (pp. 237–265). Devon: Willan.

O'Malley, T. (2013). *Sexual offences*. Dublin: Thomson Round Hall.
O'Malley, T. (2016). *Sentencing law and practice*. Dublin: Thomson Round Hall.
Penal Reform International. (2007). *Penal reform briefing No.1: Alternatives to the death penalty (1)*. Penal Reform International. Retrieved from https://www.penalreform.org/resource/penal-reform-briefing-no1-alternatives-death-penalty
Pinto de Albuquerque, P. (2015). *Life imprisonment and the European right to hope. European Court of Human Rights*. Milan: Associazone Italiana dei Constituzionalista.
Pratt, J., Brown, D., Brown, M., Wallsworth, S., & Morrison, W. (Eds.). (2005). *The new punitiveness: Trends, theories and perspectives*. Devon: Willan.
Prison Service. (2001–2016). *Annual reports*. Dublin/Longford: Irish Prison Service.
Reid, N. (2014, September 12). Killer jailed for life in 2004 to be free in two years. *Irish Times*, p. 6.
Sheleff, L. (1987). *Ultimate penalties: Capital punishment, life imprisonment, physical torture*. Columbus: Ohio State University Press.
Snacken, S. (2010). Resisting punitiveness in Europe? *Theoretical Criminology, 14*(3), 273–292.
Stokes, R. (2008). A fate worse than death? The problems with life imprisonment as an alternative to the death penalty. In J. Yorke (Ed.), *Against the death penalty: International initiatives and implications* (pp. 281–302). Farnham: Ashgate.
Tonry, M. (2007). Determinants of penal policies. *Crime and Justice: Crime, Punishment, and Politics in a Comparative Perspective, 36*(1), 1–48.
United Nations. (1994). *Life imprisonment*. Vienna: United Nations Crime Prevention and Criminal Justice Branch.
Van Hattum, W., & Meijer, S. (2016). An administrative procedure for life prisoners: Law and practice of royal pardon in the Netherlands. In D. van Zyl Smit & C. Appleton (Eds.), *Life imprisonment and human rights* (pp. 141–166). Oxford: Hart.
van Zyl Smit, D. (2001). Abolishing life imprisonment? *Punishment and Society, 3*(2), 299–306.
van Zyl Smit, D., & Appleton, C. (2016). *Life imprisonment and human rights*. Oxford: Hart.
van Zyl Smit, D., & Appleton, C. (2017, March 15). Life imprisonment worldwide webinar. University of Nottingham.

Table of Legal Instruments

Children Act 2001.
Criminal Damage Act 1991.
Criminal Justice Act 1964.
Criminal Justice Act 1984.
Criminal Justice Act 1990.
Criminal Justice Act 1999.
Criminal Justice Act 2006.
Criminal Justice (Theft and Fraud Offences) Act 2001.
Criminal Law Amendment Act 1935.
Criminal Law (Rape) Act 1981.
Criminal Law (Rape) (Amendment) Act 1990.
Criminal Law (Sexual Offences) Act 2006.
Criminal Law (Sexual Offences) Amendment Act 2007.
Criminal Law (Incest Proceedings) Act 1995.
Criminal Law (Sexual Offences) Act 2017.
Misuse of Drugs Act 1977.
Misuse of Drugs Act 1984.
Non-Fatal Offences Against the Person Act 1997.
Offences Against the State (Amendment) Act 1998.
Punishment of Incest Act 1908.
Prison Rules 2007: S.I. No. 252 of 2007.

Table of Cases

European Court of Human Rights

Vinter and Others v. United Kingdom Application Nos 66069/09, 3896/10, 130/10, Merits, 9 July 2013.

Ireland

Application of McLoughlin [1970] IR 197.
Callan v Ireland [2013] IESC 35.
Lynch and Whelan v Minister for Justice [2012] 1 IR 1.

People (Attorney General) v O'Callaghan [1966] IR 501.
People (Attorney General) v Poyning [1972] IR 408.
People (DPP) v Conroy (No.2) [1989] ILRM 139.
People (DPP) v Daniels [2014] IESC 64.
People (DPP) v Finn [2001] 2 IR 25.
People (DPP) v G [2005] IECCA 75.
People (DPP) v Griffin [2011] IECCA 62.
People (DPP) v Hennessy, unreported, Court of Criminal Appeal, 29 October 2010.
People (DPP) v Jackson, unreported, Court of Criminal Appeal, 26 April 1993.
People (DPP) v K.(G.) [2008] IECCA 110.
People (DPP) v McC [2003]
People (DPP) v McC [2008] 2 IR 92.
People (DPP) v Nash (Mark) (*Irish Times*, April 20, 2015)
People (DPP) v O'Neill [2015] IECA 327.
People (DPP) v Piotrowski (2014) IECCA 17.
People (DPP) v S.(A.) unreported, Court of Criminal Appeal, 27 March 1998.
People (DPP) v S.(P.) [2009] IECCA 1.
People (DPP) v VW (a minor), unreported, Court of Criminal Appeal, 23 March 1998.
People (DPP) v Ward, unreported, Court of Criminal Appeal, 16 January 2012.
People (DPP) v Whelan [2003] 4 IR 355.
State (Healy) v Donoghue [1976] IR 325.

USA

Miller v Alabama and *Jackson v Hobbs* (2012) 567 U.S. 460.

Table of Parliamentary Debates

205 *Dáil Debates* Cols. 323–4: Charles Haughey, 24 October 1963.
Dáil Question No. 81: Frances Fitzgerald, 8 November 2016.
Dáil Question No. 82: Frances Fitzgerald, 8 November 2016.
Dáil Question No. 112: Frances Fitzgerald, 24 January 2017.

3

The Cycle of Life

It doesn't really matter too much if it's the first review, second review, because they're not going to be released anyway.
Parole Board member 09

Introduction

There are a number of different stages to a life sentence. The first stage runs from committal to the point at which a life sentence prisoner becomes eligible for release. Normative, legal and operational considerations preclude the detention of offenders for the duration of their lives and as a result, most countries have a mechanism in place imposing a minimum term that must be served by a life sentence prisoner prior to becoming eligible for release, although the practice and the term varies cross-jurisdictionally. The point at which this temporal limit is set clearly impacts on the issue of time served. The second stage revolves around the process that determines the release or further detention of a life sentence prisoner. There are a diverse range of practices evident across different countries with decisions usually being made by either a judicial or administrative body. There has been a drive to formalise parole decision-making

D. Griffin, *Killing Time*, https://doi.org/10.1007/978-3-319-72667-0_3

in many Western jurisdictions and commonalities can be identified across release processes in terms of: the independence of the decision-making body; the criteria applied in the process; the available procedural rights; the importance of public protection; and victim input. If the determination at the first review is to further detain a life sentence prisoner, they will be eligible for further review following the passage of a period of time served in prison, thus beginning a cycle the duration of which will be country and case specific. The structure of this process and the method of determination has significant implications for the length of time a life sentence prisoner will be expected to serve. The third stage, release from prison, does not bring the sentence to an end, rather the sentence continues albeit in the community. A life sentence prisoner will remain under supervision in the community and must comply with the conditions of his release for the remainder of his life. Failure to do so could result in being returned to prison. This, in some way, resolves the ambiguity of the terms 'life sentence' and 'life imprisonment'. Those recalled to prison will continue to serve their life sentence on the inside with the offender re-entering the cycle of review in the hope of release again at a later point.

In Ireland, a life sentence prisoner serves seven years before becoming eligible for the review process. That process is informal and discretionary in nature, with decision-making operating in the political realm. The lack of discretion in relation to the mandatory life sentence for murder at sentencing is in stark contrast to the wide discretion afforded those responsible for release. Due to the informal nature of the process, individual decision-makers can influence proceedings and outcomes to a great extent. Decisions on release are not taken in isolation but are reliant upon prior decisions and judgements made at earlier stages of the process as well as the policy framing those decisions (Padfield et al. 2000, p. 33). The review process begins with a preparatory phase involving the referral and acceptance of participation, the assembling of reports on the life sentence prisoner and the conducting of an interview. This is followed by a decision-making phase based on the recommendation of the Parole Board and the decision of the Minister for Justice (Minister). A life sentence prisoner released back into the community may be recalled to prison for the breach of a condition of their release and, similar to the process of release, the system of recall is vague and discretionary. This chapter will examine the legal form and practice governing the release (and recall) of life sentence prisoners to expound on the manner by which the release process operates and its impact on life imprisonment and time served.

Parole in Ireland

It is somewhat anomalous to talk in terms of a 'parole' process in Ireland, as parole is not a legal concept. The release decision is a function of the Minister's power of temporary release contained in the Criminal Justice Act 1960 (s. 2) (as amended by the Criminal Justice (Temporary Release of Prisoners) Act 2003). Temporary release is a statutory power and does not constitute an exercise of remission or commutation of sentence (as provided for by Article 13.6 of the Constitution and conferred on the government under s. 23 of the Criminal Justice Act 1951). This power was used up until 1964 to commute the death penalty to penal servitude for life (O'Malley 2016, p. 623). Ireland also has a system of standard remission whereby those serving determinate sentences earn a reduction of up to one third of their sentence (the practice is usually 25 per cent: Rule 59, Prison Rules 2007; Prisons Act 2007, s. 35). Legally, and unlike temporary release, the practice of remission may be viewed as an entitlement (O'Malley 2011, p. 21). Standard remission is not applicable to those serving life sentences. Common examples of the use of temporary release include releasing a prisoner to receive medical attention at a hospital, allowing a prisoner attend a family occasion or release over the Christmas period. It is also a useful management tool in dealing with prison overcrowding (O'Donnell 2004). In 2016, there were 329 prisoners on temporary release (with a total 3716 persons in custody) (Prison Service 2016, p. 26). When the temporary release provisions were first being discussed by the *Oireachtas* (Irish parliament), the intention of the legislature was to provide a means of releasing prisoners for short periods (183 *Dáil Debates* Cols.559–560: Oscar Traynor, 28 June 1960). Temporary release has since become the mechanism for releasing life sentence prisoners on a full-time basis. Release is entirely at the discretion of the Minister and the process that leads to the decision of the Minister is largely a creature of policy and practice and not akin to a legal procedure. It may change at any time if the Minister so decides. The current process has existed since the establishment of the Parole Board in 2001, but its origins lie in the practices developed from the 1960s onward.

The Origins of the Process

An analysis of the history of the parole process and current release practice in Ireland is indicative of stagnation rather than change. Up until 1989, 'prison reviews' were conducted of life sentence prisoners at the institution where the offender was held. These 'prison reviews' were attended by the governor, a Department of Justice (Department) representative, prison staff, welfare chaplain, teachers, a medical officer and a psychiatrist where appropriate (393 *Dáil Debates* Col. 2624: Ray Burke, 01 December 1989). The recommendations arising from this review regarding release or detention were subsequently sent to the Minister for decision. In 1989, the Sentence Review Group was established by the then Minister, Ray Burke, to review life sentences and those serving more than seven years in prison. In announcing its establishment Ray Burke noted that he had received 'a substantial volume of representations' from life sentence prisoners, as well as 'public representatives, prominent churchmen and others' who were pressing for a review of the system (393 *Dáil Debates* Col. 2624: Ray Burke, 01 December 1989). The Sentence Review Group's function was to 'advise [the Minister] on the discharge of [her] existing statutory powers' (393 *Dáil Debates* Col. 2625, Ray Burke 01 December 1989). This followed from the recommendation of the Committee of Inquiry into the Penal System (Whitaker Committee) to establish a Sentence Review Committee (1985, paras. 6.9 and 7.12). The Minister appointed the primary author of the report, T.K. Whitaker (an economist and senior civil servant), as Chairperson (393 *Dáil Debates* Col. 2624: Ray Burke, 01 December 1989). Speaking of his appointment, he stated:

> It was the first evidence that there was going to be any notice taken of our report on the Penal System. So I said 'I can't balk at doing this job'. It was very remote from my ordinary experience and application. (Interview with T.K. Whitaker, 8 October 2008)

The Sentence Review Group was created to formalise the process surrounding the release of long-term and life sentence prisoners (393 *Dáil Debates* Cols. 2624–5: Ray Burke, 01 December 1989). The Minister stated that the establishment of the Sentence Review Group would bring our procedures of release in line with other Western democracies. In fact, parole authorities in neighbouring jurisdictions were being disaggregated, disbanded or radically reformed around this time (Bottomley 1990). The Sentence Review Group was tasked with advising the Minister having considered, amongst other factors, whether releasing an offender would constitute a threat to the community (393 *Dáil Debates* Cols. 2624–5: Ray Burke, 01 December 1989). In reality, the process was informal, with members of the group meeting at the prison to review the prisoner and make recommendations following a discussion of written reports and an interview. In terms of procedure, there appears to have been little to distinguish the process from the 'prison reviews'. The Minister remarked that the purpose of establishing this procedure was that a person serving lengthy sentences 'should have the opportunity of having his case looked at by a separate body' (393 *Dáil Debates* Cols. 2626: Ray Burke, 01 December 1989). Yet, there was little to indicate that the Sentence Review Group was an independent body, with members being appointed by the Minister. One member took a cynical view of the Group's limited influence on ministerial decision-making.

> The idea that these recommendations are made in the interests of anyone except politicians is living in cuckoo land. They're going to do what suits them. (SRG1)

T.K. Whitaker also referenced the difficulties that arose in ensuring that a recommendation was accepted by the Minister.

> Even though the Minister does represent the government, it's possible that Ministers could, as one of them was, be influenced too much by the *Garda* (police) view. And somebody has to have the guts, like I had fortunately, to go and see him and tell him, 'we are going public', unless he made a decision. (Interview with T.K. Whitaker, 8 October 2008).

Thus, what appears to have transpired through the establishment of the Sentence Review Group was a process with a veneer of officialdom through the adoption of a title, while maintaining a discretionary and political approach to decision-making.

In 2001, an 'Interim Parole Board' replaced the Sentence Review Group but again this was little more than a change in nomenclature with the Parole Board remaining a non-statutory body making recommendations to the Minister for final decision (528 *Dáil Debates* Col. 311: John O'Donoghue, 12 December 2000). The establishment of the Parole Board followed a public scandal where a man serving a life sentence for murder killed an elderly woman while on temporary release (Olden 2001; 528 *Dáil Debates* Col. 311: John O'Donoghue, 12 December 2000). A report of the incident highlighted a number of flaws in the process describing the inconsistency in the records in relation to decision-making as 'disturbing' and recommended that the procedures for the management of life sentence prisoners be tightened (Olden 2001, pp. 4–5 and 15). The establishment of the Parole Board can also be connected to a decision of the Supreme Court to reject the practice that had developed amongst trial judges where a review element was being included when the sentence was being imposed (*People (DPP) v Finn* 2001). At around the same time, public controversy resulting from political and judicial intervention to release Philip Sheedy, an offender serving a four-year sentence released early from prison, was seen to compromise the administration of justice (530 *Dáil Debates* Cols. 199–200: John O'Donoghue, 07 February 2001). These incidents served as a catalyst in placing the process of parole-type release into the public arena in a manner that had not occurred previously and contributed to the movement towards establishing the Parole Board. The then Minister, John O'Donoghue, stated that the purpose of setting up the administrative body was to draw on its operational experience prior to placing it on a statutory footing (543(2)

Dáil Debates Col. 700: John O'Donoghue, 6 November 2001). The Parole Board has been acting in an 'interim' capacity ever since, although the word 'interim' was dropped from the title by the time the Parole Board's first annual report was published. Placing the Parole Board on a statutory footing has been kept under review by successive governments. The Parole Bill 2016, an opposition bill with government support, is currently passing through the *Oireachtas* and proposes to place the Parole Board on a statutory footing (see Chap. 7).

Parole in Practice

On determining that a life sentence prisoner is eligible for review the offender is invited to participate in the parole process. During the period 2010 to 2012, 93.8 per cent of life sentence prisoners accepted an invitation to participate compared with 66.4 per cent of determinate sentence prisoners (correspondence with Parole Board, 9 April 2013). The Parole Board reviews determinate sentenced prisoners that have been sentenced to eight years or more (at the half-way point of their sentence). Those sentenced to 14 years or more have their sentence reviewed at the 7 year point (Parole Board 2003, p. 6). The lower rate of participation by determinate sentence prisoners may be explained through the operation of standard remission. Release through standard remission is automatic and unconditional meaning that the offender is not subject to supervision post-release. As remission is not applicable to life sentences, the parole process is the only viable option for release. Thus, life sentence prisoners have a strong incentive to accept an invitation to participate.

The Minimum Term

It is common practice that a life sentence prisoner is required to serve a minimum term prior to becoming eligible for release. A minimum term is often set in statute or by the sentencing court in each jurisdiction. There is little consistency in relation to temporal limits for life sentences with terms across Europe ranging from 7 years (Ireland) to

30 years (Estonia and Moldova) (*Vinter and Others v United Kingdom* 2013). Additional terms may be imposed for recidivists (Belgium: Snacken et al. 2010, p. 82) or where aggravating factors exist (New Zealand: Sentencing Act 2002, s. 104). Many of the newer members states of the European Union that abolished capital punishment more recently have adopted high minimum terms (Latvia, Poland, Albania: 25 years) while longstanding members' minimum terms tend to be at the lower range (Austria, 12 years; Germany, 15 years; Sweden, 10 years). The greatest amount of variety is perhaps to be found in England and Wales with the court imposing a tariff or minimum term representing the punitive element of the sentence with further detention on completion of the tariff being based on public protection considerations as determined through the parole process (Padfield 2016).

The Irish system has an extraordinarily low minimum term of seven years by comparison with any European or common law jurisdiction. This is a policy decision rather than a statutory requirement, which appears to have been established by former Minister Ray Burke when announcing the creation of the Sentence Review Group in 1989 (393 *Dáil Debates* Col. 2624: Ray Burke, 01 December 1989). There is no legal barrier to increasing or decreasing this minimum term of eligibility and various Ministers have stated that they will not consider release until much later than the minimum of seven years. Public statements by decision-makers indicate that anything from 10 to 20 years is the minimum a life sentence prisoner can expect to serve prior to being considered for release in reality (Parole Board 2002, p. 2; Lally 2006). The Parole Board have stated that a life sentence prisoner could get 'early parole' after 13 years but many would not be recommended for release until later due to the gravity of the offence and the risk of reoffending (Parole Board 2012, p. 5). With life sentence prisoners serving 22 years in 2016 prior to release, the minimum term of seven years and the occasional statements by decision-makers in this regard appear to be well below the reality of release. This disjoint creates confusion for those subject to the process. It also creates a lack of certainty in relation to minimum terms, placing Ireland somewhat out of step with European policy and practice (Council of Europe 2003a: Explanatory Memorandum para. 5).

The seven-year term does mark the beginning of what will become a lengthy review cycle and may be the first engagement by the life sentence prisoner with any form of sentence management (European Committee for the Prevention of Torture (CPT) 2011, p. 32; Milner 2010, p. 74). A life sentence prisoner is reviewed no more than three years after the previous review. Adopting the perspective that the minimum term is the beginning of a review cycle rather than the end of the term of imprisonment is significant. For example, if there is a legislative presumption that all life sentence prisoners will be released having reached a specified minimum term (save in exceptional cases say where the offender exhibits a risk of reoffending) then this should result in a relatively consistent approach to release. The minimum term is treated as the default point of release instead of the beginning of a review process. In many US states there are presumptive parole policies for some incarcerated offenders whereby the offender is released unless the Parole Board has cause to prolong their detention (Ghandnoosh 2017, p. 31). If the policy is to treat the minimum term as the start of the review process, as is the case in Ireland, then length of time served becomes more dependent on the discretion of the decision-makers rather than the rules. This means that time served can vary to the extent witnessed in this jurisdiction over the last number of decades.

The Review Process

The more formal parole has become, the greater the emphasis that has been placed upon procedural rules, the rights of the offender and the mechanisms for challenging the process. The Council of Europe (2003b, paras. 32–36) and the European Court of Human Rights (ECtHR) have been active in providing guidance on procedural safeguards for indeterminate sentences (*Weeks v United Kingdom* 1987; *Stafford v United Kingdom* 2002). England and Wales, and its Parole Board, has faced the greatest amount of scrutiny in this regard through the decisions of the ECtHR resulting in increased procedural safeguards for those subject to the process (Appleton and van Zyl Smit 2016, pp. 226–230). In the United States, parole processes still retain a level of informality and decision-making continues to be influenced by the political realm (Ghandnoosh 2017; Rhine et al. 2017; Ruhland et al. 2017). There are limited legal protections or enforceable rights available to those subject to the process in Ireland. The executive power of temporary release in Ireland is a privilege, not a right (*Ryan v Governor of Limerick Prison* 1988, p. 200) and the Minister has wide discretion in exercising the power of release (*Murray v Ireland* 1991, p. 472). Issues in relation to legal procedure and the formalisation of the process, such as an offender's right to legal representation, have arisen without success in judicial review proceedings (*Barry v Sentence Review Group* 2001). As a result, the procedural rights afforded to those subject to the process are scant.

The review process begins with the secretariat of the Parole Board assembling a review dossier which ordinarily includes a number of reports from: *An Garda Síochána*; the Prison Governor; the Prison Review Committee; the Probation Service; and the Prison Psychology Service. A report from a psychiatrist, a Home Circumstance Report from the Probation Service and letters from a victim or victims' family member may also be included. This review dossier is sent to all Parole Board members (members) for reading prior to the meeting at which a recommendation will be made. A copy of the report is also disclosed to the offender under review. Parole decision-makers emphasised the importance of the review dossier in their deliberations and were particularly influenced by any risk assessments available to them through the Probation Service and Prison Psychology Service (see Chap. 4). It is difficult to determine the impact of the plethora of reports available to decision-makers and what is being inferred from them. In particular, the strength of the information on risk may be diluted in the context of the vast amounts of other information presented to members and ministers for the purpose of decision-making. The discretionary nature of the process allows for a very broad interpretation and application of the available information by decision-makers.

Offender Input

The level of offender input varies significantly across jurisdictions. The Council of Europe (2003b, s. 32) states that offenders under consideration for the granting of release should have 'the right to be heard in person and to be assisted according to the law'. Where a court is determining the issue of release, as is the case in many European countries, an offender is often entitled to provide input orally, in writing or both and can be represented legally. Where the decision is by an administrative body, such as a parole board, as is the case in England and Wales, prisoners serving indeterminate sentences are often afforded a hearing before the parole authority when release is being considered (*Osborn v Parole Board* 2013). Offender input in Ireland is limited primarily to an interview conducted by two members of the Parole Board at the institution at which the offender is serving his sentence. The interview is described as 'informal' in nature and not akin to an oral hearing (Parole Board 2002, p. 9). An offender will not necessarily be interviewed for each review carried out by the Parole Board but will ordinarily be interviewed for the first review and occasionally thereafter where it is deemed appropriate. Legal representation is not permitted at the interview. When the interview is complete a written report of the interview is sent to the prisoner who must acknowledge receipt of it and may comment on the report, which is then included in the review dossier for members. In addition to this, members described providing an informal oral report on the interview at subsequent Parole Board meetings and this was deemed to be influential on recommendations made at the meeting.

> But the position is that the Board members who have interviewed the prisoner who is subject to review, they are in the best position to make recommendations. (PB05)

> I'm the person who has had the benefit of the interview, and obviously the person who does the interview has a greater insight because in addition to reading the documents they have spoken to the person. (PB08)

From the offender's perspective, the interview represents a limited opportunity to input into the decision-making process. The information given to offenders does not provide significant detail surrounding the purpose of the interview other than allowing the individual to discuss the relevant issues arising from their case (Parole Board 2002, Appendix A, V, p. 20; 2013, pp. 5–6). The scope for inquiry appears to be quite broad.

> When conducting the interview their object is to … try to ascertain, in as easy a manner as is possible, the prisoner's reaction to the crime, their abhorrence of it, their remorse for it and on this they can form an assessment of his or her intention to rehabilitate and become a normal member of society if and when released. (Parole Board 2007, p. 4)

Members were asked to indicate what they viewed as the primary purpose of the interview and while the question was specific, for members, the interview served a range of purposes. Members frequently cited the significance of having 'face-to-face' contact with the offender ('…to see the person behind the reports' PB03 (10 members)) as well as the importance of focusing on past sentence management and engagement (10 members). Members believed that the interview also facilitated a range of purposes including: examining the circumstances of, and attitude to the offence (6); exploring the contents of the review dossier (5); empowering and engaging the offender with the parole process (5); focusing on future sentence management (5); making the offender comfortable (4); addressing the release plan (4); assessing the risk level (3); identifying the attitude towards the victim(s) (2); and gauging remorse (1).

Focusing on issues surrounding past and future sentence management and addressing the contents of the review dossier is relevant subject matter to address in an interview context. Revisiting the circumstances and the attitude to the offence, using the interview to identify the risk posed and gauging the offender's level of empathy towards the victim would appear to be outside of what is appropriate content or even possible in a brief interview (interviews last from 30 minutes to an hour and 30 minutes). This is perhaps even more concerning, given the importance placed by many members on the interview and the emphasis on the 'face-to-face' encounter in subsequent decision-making at the Parole Board meeting. One member inadvertently highlighted the danger of positioning a brief, unstructured, personal interaction at the centre of a group decision-making process.

> The written dossier just gives you pages of facts, you know, your impression of me or my impression of you, you know, it tells a thousand stories I think insofar as how did we find the person, were they cold, were they willing to

> engage, were they quite monosyllabic you know, yes, no answers, were there things they just clammed up on? So you're trying to sort of see what makes this person tick, what are the issues there? (PB06)

There is potential here for interviewers to override/ignore relevant factors in the review dossier based on a compelling/poor interview impression. Interactions of this kind are subjective experiences and it is difficult to determine what weight, if any, should be given to interview impressions particularly when available data suggests that face-to-face contact may impair rather than improve judgement (Ruback and Hopper 1986; Serin 2011; Ten Brinke et al. 2012). Further, the interviewee is not given any specific direction as to the purpose of the interview or what is expected. Concerns relating to the lack of training for interviewers and lack of clarity surrounding the purpose of the interview process were identified by a number of members.

> My concern is that there could be a re-hashing of the trial at the interview process, a re-hashing of the offence, and unnecessarily so, and that really rather than looking into the past, you know, the interview board should be looking into the future, how is the prisoner going to cope with the future rather than how he or she has reacted in the past. (PB05)

> There have also [been instances] where there would have been questions asked which would have made me deeply uncomfortable, as to the appropriateness of the questions. I think that's inevitable, if you're given no training with interview techniques, you're given no training as to what's appropriate to ask during an interview, there are no guidelines as to what should or shouldn't be asked in an interview and you're just basically sent in to interview a prisoner. (PB02)

In particular revisiting the offence in the manner described would seem to conflict with what has been articulated by the courts on the role of the Parole Board:

> The Board is not there to determine the innocence or guilt of the applicant, much less to second-guess the sentence imposed by the court. To attempt to do so would be to usurp the functions which reside elsewhere under our Constitution. (McMahon J in *Grogan v Parole Board* 2008, p. 8)

It is interesting to note that members also identified the interview process as empowering for the offender, although one member was sceptical of this.

> If I were a prisoner and I had seen whatever wing I'm on and whatever cell and the yard, to be going into a huge boardroom where you sink into the carpet and you've three people on the other side of the table, I wouldn't feel that I was an equal participant in that interview. (PB02)

Given the lack of structure, the absence of legal representation or a person of support present, the free-handed approach in terms of questions and subject matter, it appears to have all the features of a process that is disempowering for offenders.

Victim Input

Parole processes have become more inclusive of victims when making a determination about release. This is in line with the development of a victims' rights discourse and the greater facilitation of victim participation in, and support by, criminal justice systems over the last number of decades. There is little by way of settled practice in terms of victim involvement in parole decision-making. Victims' rights can include the right to information, the right to be heard and the right to be present at parole hearings (Herman and Wasserman 2001, p. 433). The provision of information to victims or their families is common, but the type of information made available varies. Some countries limit disclosure to the release date while others provide personal information on the offender, details of the parole hearing and reasons for the decision (Roberts 2009). Victim input, in the form of a written or oral statement presented to the decision-making body, is a developing theme (Padfield and Roberts 2010). It appears more frequently in common than civil law jurisdictions and is perhaps indicative of the vulnerability of the political process to the victim movement and the potential for politicians to harness victims' needs and concerns in the pursuit of punitivism (Ashworth 2000). In the United States, 97.5 per cent of releasing authorities permit victim input and such input was highly ranked by parole decision-makers when considering release (Ruhland et al. 2017, p. 26). In England and Wales, a victim personal statement can be presented to the Parole Board orally or in writing (Parole Board England and Wales 2011). In Canada, victims are permitted to present prepared statements at parole hearings (Safe Streets and Communities Act, Bill C-10). Research on the impact of written and oral submissions by victims on the parole decision-making process is limited but there does appear to be a correlation between victim participation and parole denials (Morgan and Smith 2005; Parsonage et al. 1994; Polowek 2005).

The approach to victim input is more cautious in Europe, with the 'Victims' Directive' stating that a victim has a right to be notified of the release of an offender upon request (European Parliament 2012, Article 6.5 and 6.6). Civil law European countries with an apolitical approach to parole through court-like structures operate restraint on victim input. In Belgium the political system came under intense pressure to facilitate victim involvement following the arrest, in 1996, of child rapist and serial killer Marc Dutroux. Parliament successfully resisted public and political calls for victim input on decision-making and the inclusion of an expert member on victim issues on the Parole Commission (Snacken et al. 2010, pp. 81–3; Snacken 2007, pp. 186–97). Countries such as Finland and Sweden do not permit victim involvement (Schartmueller 2014; Lappi-Seppälä 2013). As Zedner (1997, p. 607) notes adopting an unstructured and unfettered approach to victim input may service punitivism over the reparative and restorative goals of the victims' rights movement. Seen in this light, it is not surprising that victim participation in the parole process is more evident in criminal justice systems more vulnerable to populist punitiveness.

Ireland fits within the European model of victim input, albeit in a characteristically informal fashion. The Victims' Charter states that the Victim Liaison Officer of the Irish Prison Service will inform the victim of the release of a prisoner, where a victim or family member requests such information (Department of Justice and Equality 2010). The Charter also states that a victim, or a family member of a victim who has died as a result of a crime, may make a submission to the Parole Board. The Criminal Justice (Victims of Crime) Act 2017 (s. 8(2)(m)(i) and (ii)), which gives effect to the Victims' Directive, states that a victim may request information on the release of the offender as well as any conditions pertaining to the victim that are relevant to release. In practice, the Parole Board receives unsolicited letters from victims and victims' families. From 2011 to 2013, 11 per cent of cases had victim representations included in the review dossier (Parole Board 2013, p. 6). The Parole Board (2015, p. 4) state that these letters are 'seriously considered' when making a decision. It is not clear how this is taken into consideration in individual cases. Members had mixed views on victim input, acknowledging that victims should be kept informed but questioned whether it was feasible or even appropriate to provide a more substantive role for victims. Further, members raised the issue of victims being informed that a life sentence prisoner is under review by the Parole Board and eligible for release after seven years. This was viewed as aggravating the suffering of victims, given that the offender is unlikely to be released until many years later.

> You have to understand the feelings of victims but personally it wouldn't sway me in terms of how I'd view a case, and I think legal precedent would say that, you know, we shouldn't be unduly influenced by actually what the victim has to say. (PB02)

> Poor victims hear that Joe Bloggs is up for review after seven years and they'll say 'what, he just killed my daughter seven years ago and now they're bloody reviewing him', and that puts them through torture. Now we know and I know that the likelihood in that probable case is that person's not going to get out for another seven years. (PB07)

Offender and victim input contributes, in some manner, to the decision-making process, which now falls for consideration.

Parole Decision-Making

For much of the twentieth century the power to pardon or commute sentences and the act of clemency, all exercised at the discretion of the state, were opaque processes with little accountability (Sebba 1977).

There is evidence that many countries have adopted a more formalised approach to parole (Bottomley 1990). Reform in parole, and criminal justice generally, has been influenced and shaped by a multitude of factors that include, but are not limited to: the decline in support for the rehabilitative ideal; the emergence of a politicised and populist approach to criminal justice; a shift in focus towards the control of those perceived to be dangerous, most often sexual and violent offenders; the emergence of a new penology and a focus on risk assessment; a perception of the ineffectiveness of parole; and a concern for standards of due process and high parole revocation rates (Garland 2001; Feeley and Simon 1992; Bottoms 1995; Cheliotis 2006). The transition to judicial and independent decision-making in the European context has often been as a result of local factors combined with a need to comply with the countries supranational obligations (Livingstone 2000). The thrust of reforms has emphasised the importance of independent decision-making and due process.

Similar to the movement towards the abolition of the death penalty, 'Europe' has been active in developing human rights standards surrounding the release of life sentence prisoners. Questions regarding the appropriateness of the use of the life sentence remain but attention has tended to focus on the practicalities of release (Council of Europe 1976, 2003b). The European Committee for the Prevention of Torture (CPT) (2012, p. 26; 2007, 2015) has emphasised the importance of establishing an appropriate procedure for release. The jurisprudence of the ECtHR has been instrumental in creating a framework for the review of indeterminate sentences and has emphasised the importance of due process in decisions on the release of life sentence prisoners (*Boulois v Luxembourg* 2012 para. 2; *Vinter and Others v United Kingdom* 2013). Ireland's process has remained political and informal with reform of the process still pending. Key elements of the review cycle will be examined including: the initial review process; the criteria employed in decision-making; the recommendation and release process; and the revocation of release. The profile of parole decision-makers will be explored first.

Parole Decision-Makers

Being a member of a parole authority requires the ability to assess, analyse and synthesise information from a range of sources in order to effectively discharge the responsibility of decision-making in a fair and equitable manner. The ability to do this is in some way dependent on the calibre of the decision-maker (Gendreau et al. 2002). Research on this in the context of parole is limited, but in other legal settings, it has been shown that factors such as political ideology and gender may be influential on decision-makers where considerable discretion exists (Hausegger et al. 2009; Hawkins 1992). In jurisdictions with a judicial process one judge or a number of judges are responsible for the decision (Italy has a 'Supervision Tribunal' consisting of four members: Gualazzi and Mancuso 2010). In parole settings that are less formalised the appointment of parole decision-makers can reflect a wider range of participants outside the legal domain. In the United States, 89 per cent of parole authorities are housed within the executive branch of government with decisions usually taken by a panel containing three members (Ruhland et al. 2017, pp. 17 and 30). Statutory requirements to qualify for parole authority membership are required in only 56 per cent of states although members were generally highly qualified in terms of educational achievement and experience (Ruhland et al. 2017, p. 21). Oral parole hearings in England and Wales are heard by three parole members or less (Padfield 2010, p. 125).

The Irish approach to the appointment of Parole Board members is consistent with the more politicised nature of parole in the United States. At the time of the establishment of the Parole Board, the Minister stated that the Board was to be 'representative of the general public as well as the relevant professional services' (541(2) *Dáil Debates* Col. 199: John O'Donoghue 3 October 2001). Since its inception, the Parole Board has comprised of approximately 12 to 14 part-time members and all members meet to discuss offenders under review. This is an unusually high number to be involved in decision-making and it is out of step with most parole authorities in other jurisdictions. Members can be divided into two separate groups, those serving in an *ex officio* capacity and 'community representatives'. The Parole Board is made up of one chairperson, four *ex officio* members and seven community representatives (Parole Board 2015, p. 9). The *ex officio* members are the director, or his/her nominee, of the Prison Service and the Probation Service and the Principal Officer in the Prison and Policy division of the Department of Justice (Department). The term 'community representative' is not defined in any publicly available document, nor is there any indication of what aspects of community is to be represented through its membership. There is a pattern in terms of the profile of appointment. Retired agents of the criminal justice system have consistently been appointed (*an Garda Síochána*, Prison Service, Probation Service, Peace Commissioners) as well as those working in non-governmental organisations related to criminal justice. The remaining members derive from diverse backgrounds such as business, retired civil and public servants and psychotherapists. Of the current 12 members, only two are female (Parole Board 2015, p. 9). Some community representatives expressed their lack of awareness of the work of the Parole Board at the time of their appointment.

> Without knowing anything at all about it at the time, I said yes I'd give it a try and I'd see how we got on. (PB08)

The inclusion of members of the community in the decision-making process is not uncommon in administrative parole processes. In England and Wales, the Parole Board is made up of: the judiciary; the psychiatric and psychological profession; the probation service; and independent members. Indeed, even where the process has been formalised into a judicial process, there may still be space for non-judicial decision-makers. The Sentence Implementation Courts in Belgium adopt a multi-disciplinary approach to composition in an attempt to enhance the quality of decision-making and to safeguard the courts independence and professionalism (Scheirs et al. 2016, p. 86). The court is comprised of one judge and two non-judicial assessors that have a relevant degree (criminology, psychology, law, sociology) and five years' experience in social integration or prisons.

Members of the Parole Board are political appointees. Up until recently, the position of Parole Board member was not publicly advertised (Department of Justice and Equality 2017). Both Chairmen stated that they received a phone call from the Minister asking whether they would accept the appointment. Community representatives were questioned on how they became members of the Parole Board. All except one stated that they were asked either by the Minister, or on her behalf by an official of the Department. Although not solicited directly in interviews, decision-makers did make reference to political association and patronage in the appointment process.

> I appointed a few people to it during my time, there were quite a number of people, I'd have to say, who would have been of my political persuasion but in fairness to them, now you hear all this thing you know, 'they're only party hacks or whatever' but in fairness to them they worked extremely hard… they were all extremely diligent and took their job very seriously. (MJ2)

> I knew the Minister for Justice and, through an associate of his… when a vacancy came up he mentioned to me would I be interested so I took the opportunity. (PB01)

> I would have had a phone call from Minister [X]'s advisor who asked me would I be interested. And then to be very open about it, I would also be a member of [a political party] which I presume is why I got that phone-call in the first place or why my name would have cropped up in the discussion. (PB02)

This is indicative of a broader approach to public appointments, criticised for their politicised nature with a lack of transparency and accountability surrounding the process (Clancy and O'Connor 2011). Ministers have wide discretion in terms of appointments to state boards and this function has often been used to serve political ends resulting in a lack of diversity in membership, limiting public representativeness (Clancy and O'Connor 2011; Institute of Directors 2012). More recently there have been moves to advertise positions to tackle these difficulties although the appointments are not confined to those who have applied for the position and the Minister may make an appointment outside of those who have expressed an interest through their application (Department of Public Expenditure and Reform 2013; Regan 2012).

On appointment, in-service training is generally not provided to members regarding the role of the Parole Board in the context of the criminal justice system or their individual role in the decision-making process

(John Costello, Sub-Committee on Penal Reform Debate, 24 October 2012). There is little indication in the annual reports of developments in terms of the performance or training of members, the improvement or maintenance of standards in decision-making or any reference to corporate governance.

> I would have received no training. I would have also, for example, have had no overview of the various different prisons, the facilities within the prisons, the services that are available. There should also have been basic information about the role of the Parole Board, which I didn't get and its remit in what should and shouldn't be taken into consideration when making a decision. None of that was provided. (PB02)

The impact of parole decision-makers on the process cannot be easily measured but it is reasonable to suppose that the method by which members are selected and subsequently organised as a body impacts on it resultant decisions. The lack of professional and educational requirements, the political nature of the appointment process and the absence of training on entry and throughout underscores the discretionary, individual and informal nature of the process.

Criteria

The Council of Europe (2003a, Explanatory Memorandum para. 18) emphasise that in the context of structuring the release process, 'the most important decision to be made is which criteria will be used to determine whether a prisoner can or cannot be granted release'. There is a broad spectrum of approaches but, generally speaking, they include such considerations as: the nature and circumstances of the offence; conduct while in custody; implementation of the sentence plan; likelihood of committing a further offence; attitude towards the victim; and the prisoner's health status. Public protection is often cited as the overarching or key criterion (see for example, Canada, England and Wales, Scotland and Northern Ireland) although many countries include considerations of risk as part of a range of different applicable criteria. Sweden determines release on the basis of: overall behaviour and development; rehabilitative efforts; risk of reoffending; offence type; and time in custody (Schartmueller 2014, p. 12). In Germany, release decisions are based primarily on the personality of the offender and the gravity of the offence. At the broader European level, there has been a focus on rehabilitation as a key component of prison policy and this is emphasised in the context of life sentences both in the jurisprudence of the ECtHR and the European Prison Rules in terms of ensuring progress towards rehabilitation (*Vinter and Others v United Kingdom* 2013, para. 115; Council of Europe 2006, rules 103.8 and 107). Irrespective of the type of criteria applied, the Council of Europe (2003a, Explanatory Memorandum para. 18) recommends that offenders are made aware of the date at which they become eligible for release and that the assessment criteria are 'clear and explicit'. Despite criteria being in place in many jurisdictions, their articulation and application can raise concerns, particularly in relation to the reliability of assessments upon which the likelihood of reoffending is determined and the uncertainty surrounding a release date (*Léger v France* 2006).

In Ireland, the Minister has as a sizable amount of statutory discretion when deciding on the temporary release of an offender and this extends to the Parole Board, a body appointed to advise the Minister. The criteria in Ireland have more in common with the European norm where the decision-making body often reviews risk alongside other factors including a review of the nature and seriousness of the offence and the rehabilitation of the prisoner (van Zyl Smit et al. 2014, p. 16). The Criminal Justice (Temporary Release of Prisoners) Act 2003 amends the Criminal Justice Act 1960 and lists 11 factors which the Minister must have regard to prior to directing release including:

1. the nature and gravity of the offence;
2. the sentence of imprisonment and any recommendations of the court;
3. the period of the sentence of imprisonment served;
4. the potential threat to the safety and security of the public (including the victim);
5. any offence of which the person was convicted before being convicted of the offence to which the sentence of imprisonment being served by him relates;
6. the risk of the person failing to return to prison upon the expiration of any period of temporary release;

7. the conduct of the person while in custody;
8. any report of, or recommendation made by: the prison governor; *an Garda Síochána*; the Probation Service; or any other person that may be of assistance.
9. the risk of committing an offence during a period of temporary release;
10. the risk of failing to comply with the conditions of temporary release and;
11. the likelihood that temporary release might accelerate the person's reintegration into society or improve prospects of obtaining employment.

While the Parole Board is not required to apply any specific criteria, it has largely adopted these legislative criteria as the 'main factors taken into account in each individual case' (Parole Board 2012, pp. 7–8; 2013, pp. 3–4). The criteria are broad in nature and look both to the past and the future. The Minister must (and the Parole Board may) take into consideration punitive or retributive aspects of the offence including its seriousness, the length of sentence imposed and served by the prisoner up to the point of review. There is also a strong focus on the future behaviour of the offender, the likelihood of the offender reintegrating successfully into the community on release and the level of risk he presents if release were to be granted. Despite the range of different criteria listed, the Parole Board and the Minister have consistently emphasised the centrality of risk and public protection to decision-making.

> The public interest dictates that until the risk of re-offending has been absolutely minimised temporary release is not an option which the Board can consider recommending. (PB04)

The selection of public protection by the Parole Board as a defining feature is at its own discretion. Interestingly, when members were discussing the factors they take into consideration when deliberating on individual cases only one member referenced the statutory criteria specifically. As will be evident in the discussion in Chaps. 4 and 5, parole decision-making is relatively unconstrained with a whole range of factors being incorporated into the decision-making process, some of which are poorly related, or completely unrelated, to the statutory criteria.

Recommendations and Decisions

The transition to formal and independent decision-making is apparent in the number of court or court-like bodies with a variety of monikers that now exist to make a determination on the issue of release (Sentence Implementation Court (Belgium); Release Board (Cyprus); Supervision Tribunal (Italy); Court of Appeal (Finland); District Court (Sweden)). The transition from executive-based decision-making to judicial is common across many countries although the point at which this formalisation took shape is specific to each. Parole in France was initially entrusted to the Minister for the Interior (1885) and subsequently the Minister of Justice (1911). This continued to be the practice for the remainder of the twentieth century until the vesting of these powers in the executive became strongly contested. In 2000, the law was reformed removing the Minister's powers and vesting them in an adversarial judicial procedure (*Léger v France* 2006). A number of countries do not make provision for the parole of life sentence prisoners (Iceland, Lithuania, Malta, the Netherlands and Ukraine) but allow for release through the commutation of life sentences *via* ministerial, presidential or royal pardon (*Vinter and Others v United Kingdom* 2013, para. 68). Of course in Ireland, decision-making is based on the recommendations of the Parole Board and the decision of the Minister.

Decisions at Parole Board level appear to occur through adopting a consensus-based approach with no voting or method of registering dissent at meetings. Members were asked how matters were resolved where there was no initial harmony on whether to release an offender and all of those interviewed remarked that such situations rarely, if ever, arise.

> I don't think we have ever had [disagreement] or had to take a vote on it. If you tease things out, and nobody takes an absolute firm line. I mean you'll get an awful cross section of opinion, one will emphasise one thing or another that will be different, but you manage to achieve it. (PB04)

> I've never seen any decision being taken in which anybody has sought to formally register their dissent because the views of everyone are taken on board. (PB11)

It seems remarkable, given the contentious nature of the subject matter that disagreement and lack of consensus does not arise more frequently amongst those in attendance. This is especially so when the number of members would suggest that obtaining consensus amongst all individuals would prove difficult. Perhaps an explanation for this can be found in the overarching approach of the Parole Board. If the Parole Board adopts a conservative approach in making recommendations it is likely that consensus is more easily reached in the context of the release and sentence management of life sentence prisoners.

> At the end of it, when it goes around the table and somebody says, I'm not too sure, we're not moving a bit quickly in this case, I'd always say we'd recommend these things in six months time or a years time, we'll try to reach agreement. (PB04)

Nonetheless, community representatives pointed to the experience of those serving as *ex officio* members as being influential in the meeting through providing 'soft' information on offenders as their other professional roles might bring them into contact with the offender under review.

> But basically he knew a lot of the prisoners personally and certainly his personal knowledge of the prisoners would be helpful in reaching a decision at Board level. (PB05)

> I think, they have a much stronger, not so much the Department, but I think the Prison Service and the Probation Service, that their opinions are given much more weight than other Board members, which is probably somewhat inevitable given that they would know the prisoner concerned or know of their history within the prison. (PB02)

The procedure followed in terms of how a decision is reached is not entirely clear, but those who have conducted the interview tend to lead the discussion on the offender under review, with the chairperson mediating and soliciting views whilst bringing the process to a conclusion in terms of a recommendation. Recommendations by the Parole Board are communicated to the Minister *via* a letter detailing the reasons for those recommendations having considered the contents of the review dossier. Since the establishment of the Parole Board recommendations made to the Minister are for the most part accepted in full (85.2 per cent) with the remainder of cases constituting: recommendations accepted in part (5 per cent); recommendations not accepted (2.3 per cent); cases referred back to the Parole Board for further consideration (1.2 per cent); a Ministerial decision is pending (6.1 per cent); or an offender released prior to a decision (0.2 per cent) (Parole Board 2002–2015). Similar to the Sentence Review Group, there appears to be space for informal dialogue between the Parole Board and the Minister outside of formal correspondence in instances where difficulties arise regarding the acceptance of recommendations by the Minister.

> It comes back to us with the reasons for it and if we want to say to the Minister, I think you are wrong about this I would ring up the Minister's secretary and ask to meet him. (PB04)

> The Chairman used to actually have an informal line of communication with me [as Minister]. He used to actually ring me up and say 'there's Mr. X's case coming up, I just want you to know what our thinking was'. (MJ1)

The decision of the Minister in relation to the recommendations is communicated to the offender *via* a letter and this is also sent to the Parole Board. Reasons are given for the decision in the letter, although a standard format is used which broadly matches the statutory criteria giving the offender little indication of the rationale for the decision.

The Review Process Cycle

Many of the recommendations surrounding the parole process relate to sentence management and the transition towards release rather than release itself as a life sentence prisoner will not be released until having served significantly longer than the minimum term of seven years. Thus, there will be a series of reviews conducted prior to the decision to release. Recommendations can relate to requesting that the offender: engage with the services available in the institution; address offence and offender related issues; and encourage the establishment of contact with family or community to facilitate re-socialisation. The Parole Board may also recommend that the offender be transferred to another institution or what might be referred to as a 'step down' facility. In terms of temporary release, the Parole Board can recommend that the Minister permit: temporary release for family purposes; escalating periods of temporary release for work or training purposes or; 'full temporary release' (i.e., parole). Members tended to adopt a different approach depending on the number of reviews conducted in an individual case. A consensus seems to exist surrounding the stages of progression towards release through the cycles of review. Those undergoing their first review were not viewed as likely to be released and the focus tended to be on sentence management, with less concern placed on the quality of the reports and the relevance of risk assessment. It was only at later stages that it appeared that members viewed the process as a mechanism for release.

> Let's say there's a review at seven years, so all you can do at seven years is to say, this is a lifer now, a murderer, say 'well done what you're doing, keep doing it and we'll see you in three years time, okay?' So you then get them to ten years, which is their second review, and then you're saying 'well done, you've really maintained all that' and then you're looking towards pushing them to two years, at twelve years. So at the third review then, you know, you're actually looking towards the door really. So you're looking towards progressing them into either the training unit, an open centre, a more step-down facility, sort of work and training. (PB07)

The parole process was viewed as incremental whereby offenders take 'quite small steps' towards release at each review (PB02). In this respect, members often associated their role with sentence management, providing a structure to offenders allowing them to progress towards release. Some members identified the lack of structured sentence management for life sentence prisoners noting that sentence management often only began at the seven-year point through the parole process. Others believed that the intervention of the Parole Board from seven years onwards served little purpose when the likelihood of release was not until much later, resulting in disillusionment and disengagement by the offender with the process over a period of reviews.

> I've seen cases where they've only begun to engage when they start thinking about the parole process, you know, so it can be an incentive in that way for them to engage. So, you know, when I think of [these] scenarios, I say 'well okay, leave it at seven'. (PB09)

> I think if anything some people are maybe coming to the system too early. Because if you've done a murder let's say and you're going to spend fifteen years in jail, well in my view now coming in at seven years is a bit too, it's too early. (PB07)

Members did comment on how they thought offenders perceived the parole process and the resultant difficulties that emerged as a result of the informality of the process, its political nature and the cycles of review that progress an individual towards release.

> Some of the prisoners, they don't think much of the parole process, I suppose because we have a kind of a grading scale towards release. (PB08)

> Now saying that, I can see where the reputation of this parole process within the prison system itself, it can be viewed in terms of the results and that's where the clash with the ministerial bit comes in, if it isn't clearer, you know, where our independence is, it's kind of 'what's the point'? You can get a 'what's the point?' engagement with the process. (PB12)

There is little information on the extent to which 'Integrated Sentence Management', a system provided by the Prison Service, is available to life sentence prisoners but there are indications that a structured plan is not in place for many that have not reached the seven-year point (CPT 2011, p. 32; Milner 2010, p. 74; Richardson 2012, p. 155; Gallagher 2017).

Release and Revocation

'Full temporary release' or 'reviewable temporary release' are terms used to describe the release of life sentence prisoners back into the community (*Dáil Question* No. 513: Alan Shatter, 26 November 2013) although, legally, this is no different to temporary release. On release, a life sentence prisoner is supervised by the Probation Service in the community for the remainder of his life. This is not the case in all jurisdictions with, for example, Finland only imposing a maximum period of three years' supervision after the release of life sentence prisoners (Penal Code of Finland, 2c: 10). 'Full temporary release' means that a life sentence prisoner will be given a specified term of release and this will be continually reviewed by the Prison Service who decide whether to grant or refuse further periods of temporary release. For this purpose, the Probation Service provides a progress report to the Prison Service reporting on reintegration, resettlement and any risk management issues arising or the breach of any conditions of release. An offender on 'full temporary release' is unlikely to be recalled or refused additional periods of temporary release unless there has been a breach of a condition. Similar to any other offender on temporary release, a life sentence prisoner is required: to keep the peace; be of good behaviour; and be of sober habits during that period (Prisoners (Temporary Release) Rules 2004). The offender must comply with any additional directions that may be set by the Minister or on his behalf by the Prison Service (Criminal Justice (Temporary Release of Prisoners) Act 2003, s. 1). O'Malley (2016, p. 637) notes that given the consequences of a breach of a condition 'it is important that any special release conditions should be realistic and capable of being fulfilled, having regard to the circumstances and characteristics of the person being released'. These conditions are communicated to the offender in writing prior to release, through a standard form, and anybody released through this process is under a statutory obligation to comply (Criminal Justice Act 1960, s. 4(2)). Breach of these conditions renders an offender 'unlawfully at large', an offence with a penalty of imprisonment of up to six months (Criminal Justice Act 1960, s. 6(1) and (2)). A member of the *Gardaí* may arrest without warrant a person suspected of being unlawfully at large and that individual will be returned to his previous place of detention (Criminal Justice Act 1960, s. 7).

Where a condition of release may have been breached, an inquiry should be instituted allowing the offender an opportunity to be heard (*State (Murphy) v Kielt* 1984). The arrest itself cannot result in automatic revocation of temporary release; rather a finding that a condition has been breached following arrest is what is pertinent (*State (Murphy) v Kielt*

1984, p. 470). An investigation should be carried out by the Minister, or his designate (most likely the prison governor of the institution from which temporary release was originally granted). The process 'does not require anything of a judicial nature' as the granting and termination of temporary release 'are clearly acts which are administrative in nature' (*State (Murphy) v Kielt* 1984, p. 472). Temporary release may be revoked where a conclusion is made, based on reasonable and objective material, that a condition has been breached (*Dowling v Minister for Justice* 2003). The standard of proof required for such an inquiry and how different breaches are to be dealt with is slightly uncertain (McDermott 2000, pp. 412–3). Nonetheless, fair procedures are necessary and the person subject to arrest must be given the opportunity to contest the grounds for the revocation of temporary release.

The discretion surrounding the revocation of temporary release for life sentence prisoners can be problematic due to the continuing and renewable nature of release that applies specifically to life sentence prisoners. In *Dowling v Minister for Justice* (2003) the applicant had been sentenced to life imprisonment in 1989 and was released on temporary release in 1999 with the Minister writing to Dowling conveying his 'best wishes to Mr Dowling for his future'. Dowling was arrested in 2001 in connection with another murder and was questioned by the *Gardaí*. He was returned to prison on the basis that the Department determined that Dowling should not be granted further periods of temporary release. In 2002 he was informed that no charges would be brought against him for the murder. Counsel on behalf of the Minister contended that as temporary release was renewable on a monthly basis it was to last only for the duration of that specified period (Dowling was required to sign on with the Prison Service every month). The Supreme Court found that Dowling was on 'full temporary release'. Fennelly J. stated that '[t]he reality is and the particular words [of the Minister] convey that the Applicant was going to be indefinitely on temporary release, provided he was of good behaviour'. Thus in the context of 'full temporary release' the refusal to renew should be interpreted as a revocation and the individual is entitled to the procedures outlined above. In *Sherlock v Governor of Mountjoy Prison* (1991) the applicant had been sentenced to penal servitude for life but had been on temporary release for 12 years. The Prison Service had renewed his temporary release on 15 occasions during that time. On the expiry of the last period, the applicant was informed that he would not be granted a further period of temporary release and was returned to prison. He was not provided with any reason for this refusal. The High Court held he had a legitimate expectation to be either provided with a further period of temporary release or, if this was not granted, to be provided with reasons for the refusal and an opportunity to be heard as set out in *State (Murphy) v Kielt* (1984). These cases must be interpreted in light of an amendment contained in s. 2(6) of the Criminal Justice Act 1960 which states that temporary release 'shall not constitute an entitlement on that person to further such release'.

The Parole Board does not have any direct involvement in the release or recall of offenders. The Prison Service manages temporary release, and the revocation thereof. From 2001 to 2016, 61 life sentence prisoners were released on 'full temporary release' while 18 life sentence prisoners were recalled to prison (see Table 1.1). There are a total of 83 life sentence prisoners living in the community (*Dáil Question* No. 112: Frances Fitzgerald, 24 January 2017). From 2001 to 2016, six of the 18 recalled had been charged with a new offence. These included theft, burglary, arson, drug and firearm offences (*Dáil Question* No. 335: Alan Shatter, 12 November 2013; *Dáil Question* No. 513: Alan Shatter, 26 November 2013; *Dáil Question* No. 513; *Dáil Question* No. 403 and 411: Alan Shatter 22 October 2014; *Dáil Question* No. 187: Frances Fitzgerald, 28 January 2017; correspondence with Department, 09 April 2015). Members highlighted the high number of recommendations accepted by the Minister annually and this was regularly referred to as a measure of success. Publicly and politically, the success (or failure) of a parole process is often based on the frequency and seriousness of reoffending on release. This type of discourse is curiously absent in the Irish context and is likely as a result of information on reoffending not coming to public attention. The number of recalls that relate to reoffending and the relative seriousness of the offences certainly raise questions as to the quality of parole decision-making and whether the process can be categorised as a success or failure on those terms.[1] Nonetheless, there is only one incident where a life sentence prisoner on temporary release has committed an additional murder on release and such was the extraordinary nature of this that an inquiry was conducted, which led, in part, to the creation of the Parole Board (Olden 2001).

The vagueness of the conditions of release and the discretion afforded the Prison Service, the Probation Service and the *Gardaí* has serious implications for life sentence prisoners living in the community. Keeping the peace, being of good behaviour and of sober habits are phrases that 'lack a precise and settled meaning' (O'Malley 2016, p. 637). The situation is exacerbated for the life sentence prisoner, who is subject to supervision for the remainder of his life and if recalled could end up serving additional lengthy periods in prison for the breach of a trivial condition. For example, three life sentence prisoners were recalled to prison for failing to be of 'sober habits' (1 in 2002; 2 in 2008) (*Dáil Question* No. 513: Alan Shatter, 26 November 2013). It is easy to envisage how anybody released could fall foul of such a condition over the course of their lifetime, particularly if this is interpreted in a stringent manner. One member identified this as a problem noting the consequences that can result from a minor breach.

> You will have cases where somebody was [on parole] for murder and is regarded entirely as low risk but may have a drink problem, and as I said they could be brought back in because of an incident over alcohol where it's part of their [release] that they shouldn't breach the terms and be found drunk on the street for example. And that has happened where somebody has messed up and they're back in and all of a sudden they're two or three years down the line back in for a slip-up involving maybe a misuse of alcohol without necessarily doing any harm to somebody. And we would have a case where, you know, somebody was arrested one night for being drunk and disorderly and was returned to prison, and the arresting Garda actually wrote in afterwards and said had he known that the person was under licence he would have treated it differently because he wasn't really posing any risk or any harm to anyone, but he just dealt with it on the street at the time. The person as a result of it remained in prison for a number of years afterwards. (PB12)

In 2016, four life sentence prisoners on 'full temporary release' were returned to prison, three for medical reasons and one for accommodation issues (*Dáil Question* No. 205: Frances Fitzgerald, 02 May 2017). It is unclear whether this was as a result of a refusal to renew temporary release or this was somehow viewed as a breach of a condition. Either way, it is difficult to see how medical matters would be better treated within the prison system than in the community. This reinforces the precariousness and uncertainty of 'full temporary release' for life sentence prisoners living in the community. Unlike determinate sentenced prisoners, release from prison does not bring the sentence to an end, with freedom waiting on the other side of the prison gate. Rather, release for a life sentence prisoner represents a fragment of freedom, which may be brought to an end through the return to prison for an array of different reasons.

Navigating the Process as a Life Sentence Prisoner

The perspectives of life sentence prisoners on their experience of imprisonment and the parole process is not well documented in this jurisdiction although the pains of imprisonment (Sykes 1958) and more specifically, the pains of indeterminacy (Sapsford 1983) have been the subject of research elsewhere. Jewkes (2005, p. 385) argues that the pains of indeterminacy and 'nightmare uncertainties' (Sapsford 1983) of the life sentence places the prisoner in a 'permanent or near permanent liminal state' which can 'intensify the experience of ageing and fears of physical and mental deterioration'. The 'fog of uncertainty' surrounding sentence management and the release process can increase insecurities, anxiety and stress where 'the route-map to freedom is by no means clear' (Crewe 2011, p. 514). The lack of certainty, legal and otherwise, experienced by Irish life sentence prisoners while navigating the parole process contributes negatively to the pains of indeterminacy with the individual decision-maker being the central factor rather than the conduit for the application of the appropriate procedure and criteria. As one life sentence prisoner stated: 'People doing life, from day one, don't know when it's going to end. There's no beginning, middle or end' (Milner 2010, p. 74). Another life sentence prisoner noted of the parole process that '[e]ven when decisions are made, lifers are not told. There is an appalling lack of communication. You have to get used to dealing with this'

(Richardson 2012, p. 155). A number of complaints were received by the CPT (2011, p. 32) from life sentence prisoners regarding the lack of a structured sentence plan making it difficult to know what the Parole Board required of them when they became eligible for release. The significant increase in the life sentence prisoner population has created operational and management difficulties for prison authorities (CPT 2011; Milner 2010).

Conclusion

In terms of time served there are a number of procedural factors that are impacting outcomes for life sentence prisoners. The seven-year minimum term now acts as the beginning of the parole process rather than a point at which a life sentence prisoner has a prospect of release. The process of appointing parole decision-makers is political and those individuals have wide discretion in terms of the factors taken into consideration upon which their recommendations are based. Similarly, the Minister, although somewhat constrained by statutory criteria, retains considerable discretion in the exercising of this executive power. The lack of legal representation or procedure surrounding the interview and review process affords the decision-makers substantial control as to outcomes leaving those subject to the process with little by way of actionable rights to challenge procedure or outcome. The parole process has developed in an *ad hoc* manner where individuals act as the agents of change rather than being restricted through stringent policies or procedures. Within this context, it is important to examine the factors that decision-makers identify as influencing their individual approach to parole outcomes.

Note

1. It is important to note that the recalls for 2001 to 2016 may relate to offenders released prior to the establishment of the Parole Board in 2001.

References

Appleton, C., & van Zyl Smit, D. (2016). The paradox of reform: Life imprisonment in England and Wales. In D. van Zyl Smit & C. Appleton (Eds.), *Life imprisonment and human rights* (pp. 217–240). Hart: Oxford.

Ashworth, A. (2000). Victims' rights, defendants' rights and criminal procedure. In A. Crawford & J. Goodey (Eds.), *Integrating a victim perspective within criminal justice* (pp. 185–204). Aldershot: Ashgate.

Bottomley, A. K. (1990). Parole in transition: A comparative study of origins, developments, and prospects for the 1990s. *Crime and Justice, 12*, 319–374.

Bottoms, A. (1995). The philosophy and politics of punishment and sentencing. In C. Clarkson & R. Morgan (Eds.), *The politics of sentencing reform* (pp. 17–49). Oxford: Clarendon Press.

Cheliotis, L. K. (2006). How iron is the iron cage of new penology? The role of human agency in the implementation of criminal justice policy. *Punishment and Society, 8*(3), 313–340.

Clancy, P., & O'Connor, N. (2011). Public appointments: Options for reform. TASC. Retrieved from https://www.tasc.ie/download/pdf/tascpublicappointments.pdf

Council of Europe. (1976). *Resolution 76/2 on the treatment of long-term prisoners.* Strasbourg: Council of Europe.

Council of Europe. (2003a). *Recommendation 22 on conditional release (parole).* Strasbourg: Council of Europe.

Council of Europe. (2003b). *Recommendation 23 on management by prison administrations of life-sentence and other long-term prisoners.* Strasbourg: Council of Europe.

Council of Europe. (2006). *Recommendation 2 of the committee of ministers to member states on the European prison rules.* Strasbourg: Council of Europe.

Crewe, B. (2011). Depth, weight, tightness: Revisiting the pains of imprisonment. *Punishment and Society, 13*(5), 509–529.

Department of Justice and Equality. (2010). *Victims charter and guide to the criminal justice system.* Dublin: Department of Justice and Law Reform.

Department of Justice and Equality. (2017). *Relevant board information.* Department of Justice and Equality. Retrieved from http://www.justice.ie/en/JELR/Parole_Board_Advertisement_December_2016.pdf/Files/Parole_Board_Advertisement_December_2016.pdf

Department of Public Expenditure and Reform. (2013). Appointments to state boards. Department of Public Expenditure and Reform. Retrieved from http://per.gov.ie/appointments-to-state-boards/

European Committee for the Prevention of Torture and Inhuman or Degrading Treatment or Punishment (CPT). (2007). *Actual/real life sentences*. Strasbourg: CPT.

European Committee for the Prevention of Torture and Inhuman or Degrading Treatment or Punishment (CPT). (2011). *Report to the government of Ireland on the visit to Ireland carried out by the European Committee for the Prevention of Torture and Inhuman or Degrading Treatment or Punishment*. Strasbourg: CPT.

European Committee for the Prevention of Torture and Inhuman or Degrading Treatment or Punishment (CPT). (2012). *Report on Switzerland*. CPT. Retrieved from http://www.cpt.coe.int/documents/che/2012-26-inf-fra.htm

European Committee for the Prevention of Torture and Inhuman or Degrading Treatment or Punishment (CPT). (2015). *25th general report of the CPT*. Strasbourg: CPT.

European Parliament. (2012). Directive 2012/29/EU establishing minimum standards on the rights, support and protection of victims of crime, and replacing council framework decision 2001/220/JHA (victims' directive). Brussels: European Parliament.

Feeley, M., & Simon, J. (1992). The new penology: Notes on the emerging strategy of corrections and its implications. *Criminology, 30*(4), 449–474.

Gallagher, C. (2017, May 2). Parole head seeks priority housing for life term prisoners. *Irish Times*. Retrieved from https://www.irishtimes.com

Garland, D. (2001). *The culture of control: Crime and social order in contemporary society*. Oxford: Oxford University Press.

Gendreau, P., Goggin, C., Cullen, F. T., & Paprozzi, M. (2002). The common-sense revolution and correctional policy. In J. McGuire (Ed.), *Offender rehabilitation and treatment: Effective programmes and policies to reduce re-offending* (pp. 359–386). Chichester: Wiley.

Ghandnoosh, N. (2017). *Delaying a second chance: The declining prospects for parole on life sentences*. Washington, DC: Sentencing Project.

Gualazzi, A., & Mancuso, C. (2010). Italy. In N. Padfield, D. van Zyl Smit, & F. Dünkel (Eds.), *Release from prison: European policy and practice* (pp. 266–299). Devon: Willan.

Hausegger, L., Hennigar, M., & Riddell, T. (2009). *Canadian courts: Law, politics, and process*. Toronto: Oxford University Press.

Hawkins, K. (1992). *The uses of discretion*. Oxford: Oxford University Press.

Herman, S., & Wasserman, C. (2001). A role for victims in offender reentry. *Crime and Delinquency, 47*(3), 428–445.

Institute of Directors in Ireland. (2012). *State boards in Ireland 2012 – Challenges for the future*. Dublin: Institute of Directors in Ireland.
Jewkes, Y. (2005). Loss, liminality and the life sentence: Managing identity through a disrupted lifecourse. In A. Liebling & S. Maruna (Eds.), *The effects of imprisonment* (pp. 366–388). Cullompton: Willan.
Lally, C. (2006, 8 March). McDowell defends length of murder sentences. *Irish Times*, p. 7.
Lappi-Seppälä, T. (2013, October 25). Parole and release from prison in Finland. Parole in Ireland – The way forward, experience from other jurisdictions. Paper presented at the Law Society of Ireland, Dublin.
Livingstone, S. (2000). Prisoner's rights in the context of the European Convention on Human Rights. *Punishment and Society, 2*(3), 309–324.
McDermott, P. A. (2000). *Prison law*. Dublin: Round Hall.
Milner, C. (2010). *The psychology of the life sentence: The subjective experiences of life sentence prisoners*. Unpublished PhD thesis: Trinity College Dublin.
Morgan, K. D., & Smith, B. (2005). Victims, punishment and parole: The effect of victim participation on parole hearings. *Criminology and Public Policy, 4*(2), 333–360.
O'Donnell, I. (2004). Imprisonment and penal policy in Ireland. *Howard Journal of Crime and Justice, 43*(3), 253–266.
O'Malley, T. (2011). *Sentencing: Towards a coherent system*. Dublin: Round Hall.
O'Malley, T. (2016). *Sentencing law and practice*. Dublin: Thomson Round Hall.
Olden, J. (2001). *Report of Mr John Olden on the management of the sentences of Thomas Murray, life sentence prisoner*. Dublin: Department of Justice and Equality.
Padfield, N. (2010). England and Wales. In N. Padfield, D. van Zyl Smit, & F. Dünkel (Eds.), *Release from prison: European policy and practice* (pp. 104–134). Devon: Willan.
Padfield, N. (2016). Justifying indefinite detention – On what grounds? *Criminal Law Review, 11*, 797–822.
Padfield, N., & Roberts, J. (2010). Victim input at parole: Probative and prejudicial? In A. Bottoms & J. Roberts (Eds.), *Hearing the victim: Adversarial justice, crime victims and the state* (pp. 255–285). Devon: Willan.
Padfield, N., Liebling, A., & Arnold, H. (2000). *An exploration of decision-making at discretionary lifer panels*. London: Home Office.
Parole Board. (2002–2015). *Annual reports*. Dublin: Parole Board.
Parole Board England and Wales. (2011). The Parole Board's commitment to victims of crime. Parole Board. Retrieved from https://www.gov.uk/guidance/the-parole-boards-commitment-to-victims-of-crime

Parsonage, W. H., Bernat, F. P., & Helfgott, J. (1994). Victim impact testimony and Pennsylvania's parole decision-making process: A pilot study. *Criminal Justice Policy Review, 6*(3), 187–206.
Polowek, K. (2005). Victim participatory rights in parole: Their role and the dynamics of victim influence as seen by board members. Doctoral Thesis. Simon Fraser University.
Prison Service. (2016). *Annual reports*. Dublin and Longford: Irish Prison Service.
Regan, M. (2012, 22 March). Majority of State board jobs go unadvertised. *Irish Examiner*. Retrieved from http://www.irishexaminer.com
Rhine, E. E., Petersilia, J., & Reitz, K. R. (2017). The future of parole release. *Crime and Justice, 46*(1), 279–338.
Richardson, M. (2012). Lifers: An exploration of coping among male life sentence prisoners. *Irish Probation Journal, 9*(1), 142–162.
Roberts, J. V. (2009). Listening to the crime victim: Evaluating victim input at sentencing and parole. *Crime and Justice, 38*(1), 347–412.
Ruback, R. B., & Hopper, C. H. (1986). Decision making by parole interviewers: The effect of case and interview factors. *Law and Human Behavior, 10*(3), 203–214.
Ruhland, E. L., Rhine, E. E., Robey, J. P., & Mitchell, K. (2017). *The continuing leverage of releasing authorities: Findings from a national survey*. Minneapolis: Robina Institute of Criminal Law and Criminal Justice.
Sapsford, R. (1983). *Life sentence prisoners: Reaction, response and change*. Milton Keynes: Open University Press.
Schartmueller, D. (2014). Too dangerous to get out? The use of individualized release mechanisms for lifetime incarcerated offenders in Sweden. *Criminal Justice Policy Review, 25*(4), 407–431.
Scheirs, V., Beyens, K., & Snacken, S. (2016). Belgian sentencing as a bifurcated practice? *Crime and Justice, 45*(1), 267–306.
Sebba, L. (1977). The pardoning power: A world survey. *Journal of Criminal Law and Criminology, 68*(1), 83–121.
Serin, R. (2011). Parole Board Canada: Pre-reading material (ATRA and decision framework). Parole Board Canada. Retrieved from http://www.ct.gov/bopp/lib/bopp/SDM.pdf
Snacken, S. (2007). Penal policy and practice in Belgium. *Crime and Justice, 36*(1), 127–215.
Snacken, S., Beyens, K., & Beernaert, M. A. (2010). Belgium. In N. Padfield, D. van Zyl Smit, & F. Dünkel (Eds.), *Release from prison: European policy and practice* (pp. 70–103). Willan: Devon.

Sykes, G. (1958). *The society of captives: A study of a maximum-security prison.* Princeton: Princeton University Press.
Ten Brinke, L., MacDonald, S., Porter, S., & O'Connor, B. (2012). Crocodile tears: Facial, verbal and body language behaviours associated with genuine and fabricated remorse. *Law and Human Behavior, 36*(1), 51–59.
van Zyl Smit, D., Weatherby, P., & Creighton, S. (2014). Whole life sentences and the tide of European human rights jurisprudence: What is to be done? *Human Rights Law Review, 14*(1), 59–84.
Whitaker Committee (Committee of Inquiry into the Penal System). (1985). Report. Dublin: Stationery Office.
Zedner, L. (1997). Victims. In M. Maguire, R. Morgan, & R. Reiner (Eds.), *The Oxford handbook of criminology*. Oxford: Clarendon Press.

Table of Legal Instruments

Criminal Justice Act 1951.
Criminal Justice Act 1960.
Criminal Justice (Temporary Release of Prisoners) Act 2003.
Criminal Justice (Victims of Crime) Act 2017.
Parole Bill 2016.
Penal Code of Finland.
Prison Rules 2007: S.I. No. 25/2007.
Prisoners (Temporary Release) Rules 2004: S.I. No. 680/2004.
Prisons Act 2007.
Rome Statute of the International Criminal Court 1998.
Safe Streets and Communities Act 2012 (Canada).
Sentencing Act 2002 (New Zealand).

Table of Cases

England and Wales

Osborn v Parole Board [2013] UKSC 61.

European Court of Human Rights

Boulois v Luxembourg Application No. 37575/04, 3 April 2012.
Léger v France Application No 19324/02, 11 April 2006.
Stafford v United Kingdom Application no 46295/99, 28 May 2002.
Vinter and Others v United Kingdom Application Nos 66069/09, 3896/10, 130/10, Merits, 9 July 2013.
Weeks v United Kingdom Application no 9787/82, 2 March 1987.

Ireland

Barry v Sentence Review Group [2001] 4 IR 167.
Dowling v Minister for Justice [2003] 2 IR 535.
Grogan v Parole Board [2008] IEHC 204.
Murray v Ireland [1991] ILRM 465.
People (DPP) v Finn [2001] 2 IR 25.
Ryan v Governor of Limerick Prison [1988] IR 198.
Sherlock v Governor of Mountjoy Prison [1991] 1 IR 451.
State (Murphy) v Kielt [1984] ILRM 141.

Table of Parliamentary Debates

183 *Dáil Debates* Cols. 559–560: Oscar Traynor, 28 June 1960.
393 *Dáil Debates* Cols. 2624–2626: Ray Burke, 1 December 1989.
528 *Dáil Debates* Col. 311: John O'Donoghue, 12 December 2000.
530 *Dáil Debates* Cols. 199–200: John O'Donoghue, 7 February 2001.
541(2) *Dáil Debates* Col. 199: John O'Donoghue, 3 October 2001.
543(2) *Dáil Debates* Col. 700: John O'Donoghue, 6 November 2001.
Dáil Question No. 187: Frances Fitzgerald, 28 January 2017.
Dáil Question No. 205: Frances Fitzgerald, 2 May 2017.
Dáil Question No. 335: Alan Shatter, 12 November 2013.
Dáil Question No. 403 and 411: Alan Shatter, 22 October 2014.
Dáil Question No. 513: Alan Shatter, 26 November 2013.
Dáil Question Nos. 112: Frances Fitzgerald, 24 January 2017.
Sub-Committee on Penal Reform Debate: John Costello, 24 October 2012.

4

The Risk Factor

There is an element of taking a chance perhaps, but that chance is almost a hundred per cent safe.
Parole Board member 03

Introduction

Risk is visible in the Irish criminal justice system but the paradigmatic shift evident in other jurisdictions has not been replicated here. Ireland did not fully subscribe to the rehabilitative ideal nor has it jumped on the risk bandwagon. Nonetheless, on the basis of the statutory framework adopted in 2003, a reorientation of the Probation Service towards risk, and the public statements of decision-makers regarding the centrality of risk in decision-making since the establishment of the Parole Board, it is clear that risk plays a central role in parole decision-making in Ireland. But there is little indication as to what this means in practice. The absence of a structured legal framework specific to the release of life sentence prisoners allows for a fluid and flexible approach to decision-making and risk is incorporated into this informal framework. Within such an environment, individual gatekeepers can impact greatly upon those subject to

D. Griffin, *Killing Time*, https://doi.org/10.1007/978-3-319-72667-0_4

the process. This is not confined to Parole Board members (members) and Ministers for Justice (Minister(s)), but all those that input into the process, such as probation and prison officers, prison psychologists and police (Padfield 2010, p. 119). As Gelsthorpe and Padfield (2003, p. 3) note 'discretion flows back and forth through all parts of agencies that make up the criminal justice 'system' and related controlling agencies'. Thus, an examination of the role of risk in the process should provide an important insight into the release of life sentence prisoners. It may also offer a rationale for the recent increase in time served by life sentence prisoners prior to release.

Risk and Risk Assessment

With the decline in support for the discretionary individualisation of rehabilitation, criminologists concerned with the governance of crime began to document significant shifts in penality over the latter part of the twentieth century. The terminology used to describe this shift has included phrases such as the 'new penology' (Feeley and Simon 1992), 'new punitiveness' (Pratt et al. 2005), 'the culture of control' (Garland 2001), 'penal populism' (Pratt 2007) and 'populist punitiveness' (Bottoms 1995). There is debate in the literature surrounding the meaning and use of these terms (Matthews 2005). A key element of this shift in criminal justice is the ascendancy of risk as an organising principle with an increasing focus on the management and control of behaviours (Cohen 1985, p. 147; Simon 1998; O'Malley 2000). Feeley and Simon (1992, p. 455; 1994) identified the emergence of a new strategic formation in penality, described as the new penology, based on the reduction of risk through the management of unruly groups. The goal of this new penology was 'not to eliminate crime but to make it tolerable through systematic coordination' (Feeley and Simon 1992, p. 455). The trends identified in criminal justice that can be linked to this include, but are not limited to: the focus in policy and practice on dangerousness and public protection; the increased use of measures of preventive detention; the development and use of actuarial risk tools to replace more discretionary measures of decision-making; a deprioritising of the rights of individuals; an increase in expressive justice; and a rise in managerialism.

The emergence of risk as central to this departure from the traditional criminal justice values of rehabilitation did not occur in isolation rather it reflects the rise of what has been described as the 'risk society' (Beck 1992). This 'risk society' is defined by an increased consciousness of risk, uncertainty and insecurity and has resulted in the development of advanced methods by which risks are measured and controlled (Ekberg 2007). There is considerable debate surrounding the extent to which the new penology is embedded in criminal justice practice or the extent to which risk and managerialism has come to dominate over penal modernism and rehabilitation (Kemshall and Maguire 2001; Garland 1996; Cheliotis 2006). While many theorists present the move towards risk and the actuarial as a movement away from the individualisation of the rehabilitative ideal, Harcourt (2007, p. 22) argues that it was the desire for greater accuracy in assessing individual cases that led to the development of actuarial justice. A further explanation of the growth of risk in criminal justice lies in the production of new technical knowledge that allowed for increasing accuracy in prediction such that models of punishment associated with the new penology grew out of 'what we began to know technically' shaping contemporary notions of justice (Harcourt 2007, pp. 32–3 and 39–45). In many respects, the goals of rehabilitation and the new penology are not dissimilar: the reduction of reoffending. However, the means by which this was to be achieved changed radically (Garland 2001, p. 174).

A key weapon in the armoury of the risk model is the risk assessment. Bonta (1996) describes risk assessments in terms of generational development beginning with clinical assessment and progressing towards what is viewed as more scientific and accurate actuarial models of assessment throughout the twentieth century. A clinical risk assessment is a subjective judgement often conducted by psychologists, psychiatrists or social workers who evaluate an individual based on their interactions with the offender and their experience as a professional (Bonta and Andrews 2007). An actuarial risk assessment uses statistical predictions about the criminality of groups to determine the outcome for an individual falling within that group. What is envisaged here is the use of group-trait statistics from large data-sets of offenders to determine that group's offending rate and then applying that assessment to the individual subject to determination (Harcourt 2007, p. 17). Actuarial risk assessment tools are frequently used in decisions made about offenders in relation to: sentencing; institutional placement; treatment planning; recommendations regarding parole; conditions in relation to supervision in the community; and the incapacitation of sex offenders after the completion of their sentence (Barbaree et al. 2001).

The prediction of the likelihood of reoffending through the use of actuarial risk assessment tools has resulted in considerable research being conducted into risk factors and their identification. This has produced what Kemshall (2006, p. 82) describes as a 'risk factorology'. Actuarial instruments include both static and dynamic factors. Static factors refer to an offender's past that can be predictive but not changed such as age, gender, race, criminal history, family criminality and social class of origin (Harcourt 2007, pp. 69–70). The majority of static factors are historical in nature and thus do not allow for the possibility of risk reduction through changes in an offender's behaviour (Bonta and Andrews 2007). Static factors do not account for criminogenic needs, targets for treatment and the dynamic nature of risk. Dynamic risk factors refer to criminogenic need and include factors such as antisocial personality, identification/socialisation with other offenders, interpersonal conflict, social achievement and substance use (Gendreau et al. 1996). 'Need' in this instance refers to problems that impact on recidivism or rule violation (rather than non-criminogenic needs such as health) and is a characteristic shared by the individual with the population statistically correlated with recidivism (Maurutto and Hannah-Moffat 2006, pp. 443–4). Advances made in the last decades of the twentieth century saw an increase in use of actuarial risk assessment methods in criminal justice and a greater focus on dynamic risk factors and criminogenic need. This was an acknowledgment that the level of risk presented is responsive to treatment and/or therapy and thus subject to change over a period of incarceration. These assessments are described as 'risk-need' instruments, some of which are theoretically based (see for example, Level of Service Inventory group of risk/need tools: Andrews and Bonta 2000, 2010). Risk assessments are increasingly being linked to the 'risk-needs-responsivity' model (Andrews et al. 1990) focusing on effective offender rehabilitation requiring the relevant agencies to respond to and address criminogenic need (Andrews et al. 2011, p. 735). The combination of static and dynamic factors allows for a 'fluid, malleable understanding of risk' (Maurutto and Hannah-Moffat 2006, p. 443) which permits the possibility of the transformation of the risk subject through correctional intervention.

Risk assessment is often conceived of as static, unified and homogenous. Research in the area undermines this interpretation (Kemshall 2003, pp. 48–56; Brown 2000, p. 95). Maurutto and Hannah-Moffat (2006) argue that risk is highly contextualised and contingent on policy, legislation and practice with decision-making being influenced by the social, cultural and institutional context. Kemshall (2003, pp. 48–56; 2006, p. 82) identifies differing conceptual approaches to risk which in turn impacts on the construction of risk assessment tools and also the framing and resolution of risk assessment problems in institutional settings. Many theorists argue that risk is a social and 'cultural product inextricably bound up with questions of value' (O'Malley 2010, p. 15; Douglas 1992). Risk can reflect the moral and political strategies of governance (Maurutto and Hannah-Moffat 2006, p. 441). It is uncommon for actuarial assessment to be implemented in pure form and thus it is important to examine how risk assessment tools are employed in practice across different institutional settings.

Research on the application of actuarial tools indicates that the organisational structure, culture and values can impact significantly upon risk assessments and decision-making (Kemshall 1998, 2003, 2006; Lynch 2000; Robinson 2001). Such findings highlight the importance of examining risk practice and the context within which recommendations and decisions are made. In their study of the purposes and use of risk/needs assessment tools in probation, Hannah-Moffat et al. (2009) found that risk assessment served purposes beyond actuarial prediction and need identification. At a policy and organisational level, the use of risk tools presents a mask of objectivity to the public and thus a layer of protection to the institution when placed under public scrutiny. At a more individual level, it can provide practitioners with a sense of security and reassurance while also mitigating some of the responsibility for the assessment and subsequent decision (Hannah-Moffat et al. 2009, p. 398). Decisions can be defended in hindsight, particularly when things go wrong. Further, the development of the risk-needs-responsivity model has allowed for 'new spaces and forms of discretionary decision-making' (Hannah-Moffat et al. 2009, pp. 299–400 and 406). Discretion within this model is systematised through risk calculation however, recommendations by assessors continue to involve 'a range of subjective judgements that are informed by practitioners' personal knowledge, experience, values and beliefs' (Hannah-Moffat et al. 2009, p. 401). Thus, it is important to be cognisant of the broader environment within which risk assessments are integrated in the Irish context.

As Ireland did not commit fully to the rehabilitative ideal it did not experience similar levels of disillusion with the apparent ineffectiveness of the penal welfare projects experienced elsewhere (Kilcommins et al. 2004). Indicators of a shift towards risk in Irish criminal justice is visible at some level although the approach remains fairly inconsistent and there is little evidence of managerialism (O'Donnell 2005; Healy 2012). At a practical level, incorporating considerations of risk, dangerousness or anything akin to preventive detention in legal decision-making presents specific issues of compatibility with the Irish constitution (O'Malley 2016, pp. 41–43). The Supreme Court in *People (Attorney General) v O'Callaghan* (1966) stated that preventive detention 'has no place in our legal system' and is 'quite contrary to the concept of personal liberty enshrined in the Constitution'. Nonetheless, the roots of a risk-based approach have emerged in areas outside of sentencing or formal decisions regarding detention, particularly in areas of decision-making surrounding prisons, probation and parole. Taking probation as an example of a service that is key to the parole process and often central in the practice of risk assessment, it appears that the Irish Probation Service resisted some of the risk-based developments evident elsewhere throughout the twentieth century (Healy 2012, p. 381). The Probation Service has been steeped in the ethos of social work since its establishment in 1907. The structure of the organisation and the practices of staff developed largely on an *ad hoc* basis. McNally (2009) notes that 'welfare' was adopted as the overarching framework at a time when many other jurisdictions were abandoning welfare for a risk-based model. A shift towards risk occurred from 2004 with Probation Officers being required to employ risk assessments in practice with risk-focused phraseology adopted at a broader policy level (Prendergast 2012; Probation Service 2008). As noted, the institutional context is crucial in how these assessments are conducted, communicated and integrated into criminal justice decision-making. Probation Officers have indicated a concern regarding the adoption of risk as an organising principle and believed that addressing the overall welfare needs of the offender to be more valuable than simply focusing on criminogenic need alone (Bracken 2010). Studies of probation in England and Wales found a continued salience in the individual and clinical approach despite the organisational drive towards 'government by numbers' (Robinson 2002, p. 13; Kemshall 1998, p. 14; 2003). This is evident in Ireland with Probation Officers valuing the ability to prioritise the clinical over the actuarial (Prendergast 2012). Probation Officers continue to enjoy an unusually high degree of autonomy when compared to the culture of managerialism now embedded in probation services elsewhere (McNally 2009; Healy 2012). Although risk may not have become the paradigm within which criminal justice decision-making in Ireland operates, there is certainly evidence that decision-making in certain contexts, including the release of life sentence prisoners, are adjusting towards a more risk-oriented approach.

Public Protection and Parole

The influence of risk is identifiable throughout the various stages of the review process for life sentence prisoners and a cursory analysis reveals that public protection is the central factor in decision-making. Risk assessments conducted by the Probation Service and the Prison Psychology Service are communicated to the Parole Board alongside a plethora of information from a variety of sources. This is a recent development as the Olden report in 2001 identified that risk assessment tools were not being employed in decisions relating to the release of life sentence prisoners at that time. Whitaker, Chairman of the Sentence Review Group stated that assessments were not available to them: 'We were just left to appraise it with our judgment' (Interview, 8 October 2008). The criteria contained in the Criminal Justice (Temporary Release of Prisoners) Act 2003 (and adopted by the Parole Board) emphasise the importance of public protection in the decision-making process. Section 2 (d, e, i and j) states that the Minister shall have regard to: 'the potential threat to the safety and security of members of the public should the person be released from prison; the risk of the person failing to return to prison upon the expiration of any period of temporary release; the risk of the person committing an offence during any period of temporary release; and the risk of the person failing to comply with any conditions attaching to his temporary release'. Successive Ministers and the Parole Board have publicly emphasised the centrality of public protection and risk in decisions surrounding the release of long-term and life sentence prisoners (541(2) *Dáil Debates* Col.199: John O'Donoghue 3/10/2001; Michael McDowell, cited in *Irish Times* 2006; 913(2) *Dáil Debates* Col.: Frances Fitzgerald 15/06/2016).

> It is important to emphasise that public safety is of paramount importance and is the key factor when the Board is reviewing a case. (Parole Board 2015, p. 5)

Twelve of fourteen members interviewed viewed public protection to be the most important consideration in their assessment of individual cases. The remaining two members stated that the balancing of public protection and individual liberty depended on each individual case. Public protection was articulated in various different ways but often included the terminology of risk and dangerousness.

> The most relevant factor is the risk of reoffending, so our primary concern I think is to the community. In other words our greatest duty, as a Board is … are we putting any member of the community in danger by allowing a prisoner out on early release or parole. That generally is the most important factor that we would look at. (PB05)

> You're there primarily to serve the public and to defend them, absolutely, so public protection would be high on the list. (PB01)

Guidelines do not exist for members in terms of how to incorporate a risk-based approach to decision-making. This is in marked contrast to other jurisdictions, which often provide decision-makers with guidelines and frameworks to structure decision-making to enhance consistency, efficiency, quality and transparency (see, e.g., the pre-reading material for Parole Board members in Canada, Serin 2011). The following examines the role of risk across the different stages of the process to determine the reality of risk in decision-making beyond the public statements of those responsible for release.

Risk Assessment and Communication

The Probation Service and Prison Psychology Service employ a range of actuarial tools when assessing a life sentence prisoner under review (for example: Level of Service Inventory-Revised (LSI-R): Andrews and Bonta 2000; Violence Risk Scale (VRS): Wong and Gordon 2006). Reports from both agencies are based on individual assessment interviews, a review of relevant files, actuarial risk assessments and other psychometric measures. Actuarial based assessments are used to supplement and support clinical assessments (Prendergast 2012). Once complete, the reports are circulated to members in the review dossier alongside other agency reports. When questioned on how members identify 'good risk' prisoners or those that do not pose a threat to the community, all members interviewed stated that the reports of the Probation Service and Prison Psychology Service assisted with their identification and quantification of risk.

> If the Probation Officer, in the final paragraph of their report, normally it says conclusions and recommendations, and if a person puts pen to paper and says [they are a risk], well I think it's a very, very foolish person that would ignore such a comment or such a recommendation. (PB14)

While it was evident that assessments contained in these reports were influential at an individual and Board level, other expressions of risk in the review dossier from outside of the Probation Service and Prison

Psychology Service were identified as having a role in this regard (for example, reports from the *Gardaí* (Irish police), Governor of the Prison and Prison Review Committee).

> Well the risk assessment, you're looking at it I suppose from the whole report. I suppose from the professional point of view you're looking at psychology reports, probation reports, the report from the prison governor, you're looking at what the *Gardaí* may be saying in relation to the particular offence, or whether or not, you know, he or she might be a risk to the community on release, and then you're trying to also then from the [Prison Review Committee] report, which really is a current assessment from all of the therapeutic services combined as to how they feel this person is doing, you know, so they're the sort of things I'd be looking at. (PB06)

The lexicon of risk did not come freely to some members. Only one member interviewed referenced a risk assessment. Members did articulate how risk assessments were presented to them.

> They've various academic means of assessing risk that they apply, and they would say 'this person is in the category of 20 per cent, 40 per cent, 50 per cent of reoffending within a given period of release, or reoffending violently within a period'. (PB08)

> It's normally categorised as high, medium and low risk. (PB05)

It is a matter of concern that a number of members appeared to have little understanding of risk assessment, as is evidenced through the following circuitous dialogue:

> *Interviewer:* *Were there actuarial risk assessments available to you?*
> *Interviewee*: No, no.
> *Interviewer:* *No statistical instruments…*
> *Interviewee*: No, no.
> *Interviewer:* *In the reports from the psychology service even…*
> *Interviewee*: No, no
> *Interviewer:* *Was the risk, let's say in the reports just a clinical…*

Interviewee: Clinical, it was yeah
Interviewer: Like high, medium, low categories?
Interviewee: Yeah. They had their own particular tests, yeah, and they gave us the results of those particular tests...
Interviewer: In percentage form?
Interviewee: Percentage, yeah, yeah, but there was no actuarial. (PB09)

Members themselves identified their own difficulties in interpreting risk assessments and the integration of same into their role as decision-makers. The communication of assessments by experts to other decision-makers is of critical importance when the professional carrying out the risk assessment is not the key decision-maker (Monahan 1993, p. 242). The style of risk communication can be as important a consideration as the content of the assessment. This is crucial in contexts, such as parole, where decisions are being made on the basis of such data but those making the decision have a limited ability in interpreting information presented in a statistical format and from a discipline with which they are not familiar (Heilbrun et al. 2004). Difficulties arise when making predictions of individuals based on statistical models despite the widespread acceptance of the prediction paradigm (Hart and Cooke 2013). The score resulting from a risk assessment is not a prediction of that offender's likelihood of reoffending, rather it is an estimate of the rate of reoffending that can be expected of a group of offenders with matching covariates to that individual (Copas and Marshall 1998). Risk assessments rely on analogical or inferential reasoning: 'This man *resembles* offenders who were likely to recidivate, therefore he is *likely* to recidivate' [emphasis in original] (Hart 2003, p. 385). Faigman et al. (2014) identify a basic cultural and language gap between the scientific and legal world, the former focused on the phenomenon of groups, the latter focused on the individual, such that reasoning from group data to individual decisions can be highly problematic. An understanding of this dynamic is important in parole decision-making where actuarial risk assessments are being applied to individual cases to assist parole decision-makers with little training on risk assessment. There is potential for members, as untrained decision-makers, to draw inferences from the data in an individual case at hand that may not be appropriate or accurate.

> On occasion, you can find that some of the reports tend to be overly professional, but in fairness to them, you know, when you look at the recommendations that are made in those reports, those recommendations tend to be clear-cut. (PB03)

> [The risk assessments] probably could have been better. It's a very difficult area, very subjective, and you are relying on those experts and those people who are cheek-to-jowl with those prisoners on a daily basis. (PB09)

> There would have been a presentation to the Board around risk assessment within the Probation Service, but it just happened to be my second or third meeting. There were other people who were on the Board for years who wouldn't have had it until then either, so there's an absolute lack of information provided beforehand. (PB02)

The decision-makers competency in understanding the risk assessment may be lost due to the 'Chinese whispers' of communication, thus reducing the overall quality of decision-making (Carson and Carson 2010, pp. 164–5). The margin of error that can occur as a result of this decision relates to the number of false positives (incorrectly assessing an offender as high risk) or false negatives (incorrectly assessing an offender as low risk) (Moore 1996). A culture of decision-making that is accepting of false positives fits with a penal system primarily concerned with the protection of the public and the containment of danger but is not necessarily consistent with a risk-based approach in the actuarial sense. Within the punitive realm, false positives are tolerable, false negatives are not.

Common Sense, Good and Bad

Despite the emphasis on the importance of risk there appears to be some level of resistance to, and scepticism of the risk assessments generated by the Probation Service and Prison Psychology Service. Some members appeared to question the value of risk assessments placing what can be termed a 'common sense' approach on at least an equal footing with the empirically based data contained in the assessments.

> When you look at all the other factors combined and, you know, frequently when you meet with prisoners and see how they behave in prison, any common sense approach by-and-large would let you know whether or not the person presents a risk. (PB03)

> We get psychological reports in all cases which require it and we make our best guess at the end of that. But there isn't a magic formula. It's all educated guess work. I think we're good at it. They will quote the statistical risks when making their own assessment. They are a factor in [the decision] but they are not the deciding factor in it. (PB04)

> At the end of the day what you want is common sense. (PB06)

The creation, communication and assimilation of risk assessment into decision-making is a complex process, mediated through individuals, who may be sceptical as to whether the professional risk assessment is more accurate than their own assessment. Questions as to the validity and reliability of risk assessments raised by members related to a perception that the assessment was not objective ('It's very far from an exact science' (PB05)), concern over the formulaic nature of the assessments and the limited range of factors taken into consideration.

The common sense approach has been identified as being influential at many different levels in correctional contexts resulting in what has been termed 'correctional quackery' (Gendreau et al. 2002, 2009). Gendreau et al. (2002, pp. 365–71; 2009, p. 387) argue that what is routinely employed is 'bad' common sense, the type ingrained in everyone deriving from anecdotal and personal experience while engaging with 'simple-minded' declarations. 'Good' common sense, a careful and systematic approach to decision-making based on the available empirical evidence while controlling for validity and reliability, is identified as a less frequent approach for those involved in professional quackery of this nature. Members are correct to question issues such as the validity and reliability of the information provided to them as the literature on risk continues to assess and re-assess the predictive accuracy of risk assessments. However, this is not what was presented in interview. Rather, risk assessments were at times being placed in conflict with their individual common sense assessment. It is not entirely obvious which approach prevails if these assessments are incongruous. There are two key possibilities that might arise when members are attempting to reconcile discordant information. A risk assessment indicating that a life sentence prisoner is low risk and suitable for release might be overridden by the common sense approach of members placing the offender in a higher category of risk and resulting in a recommendation to further detain the individual. This could result in false positives. An assessment indicating medium or high risk but a common sense approach categorising as low risk could result in false negatives. It is suggested, given the cautious approach adopted by members when dealing with issues of risk, and the increase in time served by life sentence prisoners, that it is the former that is a more likely occurrence.

A Culture of Cautiousness

Parole Board members adopted a cautious and conservative approach to decision-making and viewed the collective approach of their colleagues as 'more risk averse than risk takers' (PB01). It appears that only where all available information indicated a low level of risk and this was consistent with the individual and group deliberations of the Parole Board, was release considered a realistic option to recommend to the Minister. Padfield et al.'s (2000, p. 53) analysis of 'discretionary lifer panels' found that panels operated with 'extreme caution' in their decision-making and this approach may be replicated in the Irish context. Despite acknowledging the benefits of temporary release, the risk of reoffending was often interpreted as something to be managed within the prison system and only those whose risk was absolutely minimised were viewed as being suitable for release (Parole Board 2004, p. 7). Risk taking to facilitate the process of reintegration and management in the community was not viewed favourably. Risk management and reduction is a process that continues on re-entry (Kubrin and Stewart 2006; Kemshall 2008) and perhaps this conservative approach fits more neatly with the punitive component where public protection based on the exclusion of those perceived to be dangerous is central (see Chap. 5). Yet, this risk averse practice is not static and can operate in the opposite direction, depending on the individual and overarching approach adopted.

> And as a member of the Board, any indication whatsoever that a person is a risk I would be very, very slow personally to, add my name I suppose really, add my voice to a recommendation to release that person. (PB14)

> The problem is the Board has been criticised by saying that it's too conservative … and maybe the Board has been conservative in the past. (PB05)

> There has been a notable shift in terms of the approach towards risk and I think the group might be becoming slightly less risk averse. We've agreed we're looking at things in terms of risk and this person we believe is low risk so this is something we need to be pushing. (PB02)

> An individual has to jump through so many hoops to get parole that I think maybe by the time they get it, you know, the likelihood of them reoffending is probably small, you know? (PB10)

Members are not specifically focused on the risk of violent reoffending; rather the risk they are concerned with can relate to any behaviour that might result in the revocation of temporary release.

> And sometimes you have a case of somebody who is low risk of violent offending but they're a high risk of reoffending by way of, you know, they could be a chronic alcoholic, they're more of a nuisance, and they'll do something stupid, they might go in and, you know, rob a shop or something or be a general nuisance in society, but they're not posing necessarily any physical harm to others. There are a number of cases like that where you can kind of see this person we're going to see again because they just don't have the capacity to turn around that issue. (PB12)

> I really feel any risk of reoffending, that's the first thing I would say, any risk of reoffending must be taken very seriously. (PB14)

> If you have a person who has been convicted of murder, some people who were released from murder after very many years, committed other offences, but they are way down the scale if you like. I remember one committed shoplifting just when they were about to come before us they were given a period of temporary release by the prison service and they shoplifted. Now how do you equate shoplifting to murder? You can't. So it's a very difficult question and I think you'd have to look into each case on its own. (PB04)

The cautious approach was particularly evident when members discussed cases they viewed as presenting an unacceptably high risk. Five of fourteen members stated that they were involved in reviewing cases where they believed that the offender should never be released. This assessment was related to the offender's perceived dangerousness and the difficulties encountered in reducing their risk of reoffending. Thus, as noted by these decision-makers, a life sentence prisoner may serve life in prison in the real sense.

> I think there are a small group of people who probably will remain in prison for the rest of their lives, they are very small but I think they are there. I think it's their overall risk to reoffending and the fact that they haven't, over a prolonged period of time, taken any responsibility for what they have actually done. (PB06)

Interviewee: I think a small few people they're just so dangerous, so bad that I can't see how anybody could justify their actual exit from prison – a very small few now. And you know them when you've read their files, they jump right out at you and hit you.

Interviewer: What would indicate that?

Interviewee: Oh just the level, just the whole, the crime, the crimes usually, the sadistic nature of the crimes, the lack of empathy, lack of ownership, and then their subsequent denial, and then their behaviour in prison… and I suppose how, how messed up they are usually, you know?

Interviewer: So they would be considered as an unacceptably high risk?

Interviewee: Yeah, they'd be just too violent, you know? Usually mostly men now… and often in that scenario, it's not like bank robbers, it's mostly in the domestic scene, you know, that you'd really wonder that if they came out and met another unfortunate woman who hooked up with them – they'd kill her – when things weren't going right for them, because they know no other mechanisms, you know? (PB07)

The indeterminate nature of the life sentence and the discretion within the parole process was seen as instrumental in facilitating the incapacitation of those that present a level of dangerousness beyond what members viewed as acceptable in society.

Risk Assessment, Parole Board Style

A positive assessment by the Probation Service or Prison Psychology Service indicating that a life sentence prisoner is at a low risk of reoffending is not the only risk-based hurdle that must be overcome to secure a release recommendation. In addition, the offender must satisfy the Parole Board's own style of risk assessment. Members identified a range of risk factors that they viewed as relevant to their deliberations. Members were asked for their individual view of risk, rather than the factors they believed were taken into account in the risk assessments available to them. In that sense, what is presented is their individual assessment of the factors relevant to their deliberative process. When discussing how to identify and quantify risk, many of the factors identified by members map onto the static and dynamic factors incorporated in risk assessment tools as well as the statutory criteria in the Criminal Justice (Temporary Release of Prisoners) Act 2003 (see Fig. 4.1). Four of the most referenced criteria were statutory in nature (criminal history; nature of the offence; treatment participation; offender re-entry). This is unsurprising given the broad nature of the statutory criteria, despite the lack of explicit references by members to the statute itself. Non-statutory factors such as educational attainment and substance use include some references to treatment participation and offender re-entry. Members subscribed to the view that risk can be reduced through intervention and this is evidenced through the frequent reference to dynamic risk factors. Many of the factors referenced have been found to influence parole decision-making elsewhere (see for example: Caplan 2007; Hood and Shute 2000; Hood et al. 2000; Huebner and Bynum 2006; Padfield et al. 2000). Nonetheless, members did not feel constrained by any framework taking somewhat of a *carte blanche* approach to their deliberative process.

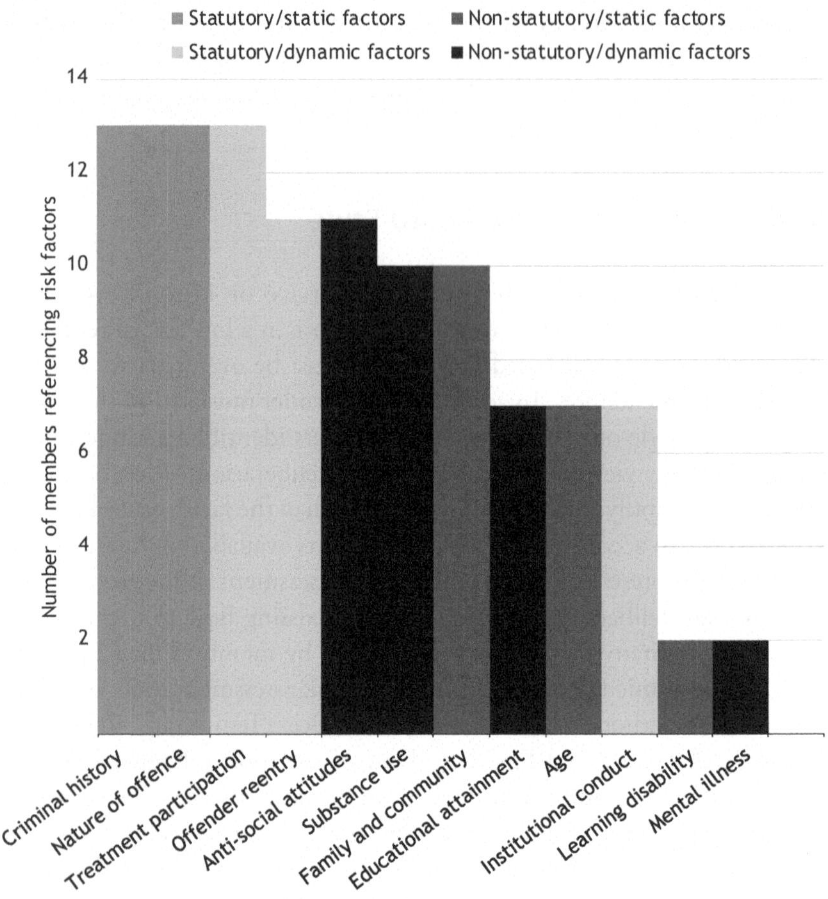

Fig. 4.1 Risk factors identified by Parole Board members in decision-making

Caution should be exercised when interpreting some of these risk factors. For example, the nature and gravity of the offence was one of the most frequently referenced factors by members. This is also ordinarily taken into consideration by a trial judge at sentencing. As already noted, the majority of life sentences are imposed for the same offence, murder. It is not possible at sentencing stage to distinguish between different types of murders based on culpability or depravity. Members tended to draw distinctions between certain types of murders in determining the risk of reoffending depending on a number of factors and it is certainly possible that issues of risk and the gravity of the offence are being conflated here. This raises a question as to whether the Parole Board is engaging in a form of risk assessment or a resentencing of sorts. In terms of the increase in time served, members were keen to identify the older an offender the lower the risk they presented. Paradoxically, members commented on the difficulties created through the length of time those participating in the process spend in prison and its concomitant impact on the risk of reoffending.

> Then they might stand still and you might actually be re-categorising them as more at risk of literally just stagnating and becoming institutionalised within the prison system. (PB06)

The institutionalisation that results from the increasing length of time a life sentence prisoner is required to serve prior to release may be impacting on the likelihood of being recommended for release. If this is considered relevant to the likelihood of reoffending then it is a factor created through the organisational structure of the process, to which members contribute and over which they exert some level of control. Even when an offender has been identified as low risk this will not necessarily result in a recommendation to release. There are practical constraints that might frustrate such a recommendation including difficulties in sourcing appropriate housing and community supports (Parole Board 2015, p. 4; Gallagher 2017).

Given the array of factors, the Parole Board's approach is, perhaps, not easily aligned with formal risk assessments designed to quantify, classify and control risk. It is a challenge to place the risk factors in any order or system to elucidate their impact on decision-making. There is a vagueness surrounding the Parole Board approach and this can enhance rather than reduce uncertainty when analysing the decision-making process. Given the unconstrained approach there is a danger that assumptions are being mistaken for assessments (Padfield et al. 2000, p. 140). Nonetheless, the factors identified by members in their version of risk assessment are significant to the recommendation process and will ultimately impact on those under review.

Previous Criminal History

Previous criminal history is a statutory factor taken into consideration by the Minister (s. 2(e)) and the Parole Board (2002, p. 10). It is a static factor in risk assessment tools and is viewed as such by members. It can also be a factor in sentencing an offender, with a lack of previous convictions treated as a mitigating factor (O'Malley 2016, pp. 172–177). A history of violence is a strong predictor of future violent behaviour (Klassen and O'Connor 1988), with the frequency of the violence increasing the risk of future violence (Borum et al. 1996). Criminal history or violence throughout the lifespan was identified by thirteen of fourteen members as a factor of significance when attempting to assess whether an offender poses a threat to the community on release. Where the offender's index offence was the only offence committed and no other previous criminal history was evident, members tended to place such an individual in the low-risk category. The 'once-off' offender who committed a 'crime of passion' (often a murder) was described as regularly appearing before the Parole Board. Seven of fourteen members referred specifically to a 'once-off' murder when asked to identify a low-risk offender.

> Low risk, a person who was never involved in trouble, never involved in crime in their lives, and committed some desperate crime and prior to that had no stain on their character whatsoever. (PB14)
>
> We'll say in murder for example, you could have a murder case which, you know, was a crime of passion or almost wasn't meant to happen, you know, just the circumstances, and you might say that the chances of that person reoffending are probably slim. (PB06)

By way of contrast, 11 members of the Parole Board placed those with a history of offending in the high-risk category.

> If a person has a long list of convictions, and particularly convictions for violence and eventually he commits a very serious offence, manslaughter or murder, I would feel in his case that probably I'd rate a risk of him reoffending. He's a bigger risk, in my opinion, than the guy who has no previous record, whose family are law-abiding people, who commits a once-off very serious offence and who has served his sentence and is coming towards the end of it. (PB14)

This approach to level of risk based on previous criminal history is consistent with social psychological explanations of crime that behavioural habits and histories, and the number and frequency of previous convictions, can be predictive of future offending behaviour (Gendreau et al. 1996; O'Donnell et al. 2008, pp. 135–136). Interviews conducted with 98 life sentence prisoners and 340 determinate sentence prisoners indicated that 63 per cent of life sentence prisoners had no previous convictions (in comparison with 37 per cent of determinate sentence offenders) (Kennedy et al. 2005, p. 44).

Nature and Gravity of the Offence

The nature and gravity of the offence forms part of the statutory criteria taken into consideration by the Minister (s. 2(a)) and the Parole Board (2002, p. 10). It forms a key part of one aspect of the proportionality principle that governs Irish sentencing. Offence type can also be predictive of the likelihood of reoffending (Steadman et al. 2000). Thirteen of fourteen members identified the nature and gravity of the offence as a relevant, static factor in their determination of the likelihood of an individual reoffending when considering an offender for recommendation to release.

> You see, sometimes the very depravity of the offence worries you about the fact if they had their freedom, would they do it again? (PB04)
>
> So if anyone has committed a very serious offence, you know, you're going to be concerned, if you like, about their future behaviour. (PB05)
>
> The type of crime it was, the degree of violence that was used. (PB08)

With all murderers sentenced to a mandatory life sentence, members employed the discretion afforded them within the parole process to draw distinctions between different types of murders. They categorised cases under review in terms of high and low risk on the basis of offence type, the circumstances surrounding the commission of the offence, whether the offence was an isolated incident and the relationship between the victim and perpetrator. An intra-familial murder, a 'crime of passion', or a conflict arising out of an unusual set of circumstances were described as low risk. The relationships characterised as low risk related to murders involving family, spouses, friends and acquaintances (which account for 76 per cent of homicides) (Dooley 2001, p. 12; O'Donnell 2005, p. 105).

> In a domestic situation the probability is the person will not reoffend, will never reoffend. (PB03)

> You know, a neighbour dispute involving a gun and a fatality, and when you understand what the triggers were to that dispute, a land dispute, you know, you can see that farmer will probably never do that again. So some are low [risk]. (PB07)

> We'll say in murder for example, you could have a murder case which, you know, was a crime of passion or, you know, almost wasn't meant to happen, you know, just the circumstances, and you might say that the chances of that person reoffending are probably slim. (PB06)

Age and substance use were identified as contributing factors in the commission of a violent offence and such offences were often placed in the 'once-off' category. There is a paucity of information on the correlation between the commission of an offence and psychoactive substances in Ireland although it does appear to be a contributing factor in homicide offences (Dooley 1995, 2001).

> Now quite honestly it is stunning, when you review eighty or ninety cases a year and have reviewed them for five years, the huge element of alcohol and drugs as the flash that makes somebody do something that's mad, as in beat a woman over the head, kill her, rape her, dump her over a wall – all sorts of really crazy crimes that when you think in the cold light of day probably would never have happened, but it had happened in that flash. (PB07)

> There are quite a number of cases that I would come across where you would see factors such as alcohol involved where if alcohol were not involved would this person be here in front of us? Possibly not. (PB03)

> These were all once-off incidences in a lot of cases, in eighty, seventy-five per cent where young people went out, got drunk, got into an argument or an altercation and it got out of hand. (PB01)

Despite categorising the 'once-off' murder as low risk, this did not necessarily translate into a view that there was no risk.

> So even if it's a situation where somebody, it was a moment of, you know, [*snaps fingers*] one moment of madness that's never going to occur again, it still needs to be addressed. (PB12)

By way of contrast, members placed homicides related to what might be referred to as 'gangland' or 'organised' crime activity in the high-risk category. Homicides connected to the illegal drugs trade are fairly new to the Irish penal landscape (Dooley 2001, pp. 16–17). There has been an increase in gun-related homicides where the perpetrator was 'known to the *Gardaí*' since the 1990s (Campbell 2010).

> But I will say to you the ones you worry about are the ones that belong to a gang and who are part of that gang and have been sent out to commit murder, who were paid for it in some shape or form whether it was in hard cash or in drugs or whatever. They're the ones you worry about and these would be generally young men, and these can be the difficult ones. (PB09)

Members were not questioned specifically about those that committed a sexual offence, however, sexual offences and sexual deviancy associated with an offence were frequently referenced when categorising high-risk offenders.

> The offender would have said quite openly that he still had sexual fantasies about the particular person, who still lived in their own locality which he planned to return to and felt that this person, who was a child when the original offence was committed, was still in love with him and people just didn't understand that they were in love with each other. To me, somebody who's fantasising about having a sexual relationship with the person they have tried to kill and he wants to return and have a sexual relationship with that person, to me that is a very high risk. (PB02)

There were 12 prisoners serving a life sentence for a sex offence in 2015, accounting for 3.5 per cent of the total life sentence prisoner population (*Dáil Question* No. 81: Frances Fitzgerald 08/11/2016). On a general note, those convicted of homicide have a lower rate of recidivism on release (26.2 per cent) when compared with the general recidivism rate across all offences (62.3 per cent) and the offence type for reconviction tends to be non-violent in nature (Prison Service 2013, pp. 13 and 16).

Treatment Participation

Thirteen of fourteen members viewed an offender's engagement with the available therapeutic services as important in mitigating future risk. While treatment participation is not referred to specifically in the statutory criteria, conduct in custody (s. 2(g)) and the recommendations of the relevant prison governor and Probation Officer, are taken into consideration by the Minister (s. 2(h)(i) and (iii)). It is also a factor that has been adopted by the Parole Board (2002, p. 10). Treatment participation was considered to be a dynamic factor by members and this is consistent with risk assessment tools. Members identified level of engagement with the available therapeutic services as important in assessing risk reduction when deliberating on individual cases.

> But you can also gauge [risk] by the level of engagement that a person has done while they're in prison. (PB03)
>
> I suppose low risk would be somebody who has done all that he or she can do within the prison system. (PB06)
>
> [An unacceptably high-risk case] that does come to mind is that if a prisoner, wasn't engaging with the services, that he was refusing the various rehabilitation courses that they can do, if he has an alcohol problem or drug problem and he's not dealing with it, if he's not engaging in any of the services and he just won't participate. (PB05)

The purpose of engagement, as viewed by members, ranged significantly but related primarily to addressing: offending behaviour; substance use issues; education; employment and life skills; and violent behaviour generally.

> Addressing the issues which revolved around the offending behaviour. (PB11)
>
> If they have a drug problem they've participated, for example a lot of prisoners they go on Methadone treatment, so if they're on Methadone

> treatment and they're following that and even if they got off the Methadone that would be a major plus, if they've an alcohol problem and they're going to AA. (PB04)

> Their engagement with the education services ... employment, or potential for employment afterwards. (PB02)

> Someone that wouldn't be showing any aggressive tendencies at all, even when they're put under pressure by a question, that there's an acceptance there and also that you can see a change in their ... you know, what must have been there previously. (PB01)

Members stated that they would be very reluctant to release an offender who did not engage with the available rehabilitative services.

> I would not entertain a guy like that for parole or for early release of any kind – is that simple enough? (PB08)

> I would be concerned about that prisoner's risk, if they're refusing point blank to engage with services because whatever led to the initial offence hasn't been explored or managed or addressed and it's impossible to know could the same circumstances or that same scenario arise and how that prisoner would in turn manage it. (PB02)

Despite the emphasis on the importance of engagement with the relevant services some members questioned the sincerity of the engagement of some offenders.

> I mean there's a bit of window-dressing involved with certain individuals. We come across scenarios where you'd have somebody who's doing all the courses, he's doing this, he's doing that, but then you might go and meet someone and then you would just see, 'oh this is only window-dressing to get out'. Some people are good at playing the game. (PB10)

Thus, while non-engagement raised concern and was viewed as an indication of increased risk, it did not necessarily result in engagement being equated with low risk.

Offender Re-entry and Community Support

Eleven of fourteen members identified the importance of factors surrounding offender re-entry on recidivism. In addition to taking into account the likelihood of a person reoffending or breaching their conditions on release, the Minister must have regard to whether temporary release 'might accelerate the person's reintegration into society or improve his prospects of obtaining employment' (s. 2(k)). These factors are also taken into consideration by the Parole Board (2002, p. 10) and can be considered dynamic in nature (Moore et al. 2013). Studies tend to focus on the individual factors associated with reoffending, but there is also interest in the community and neighbourhood contexts and the correlates with recidivism (Kubrin and Stewart 2006). The range of areas covered by risk assessment tools such as education, employment, financial situation, family/marital context, accommodation, companions and alcohol drug/problems, can be identified as dynamic factors that impact on offender re-entry and the likelihood of recidivism (Kazemian and Maruna 2009). The limited data on the general prison population indicates that the families and communities to which offenders return on release are often characterised by some level of socioeconomic deprivation (O'Mahony 1997; Seymour and Costello 2005; Bacik and O'Connell 1998). An offender with prospects of employment, strong family support, who has distanced himself from any criminal associations and has secured accommodation was viewed as being at a low risk of reoffending. Those with weak employment prospects, poor family support, lack of accommodation and continued associations with criminal peers were viewed as high risk.

> A source of income, if they have a trade that they can use and earn a living from, that is a difference. (PB01)

> What would be relevant is whether the prisoner is going to live with a family member, whether he or she would have family support, I think we'd be more concerned if they didn't have any fixed location to go to and they were going to be wandering around the community. (PB05)

> If they go back into the environment they came from, if they're still involved in drugs, if they go back to their criminal friends and they say … they're drinking and they say 'will we do a job, I know where there's easy money to be picked up' – will they go along? – yes they will, a lot of them, yes they will. (PB08)

One member questioned whether it was appropriate to take into consideration factors that were not within the control of the offender.

> Some of the risk factors for example would be family support, or something like that, they're very static things that the offender can do little to change or little to address and they can have done huge work in other areas but they can't change the fact that they have little or no family support. (PB02)

Antisocial Attitudes

Eleven of fourteen members described the attitude of the offender as significant in assessing the likelihood of recidivism and viewed it as a factor appropriate for intervention to reduce reoffending. Attitudes are not included as a statutory factor but antisocial attitudes, which can include the attitude of the offender towards the offence, offending generally, legal institutions and criminal others are included as dynamic factors in risk assessments (Mills et al. 2004). As a dynamic factor, antisocial attitudes allow for the provision of an explanation for the index offence as well as acting as a measure for change. Members viewed acknowledgement of the offending behaviour as crucial in terms of risk assessment as well as providing the means to address broader issues through engagement with the available services. Members were questioned on their approach to individuals that maintain their innocence throughout the parole process. All members stated that it would not be appropriate for the Parole Board to retry the offence and that the appropriate domain to challenge this was through the courts. They were also of the view that the maintenance of innocence should not preclude considering an offender for release. Nonetheless, there was a concern that the failure to acknowledge the offending behaviour served to frustrate the relevant services from conducting offence-related work. Refusal to accept responsibility for the index offence was also viewed as contributing to the level of risk posed by the offender resulting in a reluctance to release in these cases. This may result in a paradoxical situation whereby the 'innocent' life sentence prisoner is unlikely to be released, while the 'guilty' life sentence prisoner will be released (Samuels 2003, p. 179).

> That happened a couple of times, you know, where you'd have someone who said 'look, I'm innocent', you know. There's really very little that the Board then can do. It's very hard like because you do wonder then miscarriage of justice, whatever, but your hands are kind of tied. (PB10)

> Yes, they're maintaining their innocence but, you know, they've reached a point whereby they no longer represent or they do not represent a threat to society as far as we can gauge, and the recommendation could well be to prepare them for release. (PB03)

> The risk unacceptably high would be one where perhaps the person didn't even accept that he had done the offence, had done the crime, and so therefore non-acceptance of that fact actually militated against working on victim empathy aspects, working on issues that might be considered from all of the reports to have contributed to the crime. I would have grave concerns about that type of case. (PB06)

Members identified the attitude of the offender towards the victim deeming remorse and attitudes towards victimisation important in the assessment of risk. Targeting the capacity for empathy has been identified as important for treatment, particularly for sex offenders (Carich et al. 2004).

> Their ability to identify with the victim, to apologise, to make good, to do some reparation, you know that kind of thing, they're always good bets. (PB07)

In addition, six of fourteen members identified an offender's attitude towards peers and particularly an individual's association with the illegal drugs trade as contributing to the level of risk presented by an individual.

Whether an individual persisted in maintaining links with 'gang' activity or distanced himself from his criminal associations was deemed to be of significance. 'Gang' membership and peer association has been shown to be predictive of recidivism (Huebner et al. 2007).

> There was a case there when someone had been in for subversive organising. He went on and did a third-level degree. He came from a very well supported family background. He renounced the organisation he was associated with and that individual wants to get on and study [for] a degree and start a business of his own. (PB01)

Substance Use

Ten of fourteen members believed that offenders with on-going issues involving drugs and alcohol contributed to their likelihood of reoffending. Substance use is not addressed in the statutory criteria although an offender is required to be of 'sober habits' on release. Issues surrounding substance dependence have been identified in the Parole Board annual reports as a factor of importance (2005, pp. 3–4), noting that it is a barrier to recommending release where these issues have not been addressed through engagement with services.

> It is virtually impossible to see how the Board could recommend temporary release in respect of a prisoner who still requires to feed a drug addiction. (2006, p. 4)

Use of drugs and alcohol is a dynamic risk factor and is appropriate for intervention consistent with the risk-needs-responsivity model for offender assessment and rehabilitation, while the association between substance use and violence is well established in the literature (Abracen et al. 2000). In a 2005 study, 47 per cent of life sentence prisoners reported a current alcohol problem while 29 per cent reported a current drug problem (Kennedy et al. 2005, pp. 55–6). In the views of members, an offender who failed to address substance use issues through availing of the therapeutic services in prison presented a high risk of reoffending.

> [A high-risk offender is] someone who hasn't dealt with their drug abuse and has been in [prison] in relation to a drug related crime. The likelihood is that they will reoffend because they haven't addressed the issues that had them there in the first place, to cause their crime. (PB01)

Family and Community Influences

Ten of fourteen members identified factors related to an individual's childhood, family and community upbringing as relevant in the commission of the principal offence and these continued to be a factor for members when assessing an individual for recommendation to the Minster. Family risk factors are significant in the prediction of violent and sexual offending and predictors include: poor parental supervision; parental rejection; large family size; parental neglect and disrupted parental care; parental conflict; antisocial parents; and physical and sexual abuse (Farrington et al. 2012). Community level influences on crime and offending are well documented with social organisation and structural characteristics of communities playing a role in producing criminal acts (Wikström and Sampson 2003). While not a statutory factor, family and community influences can be considered a dynamic risk factor. Members tended to view family and community as static and historic over which the life sentence prisoner had little agency. Members placed those with what might be described as a 'difficult' childhood resulting from the influence of family or community into a high-risk category.

> What led to that flash, what led to that violence… usually those people have had rejection in the past, have been beaten up by their dads, have been abused as kids, have a very low self-image, self-esteem, so you're also looking to that, you know, to see would that happen again, you know? So it's about the circumstances of the individual profile, you know? (PB07)

> I think it would be incorrect to say that a deprived background or coming from a deprived area, necessarily makes you an offender, I don't believe that for one moment. But I think the whole family background and parenting and the controls that are with children and with young families, people falling out of school, all of those issues all contribute perhaps to moving into that alcohol, sort of drugs area, at a much earlier age than perhaps other people might actually do it. (PB06)

Educational Attainment

Seven of fourteen members referenced educational attainment when discussing release and reoffending. Educational attainment is not a statutory factor but is included as a dynamic risk factor (Andrews and Bonta 2000). Levels of educational attainment are significantly lower amongst the prison population than the general population (Central Statistics Office 2011; O'Mahony 1997, p. 53). Educational attainment may be higher for those serving life sentences as an assessment of 26 life sentence prisoners indicated that 21 of those surveyed had attained lower secondary education or above (the survey did not account for whether this education was attained prior to or during imprisonment) (Milner 2010, p. 47). Engagement with educational programmes while incarcerated has a positive impact on recidivism on release (Farrington et al. 2012, pp. 50–51). An Irish study found that recidivism rates were higher amongst those who had less formal education or were illiterate (O'Donnell et al. 2008, pp. 134–5). Members were cognisant of low levels of education on entry and viewed engagement with the available education services as significant in reducing the level of risk posed by the offender.

> And it's very enlightening for example when you see somebody who comes into the system who is maybe illiterate and see how they have gone on to do their Leaving Cert or indeed Open University et cetera. So it's really I suppose the balance between the offence that the person is in for and how they've used their time in the prison system, really to me they would be the factors that would influence. (PB06)

Age

Age is not a statutory factor yet seven of fourteen members believed that the age of an offender at the time of review to be of significance in identifying good risk prisoners, acknowledging that it played a role in the decision-making process. 'Aging out' or the maturation out of crime is well recognised in criminology (Gottfredson and Hirschi 1990) although our understanding of this process in Ireland is rather limited (Healy and O'Donnell 2008). Recidivism data from the Prison Service (2013, p. 11) evidences that maturation out of crime does occur in the Irish context. As offenders age, the influence of social factors such as family and employment can have a cumulative effect resulting in desistance from crime (Laub and Sampson 1993). Age is incorporated as a static factor in assessment tools when considering the commission of the offence and in the context of the parole process (Andrews and Bonta 2000). Members tended to view age as a dynamic factor although it is a static factor in assessment tools. This can be linked to the length of time served by a life sentence prisoner prior to release. In 2016, the average age of life sentence prisoners committed was 29 years while the average age on release was 54.5 years (*Dáil Question* No. 827: Frances Fitzgerald 20 June 2017). Consistent with research on 'aging out', members tended to place the middle-aged and elderly offender into the low-risk category.

> You look at the statistics, you see the risk of it, you see what age they are, people grow too old to commit some of these crimes. A person whose profile would be much more in danger of losing their temper at 26 than they would be at the age of 56. (PB04)

> These guys do improve as the years go by, they do mature, they do cop on, families might get at them, their own minds get at them. (PB09)

In addition to taking into consideration the age of an offender, physical health problems were identified by members as a factor that might facilitate release. The statutory framework makes specific provision for the Minister to release an offender for health or humanitarian reasons (s. 1(b)). Members placed those with physical health difficulties, often associated with the ageing process, into the low-risk category.

> We interviewed a man, again last month, he was convicted of killing his wife, he has spent eighteen years in jail, he has a serious, serious lung problem, he can barely walk ten steps without looking for breath, he'll probably have to go around in a wheelchair – the likelihood of him committing a crime is very slim. (PB01)

An ageing prison population is presenting administrative challenges in many jurisdictions (Human Rights Watch 2012) with the Council of Europe (2003, paras. 10–37) recommending that elderly prisoners be assisted in maintaining standards of good physical and mental health. In Ireland, there has been an increase of those over the age of 50 in the general prison population (from 5 per cent in 2001 to 9.7 per cent in 2016) (Prison Service 2001, pp. 94–95; 2016, p. 34) and the management of older persons has been identified for strategic action (Prison Service 2010, p. 49; IPRT 2016).

Institutional Conduct

Regard is to be had of an offender's conduct in custody when being considered for release (s. 2(g); Parole Board 2002, p. 10). Members identified prison discipline as particularly important when considering an offender for recommendation to the Minister. Institutional misconduct can be predictive of reoffending on release (Heil et al. 2009) but this is a complicated matter as environmental factors might influence aggressive behaviour (see for example: the composition of the prison population; turnover of the population; prison overcrowding: Gendreau et al. 1997). There is evidence to suggest that those serving short-term prison sentences engage in misconduct more frequently than long-term offenders, such that there may be an inverse relationship between sentence length and prison misconduct (Mooney and Daffern 2011; Cunningham and Sorensen 2007). It is difficult to assess whether institutional conduct should impact on decision-making when assessing the risk of recidivism for long-term offenders yet it appears to play an important role in parole decision-making (Caplan 2007). Seven of fourteen members identified issues of prison misconduct as contributing to their assessment of the risk of reoffending on release. Members viewed those who could be described as the 'model prisoner' positively and low risk, while those in receipt of 'P19s' were viewed negatively and high risk ('P19' refers to the form completed by the Governor where a breach of discipline has occurred) (Part 3 of the Prisons Act 2007; rules 66–8 of the Prison Rules 2007). A breach of prison discipline does not necessitate an act of aggression by a prisoner and the behaviour involved can be relatively trivial such as intoxication, disrespect to a prison officer or offences against good order or discipline. Members were aware that they had a role in prison discipline and that their approach had influence on other life sentence prisoners eligible within the system. In essence, they were keen not to condone the institutional troublemaker through progressing them towards release (Hawkins 1983, p. 112). Given that three years can pass between reviews, there is potential for an offender's institutional behaviour to improve or disimprove considerably over time and members accounted for this throughout the cycles of review.

> The number of P19s is very telling. If somebody had no P19s in three or four years it indicates a level of consistent good behaviour. If someone is consistently having P19s, disagreements with other prisoners, disagreements with prison officers, abusing the system, well that's very important. If somebody says 'oh, I don't do this, I don't do that' yet they've proved positive for drugs in the last three months, they've had a fight with a fellow prisoner, they've been uncooperative with staff, well again, it tells its own tale. (PB01)

Learning Disability

Research indicates that the use of risk assessments on groups of offenders with learning disabilities demonstrates predictive and discriminative validity (Lindsay et al. 2008). Learning disability is considered to be a static factor and while it may be relevant for the purpose of risk assessment, it is not included in the statutory criteria. Low intelligence and attainment, which may fit with a pattern of cognitive and neuropsychological deficits, can also be predictive of offending behaviour (Farrington 2002, pp. 678–9). A former Chairperson of the Parole Board identified the difficulties presented by 'intellectually disabled offenders' and noted the reluctance of the 'ordinary services' in engaging with offenders presenting with such issues (Parole Board 2007, p. 6). The inconsistent use of terminology (intellectual disability, intellectual capacity, learning disability, developmental disability, cognitive impairment) results in a lack of consensus and clarity in terms of categorising behaviour. Nonetheless, three of fourteen members connected the risk of reoffending with what can broadly be understood to fall within the realm of intellectual and learning disability (as distinct from educational deficits).

> And sometimes we would ask for a mental assessment, an intelligence assessment to see is he capable of learning from these experiences, sometimes they'll come back and they'll say 'no, no we've gone as far as we can'. Now, those people could be risky guys. (PB08)

> He [committed] a very violent crime, he didn't kill someone but he could very well have killed someone, he is very badly mentally challenged, he would have a very low IQ and would be very easily led. I reckon he's a very high risk. (PB01)

Mental Illness

Research indicates that mental illness impacts negatively on the likelihood of parole release by decision-makers (Caplan 2007; Hannah-Moffat 2004). An Irish study in 2005 (Kennedy et al., p. 49) found a higher prevalence of mental illness[1] and psychosis[2] across the lifetime of life sentence prisoners (50 per cent) when compared with fixed-term sentence prisoners (34 per cent). Interestingly, members tended not to make overt references to terminology related to mental illness although members did reference psychological factors with those perceived to be high risk. For example, one member referenced psychopathy directly when describing high-risk offenders.

> Then there's some very high risk and you think, "Jesus, that's a really dangerous person, I can definitely see that person doing that again" because they're sadistic, because they're psychopathic. (PB07)

The term 'psychopath' has a defined meaning within the field of psychology (Hare 2003) and an ill-defined colloquial meaning, thus rendering any assessment of its use by criminal justice authorities, including parole decision-makers, replete with difficulties.

Conclusion

The analysis presented in this chapter indicates that members adopt a conservative and risk averse approach when deliberating on a life sentence prisoner under review. Members identified public protection as the key consideration in their assessment of life sentence prisoners and articulated the factors they believed to impact on the level of risk presented by an offender. These factors are employed to determine outcomes within a fluid and malleable system where the overarching culture of cautiousness only permits those considered to be 'safe bets' as suitable for a release recommendation. Thus members appear to adopt a defensive rather than defensible framework when making recommendations in individual cases. Defensible decisions are based on the appropriate use of information grounded on the available evidence. Defensive decisions focus on the 'worst case scenario' and are intolerant of errors (Kemshall 2001). The origin of this form of groupthink is hazy, but it is reasonable to surmise that the escalation in time served by life sentence prisoners may, in part, reflect an increased focus on risk assessment over the last decade. The tendency towards cautiousness may also be a reaction to the heightened public and political scrutiny of Parole Board decision-making since its establishment in 2001 (see Chap. 5).

In the context of life sentence prisoners, parole decision-makers must assimilate and interpret information on risk while being cognisant of the dangerousness associated with the population under review, as well as public perceptions of dangerousness, which may run counter to the risk assessments presented. Such a disjoint between public perception, the knowledge of experts and the assumptions of decision-makers raise questions as to how decisions surrounding risk and security are made and whether risk can truly be described as central to the process. This is particularly concerning when the legal framework gives decision-makers broad discretionary powers, as is the case with the administration of life sentences in Ireland. Risk and public protection may be presented externally to the public as the issue of paramount importance. But it may also represent an acceptable facade to decision-making behind which a myriad of factors can impact upon the release decision. As will become evident, there are other considerations operating to influence parole outcomes, many of which are incongruous with the objectives of the risk paradigm.

Notes

1. 'Mental illness' includes psychosis, affective disorder, anxiety disorder but excludes substance use disorder (Kennedy et al. 2005, pp. 47–48).
2. 'Psychosis' includes schizophrenia, psychotic mood disorder, substance induced psychosis and other psychotic disorders (Kennedy et al. 2005, pp. 47–48).

References

Abracen, J., Looman, J., & Anderson, D. (2000). Alcohol and drug abuse in sexual and nonsexual violent offenders. *Sexual Abuse, 12*(4), 263–274.

Andrews, D. A., & Bonta, J. (2000). *The level of service inventory-revised.* Toronto: Multi-Health Systems.

Andrews, D. A., & Bonta, J. (2010). *The psychology of criminal conduct.* London: Routledge.

Andrews, D. A., Bonta, J., & Hoge, R. D. (1990). Classification for effective rehabilitation: Rediscovering psychology. *Criminal Justice and Behavior, 17*(1), 19–52.

Andrews, D. A., Bonta, J., & Wormith, J. S. (2011). The risk-need-responsivity (RNR) model: Does adding the good lives model contribute to effective crime prevention? *Criminal Justice and Behavior, 38*(7), 735–755.

Bacik, I., & O'Connell, M. (1998). *Crime and poverty in Ireland.* Dublin: Sweet and Maxwell.

Barbaree, H. E., Seto, M. C., Langton, C. M., & Peacock, E. J. (2001). Evaluating the predictive accuracy of six risk assessment instruments for adult sex offenders. *Criminal Justice and Behavior, 28*(4), 490–521.

Beck, U. (1992). *Risk society: Towards a new modernity.* London: Sage.

Bonta, J. (1996). Risk-needs assessment and treatment. In A. T. Hartland (Ed.), *Choosing correctional options that work: Defining the demand and evaluating the supply* (pp. 18–32). Thousand Oaks: Sage.

Bonta, J., & Andrews, D. A. (2007). Risk-need-responsivity model for offender assessment and rehabilitation. *Rehabilitation, 6*(1), 1–22.

Borum, R., Swartz, M., & Swanson, J. (1996). Assessing and managing violence risk in clinical practice. *Journal of Psychiatric Practice, 2*(4), 205–215.

Bottoms, A. (1995). The philosophy and politics of punishment and sentencing. In C. Clarkson & R. Morgan (Eds.), *The politics of sentencing reform* (pp. 17–49). Oxford: Clarendon Press.

Bracken, D. C. (2010). Differing conceptions of risk and need in Irish probation officers. *Irish Probation Journal, 7*(1), 108–118.

Brown, M. (2000). Calculations of risk in contemporary penal practice. In M. Brown & J. Pratt (Eds.), *Dangerous offenders: Punishment and social order* (pp. 93–108). London: Routledge.

Campbell, L. (2010). Responding to gun crime in Ireland. *British Journal of Criminology, 50*(3), 414–434.

Caplan, J. M. (2007). What factors affect parole – A review of empirical research. *Federal Probation, 71*(1), 16–19.

Carich, M. S., Metzger, C. K., Baig, M. S., & Harper, J. J. (2004). Enhancing victim empathy for sex offenders. *Journal of Child Sexual Abuse, 12*(3–4), 255–276.

Carson, D., & Carson, T. (2010). Public protection: Perpetrators, predictions, prevention and performance. In M. Nash & A. Williams (Eds.), *Handbook of public protection* (pp. 162–180). Oxon: Willan.

Central Statistics Office. (2011). *Quarterly national household survey: Educational attainment thematic report 2011*. Dublin: Central Statistics Office.

Cheliotis, L. K. (2006). How iron is the iron cage of new penology? The role of human agency in the implementation of criminal justice policy. *Punishment and Society, 8*(3), 313–340.

Cohen, S. (1985). *Visions of social control: Crime, punishment and classification*. Cambridge: Polity Press.

Copas, J., & Marshall, P. (1998). The offender group reconviction scale: A statistical reconviction score for use by probation officers. *Journal of the Royal Statistical Society Series, 47*(1), 159–171.

Council of Europe. (2003). *Recommendation 23 on management by prison administrations of life-sentence and other long-term prisoners*. Strasbourg: Council of Europe.

Cunningham, M. D., & Sorensen, J. R. (2007). Predictive factors for violent misconduct in close custody. *The Prison Journal, 87*(2), 241–253.

Dooley, E. (1995). *Homicide in Ireland 1972–1991*. Dublin: Stationery Office.

Dooley, E. (2001). *Homicide in Ireland 1992–1996*. Dublin: Stationery Office.

Douglas, M. (1992). *Risk and blame: Essays in cultural theory*. London: Routledge.

Ekberg, M. (2007). The parameters of the risk society: A review and exploration. *Current Sociology, 55*(3), 343–366.

Faigman, D. L., Monahan, J., & Slobogin, C. (2014). Group to individual (G2i) inference in scientific expert testimony. *University of Chicago Law Review, 1*, 417–480.

Farrington, D. P. (2002). Developmental criminology and risk focused prevention. In M. Maguire, R. Morgan, & R. Reiner (Eds.), *The Oxford handbook of criminology* (pp. 657–701). Oxford: Oxford University Press.

Farrington, D. P., Loeber, R., & Ttofi, M. M. (2012). Risk and protective factors for offending. In D. P. Farrington & B. C. Welsh (Eds.), *The Oxford handbook of crime prevention* (pp. 46–49). Oxford: Oxford University Press.

Feeley, M. M., & Simon, J. (1992). The new penology: Notes on the emerging strategy of corrections and its implications. *Criminology, 30*(4), 449–474.

Feeley, M., & Simon, J. (1994). Actuarial justice: The emerging new criminal law. In D. Nelken (Ed.), *The futures of criminology* (pp. 173–201). New York: Sage.

Gallagher, C. (2017, May 2). Parole head seeks priority housing for life term prisoners. *Irish Times*. Retrieved from https://www.irishtimes.com

Garland, D. (1996). The limits of the sovereign state strategy: Strategies of crime control in contemporary society. *British Journal of Criminology, 36*(4), 445–471.

Garland, D. (2001). *The culture of control: Crime and social order in contemporary society*. Oxford: Oxford University Press.

Gelsthorpe, L., & Padfield, P. (Eds.). (2003). *Exercising discretion: Decision-making in the criminal justice system and beyond*. Devon: Willan.

Gendreau, P., Little, T., & Goggin, C. (1996). A meta-analysis of the predictors of adult offender recidivism: What works! *Criminology, 34*(4), 575–608.

Gendreau, P., Goggin, C. E., & Law, M. A. (1997). Predicting prison misconducts. *Criminal Justice and Behavior, 24*(4), 414–431.

Gendreau, P., Goggin, C., Cullen, F. T., & Paparozzi, M. (2002). The common-sense revolution and correctional policy. In J. McGuire (Ed.), *Offender rehabilitation and treatment* (pp. 359–386). Chichester: Wiley.

Gendreau, P., Smith, P., & Thériault, Y. L. (2009). Chaos theory and correctional treatment: Common sense, correctional quackery, and the law of fartcatchers. *Journal of Contemporary Criminal Justice, 25*(4), 384–396.

Gottfredson, M., & Hirschi, T. (1990). *A general theory of crime*. Stanford: Stanford University Press.

Hannah-Moffat, K. (2004). Losing ground: Gendered knowledge, parole risk, and responsibility. *Social Politics: International Studies in Gender, State & Society, 11*(3), 363–385.

Hannah-Moffat, K., Maurutto, P., & Turnbull, S. (2009). Negotiated risk: Actuarial illusions and discretion in probation. *Canadian Journal of Law & Society/La Revue Canadienne Droit et Société, 24*(3), 391–409.

Harcourt, B. E. (2007). *Against prediction: Profiling, policing and punishing in an actuarial age*. Chicago: University of Chicago Press.

Hare, R. D. (2003). *Manual for the revised psychopathy checklist*. Toronto: Multi-Health Systems.

Hart, S. D. (2003). Actuarial risk assessment: Commentary on Berlin *et al. Sexual Abuse: A Journal of Research and Treatment, 15*(4), 383–388.

Hart, S. D., & Cooke, D. J. (2013). Another look at the (im-)precision of individual risk estimates made using actuarial risk assessment instruments. *Behavioral Sciences & the Law, 31*(1), 81–102.

Hawkins, K. (1983). Assessing evil: Decision behaviour and Parole Board justice. *British Journal of Criminology, 23*(2), 101–127.

Healy, D. (2012). Advise, assist and befriend: Can probation supervision support desistance? *Social Policy & Administration, 46*(4), 377–394.

Healy, D., & O'Donnell, I. (2008). Calling time on crime: Motivation, generativity and agency in Irish probationers. *Probation Journal, 55*(1), 25–38.

Heil, P., Harrison, L., English, K., & Ahlmeyer, S. (2009). Is prison sexual offending indicative of community risk? *Criminal Justice and Behavior, 36*(9), 892–908.

Heilbrun, K., O'Neill, M. L., Stevens, T. N., Strohman, L. K., Bowman, Q., & Lo, Y. W. (2004). Assessing normative approaches to communicating violence risk: A national survey of psychologists. *Behavioral Sciences & the Law, 22*(2), 187–196.

Hood, R., & Shute, S. (2000). *Parole decision-making: Weighing the risk to the public*. London: Home Office.

Hood, R., Shute, S., & Wilcox, A. (2000). *The parole system at work: A study of risk based decision-making*. London: Home Office.

Huebner, B. M., & Bynum, T. S. (2006). An analysis of parole decision making using a sample of sex offenders: A focal concerns perspective. *Criminology, 44*(4), 961–991.

Huebner, B. M., Varano, S. P., & Bynum, T. S. (2007). Gangs, guns, and drugs: Recidivism among serious, young offenders. *Criminology & Public Policy, 6*(2), 187–221.

Human Rights Watch. (2012). *Old behind bars: The aging prison population in the United States.* New York: Human Rights Watch.

Irish Penal Reform Trust. (2016). *'I'm here, time stands still': The rights, needs and experiences of older people in prison.* Dublin: IPRT.

Irish Times. (2006, March 9). McDowell defends length of murder sentences. *Irish Times*, p. 7.

Kazemian, L., & Maruna, S. (2009). Desistance from crime. In M. D. Krohn, A. J. Lizotte, & G. Penly Hall (Eds.), *Handbook on crime and deviance* (pp. 277–295). New York: Springer.

Kemshall, H. (1998). *Risk in probation practice.* Aldershot: Ashgate.

Kemshall, H. (2001). *Risk assessment and management of known violent and sexual offenders: A review of current issues.* London: Home Office.

Kemshall, H. (2003). *Understanding risk in criminal justice.* Maidenhead: Open University Press.

Kemshall, H. (2006). Crime and risk. In P. Taylor-Goodby & J. Zinn (Eds.), *Risk in social science* (pp. 76–93). Oxford: Oxford University Press.

Kemshall, H. (2008). *Understanding the managements of high risk offenders in the community.* Maidenhead: Open University Press.

Kemshall, H., & Maguire, M. (2001). Public protection, partnership and risk penality: The multi-agency risk management of sexual and violent offenders. *Punishment and Society, 3*(2), 237–264.

Kennedy, H. G., Monks, S., Curtin, K., Wright, B., Linehan, S., Duffy, D., Telijeur, C., & Kelly, A. (2005). *Mental illness in Irish prisoners: Psychiatric morbidity in sentenced, remanded, and newly committed prisoners.* Dublin: National Forensic Mental Health Service.

Kilcommins, S., O'Donnell, I., O'Sullivan, E., & Vaughan, B. (2004). *Crime, punishment and the search for order in Ireland.* Dublin: Institute of Public Administration.

Klassen, D., & O'Connor, W. A. (1988). A prospective study of predictors of violence in adult male mental health admissions. *Law and Human Behavior, 12*(2), 143–158.

Kubrin, C. E., & Stewart, E. A. (2006). Predicting who reoffends: The neglected role of neighborhood context in recidivism studies. *Criminology, 44*(1), 165–197.

Laub, J. H., & Sampson, R. J. (1993). Turning points in the life course: Why change matters to the study of crime. *Criminology, 31*(3), 301–325.
Lindsay, W. R., Hogue, T. E., Taylor, J. L., Steptoe, L., Mooney, P., O'Brien, G., Johnston, S., & Smith, A. H. (2008). Risk assessment in offenders with intellectual disability: A comparison across three levels of security. *International Journal of Offender Therapy and Comparative Criminology, 52*(1), 90–111.
Lynch, M. (2000). Rehabilitation as rhetoric: The ideal of reformation in contemporary parole discourse and practices. *Punishment and Society, 2*(1), 40–65.
Matthews, R. (2005). The myth of punitiveness. *Theoretical Criminology, 9*(2), 175–201.
Maurutto, P., & Hannah-Moffat, K. (2006). Assembling risk and the restructuring of penal control. *British Journal of Criminology, 46*(3), 438–454.
McNally, G. (2009). Probation in Ireland, part 2: The modern age, 1960s to 2000. *Irish Probation Journal, 6*(1), 187–228.
Mills, J. F., Kroner, D. G., & Hemmati, T. (2004). The measures of criminal attitudes and associates (MCAA) the prediction of general and violent recidivism. *Criminal Justice and Behavior, 31*(6), 717–733.
Milner, C. (2010). *The psychology of the life sentence: The subjective experiences of life sentence prisoners*. Unpublished PhD thesis, Trinity College Dublin.
Monahan, J. (1993). Limiting therapist exposure to Tarasoff liability: Guidelines for risk containment. *American Psychologist, 48*(3), 242–250.
Mooney, J. L., & Daffern, M. (2011). Institutional aggression as a predictor of violent recidivism: Implications for parole decision making. *International Journal of Forensic Mental Health, 10*(1), 52–63.
Moore, B. (1996). *Risk assessment: A practitioner's guide to predicting harmful behaviour*. London: Whiting and Birch.
Moore, R., Gray, E., Roberts, C., Taylor, E., & Merrington, S. (2013). *Managing persistent and serious offenders in the community*. London: Routledge.
O'Donnell, I. (2005). Crime and justice in the Republic of Ireland. *European Journal of Criminology, 2*(1), 99–131.
O'Donnell, I., Baumer, E. P., & Hughes, N. (2008). Recidivism in the Republic of Ireland. *Criminology & Criminal Justice, 8*(2), 123–146.
O'Mahony, P. (1997). *Mountjoy prisoners: A sociological and criminological profile*. Dublin: Stationery Office.
O'Malley, P. (2000). Risk societies and the government of crime. In M. Brown & J. Pratt (Eds.), *Dangerous offenders: Punishment and social order, Dangerousness, risk and modern society* (pp. 189–208). London: Routledge.

O'Malley, P. (2010). *Crime and risk*. London: Sage.

O'Malley, T. (2016). *Sentencing law and practice*. Dublin: Thomson Round Hall.

Olden, J. (2001). *Report of Mr John Olden on the management of the sentences of Thomas Murray, life sentence prisoner*. Dublin: Department of Justice and Equality.

Padfield, N. (2010). Discretion and decision-making in public protection. In M. Nash & A. Williams (Eds.), *Handbook of public protection* (pp. 103–132). Oxon: Willan.

Padfield, N., Liebling, A., & Arnold, H. (2000). *An exploration of decision-making at discretionary lifer panels*. London: Home Office.

Parole Board. (2002–2015). *Annual reports*. Dublin: Parole Board.

Pratt, J. (2007). *Penal populism*. New York: Routledge.

Pratt, J., Brown, D., Brown, M., Hallsworth, S., & Morrison, W. (2005). *The new punitiveness. Trends, theories and perspective*. Devon: Willan.

Prendergast, M. (2012). Practitioner perceptions on the merits, challenges and ethical dilemmas of LSI-R in practice. *Irish Probation Journal, 9*(1), 111–131.

Prison Service. (2001–2016). Annual reports. Dublin/Longford: Irish Prison.

Probation Service. (2008). *Strategy statement 2008–2010*. Dublin: Stationery Office.

Robinson, G. (2001). Power, knowledge and "what works" in probation. *Howard Journal of Crime and Justice, 40*(3), 235–254.

Robinson, G. (2002). A rationality of risk in the Probation Service: Its evolution and contemporary profile. *Punishment and Society, 4*(1), 5–25.

Samuels, A. (2003). In denial of murder: No parole. *Howard Journal of Crime and Justice, 42*(2), 176–180.

Serin, R. (2011). *Parole Board Canada: Pre-reading material (ATRA and decision framework)*. Parole Board Canada. Retrieved from http://www.ct.gov/bopp/lib/bopp/SDM.pdf

Seymour, M., & Costello, L. (2005). *A study of the number, profile and progression routes of homeless persons before the court and in custody in Dublin*. Dublin: Probation and Welfare Service/Department of Justice and Equality.

Simon, J. (1998). Managing the monstrous: Sex offenders and the new penology. *Psychology, Public Policy and Law, 4*(1–2), 452–467.

Steadman, H. J., Silver, E., Monahan, J., Appelbaum, P. S., Clark Robbins, P., Mulvey, E. P., Grisson, T., Roth, L. H., & Banks, S. (2000). A classification tree approach to the development of actuarial violence risk assessment tools. *Law and Human Behavior, 24*(1), 83–100.

Wikström, P. O. H., & Sampson, R. J. (2003). Social mechanisms of community influences on crime and pathways in criminality. In B. B. Lahey, T. E. Moffitt, & A. Caspi (Eds.), *Causes of conduct disorder and juvenile delinquency* (pp. 118–148). New York: Guilford Press.
Wong, S. C., & Gordon, A. (2006). The validity and reliability of the Violence Risk Scale: A treatment-friendly violence risk assessment tool. *Psychology, Public Policy, and Law, 12*(3), 279–309.

Table of Legal Instruments

Criminal Justice (Temporary Release of Prisoners) Act 2003.
Prison Rules 2007: S.I. No. 25/2007.
Prisons Act 2007.

Table of Cases

Ireland

People (Attorney General) v O'Callaghan [1966] IR 501.

Table of Parliamentary Debates

541 (2) *Dáil Debates* Col.199: John O'Donoghue, 3 October 2001.
913(2) *Dáil Debates* Col.: Frances Fitzgerald, 15 June 2016.
Dáil Question No. 81: Frances Fitzgerald, 08 November 2016.
Dáil Question No. 827: Frances Fitzgerald, 20 June 2017.

5

Punishment, Public Opinion and Politics

Anyone who says they wouldn't have a political agenda, or a sort of a public perception or agenda in the back of their mind is talking horseshit to be honest, you know?
Minister for Justice 2

Introduction

This chapter explores the range of factors outside of risk that impact on parole decision-makers. Hawkins (1983a, p. 102) describes the decision of a parole authority as symbolically significant as 'a parole board is engaged in the appearance of condoning or condemning criminal behaviour; it is making statements about good and evil, desert and punishment, to the prisoner, the institutions, and the wider community'. The symbolic significance of the process was evident amongst decision-makers and clearly impacted on outcomes, although the strength and consistency of statements in relation to this varied considerably when compared to the concreteness in identifying risk factors. Nonetheless, this challenges the presentation by the Parole Board that risk is the central factor in the decision-making process. This is particularly relevant in Ireland where

D. Griffin, *Killing Time*, https://doi.org/10.1007/978-3-319-72667-0_5

what constitutes 'risk' for parole decision-makers can be so imprecise and the discretionary nature of the process allows for an unconstrained approach to outcomes. This chapter reveals that decision-makers are incorporating their perceptions of the purposes of punishment, public opinion, and the political regime *du jour* when deliberating on the case of a life sentence prisoner. Risk assessment and the statutory criteria are being supplemented by these considerations. Parole Board members (members) and Ministers for Justice (Minister(s)) viewed their role as reaching beyond a binary decision of release or restraint dictated by public protection. This chapter also provides an insight into the decision-making of a number of former Ministers. Ministers were open in acknowledging that their decision-making was influenced by politics and public opinion with little evidence that the statutory criteria placed any constraint on their decision-making process. The incorporation of such factors may be indicative of a punitive shift in parole decision-making.

Evidence of Punitivism

Punitiveness is a poorly understood, 'thin' theoretical concept with little consensus surrounding its definition (Matthews 2005, p. 178). While the jurisdictional measure of punitiveness is often the imprisonment rate, what is being described is 'an unspecified mix of attitudes, enactments, motivations, policies, practices, and ways of thinking that, taken together, express greater intolerance of deviance and deviants, and greater support for harsher policies and severer punishments' (Tonry 2007, p. 7). Matters are further complicated by the diverse practices evident across a range of Western jurisdictions. It is increasingly being argued that the factors that are deemed to contribute to punitivism (such as high crime rates, harsher public attitudes, cynical politicians, ethnic tensions, rapid social and economic change, postmodernist angst and 'penal populism'), have little to do with the adoption of punitive policies in individual countries and fail to explain the increasing divide between the United States and other democratic societies in terms of penal policy (Cavadino and Dignan 2006; Tonry 2001; Nelken 2009). Rather, Zimring and Johnson (2006,

p. 271) argue that 'what sets the United States apart from other countries in terms of punitiveness is both the greater political importance of crime and the larger structural vulnerability of criminal justice to the political process'. Common law countries, including the United States, United Kingdom, Canada, Australia and New Zealand are at the higher end of the international imprisonment rate in comparison with other countries in Western Europe (Walmsley 2016) and appear to be more susceptible to punitive 'policy transfer'; however, categorising a criminal justice system as 'punitive' is a complex task and providing an explanation even more so (Tonry 2007, p. 30). Tonry (2001, p. 518) accepts that ultimately, explanations of penal policy and practice in individual jurisdictions remain 'parochially national and cultural'.

Up until relatively recently, Ireland could be considered an anomaly amongst other common law countries in terms of its resistance to punitivism (Griffin and O'Donnell 2012). This resistance may be associated with trends specific to the Irish criminal justice system such as: traditionally low rates of crime and imprisonment; the absence of public or political concern about crime until the 1990s; an individualised sentencing system and a fiercely independent judiciary; little concern regarding monitoring, control and punishment; satisfaction with the police; and the absence of a criminological discourse (for a discussion, see Kilcommins et al. 2004). Nonetheless, the veracity of Adler's (1983) description of Ireland as a nation 'not obsessed with crime' can certainly now be challenged with evidence of a hardening of public attitudes, an increasingly politicised approach towards issues of law and order and a media characterised by populist punitiveness (O'Donnell and O'Sullivan 2003; O'Donnell 2005, 2011; O'Connell 1999). June 1996 is considered a tipping point in Irish criminal justice, with the murder of a crime journalist and a Garda detective becoming defining moments in the debate on law and order (O'Donnell 2005). Crime became an issue of public and political concern in a manner not witnessed previously. While the level of public concern about crime and disorder has since abated, issues of law and order continue to occupy a space in the public and political consciousness. This has been assisted by an increase in the rate of lethal violence, its association with 'gangland' crime (Campbell 2010) and the distorted media coverage given to this type of crime

(O'Connell 1999). The imprisonment rate increased significantly in the mid-1990s coinciding with a decrease in the crime rate. Although there was a combination of factors that led to these contradictory trends, a key component was the politicisation of crime during this period (O'Donnell 2004). But, there has been an overall decrease in the prison population since 2014 (Prison Service 2014–2016) and this may be reflective of a more strategic approach to penal policy (Rogan 2015).

The public and political view on crime cannot now be simply categorised as punitive, particularly given the history of moderation in relation to criminal justice issues (O'Donnell and Jewkes 2011; O'Donnell and O'Sullivan 2001). Politicians take an occasional interest in issues of law and order but the tendency to use crime as a tool in political discourse is minimal and the Irish approach does not easily align with the politicisation of crime control that Garland (2001) argues is instrumental in the transition towards punitivism. For example, legislation introducing the right to vote for the prison population was met with little opposition politically in Ireland (Behan and O'Donnell 2008), whereas it was the subject of fierce debate in the United Kingdom (Murray 2012). On examining the temporary release of prisoners at Christmas in the United Kingdom and Ireland, O'Donnell and Jewkes (2011) noted the difference in tone and style in media reports. Unlike the United Kingdom, which linked the practice to themes of recidivism, pampered (and dangerous) prisoners, and misplaced political correctness, in Ireland the situation was presented in a factual and uncontroversial manner. Irish politicians tended not to make capital by taking a law-and-order approach to temporary release, instead supporting the system of trust that such a practice necessitated. An examination of political manifestos from 1977 to 1992 indicates that political parties did not focus on crime with the electorate being primarily concerned with economic conditions and levels of unemployment (Hamilton 2014, p. 32). There is evidence that the political mood hardens from the 1990s onwards with references to crime in parliamentary debates steadily increasing during this period (p. 33).

The indeterminate nature of the life sentence, its increasing application as a discretionary sentence for a range of offences outside of its mandatory application in cases of murder and an overall increase in time served certainly fits within a drive towards increased punitiveness (Mauer et al. 2004;

Simon 2007). Garland (2001, pp. 111–135) argues that austere measures and the tightening of controls have been applied to those who commit the most serious offences and those perceived to be dangerous. Nash and Williams (2010, p. 83) state that while risk and risk management has become a preoccupation of public protection, 'discourses of risk are often used to mask draconian policies, especially around extended and indeterminate sentences'. Garland (2001) identifies the contradictory nature of the overall drive towards efficiency and effectiveness whilst imposing harsh, expressive and expensive sanctions for certain categories of offenders. While the critics of rehabilitation in the latter decades of the twentieth century focused on the importance of retribution and deterrence as penal rationales, Zimring and Hawkins (1995) argue it was the incapacitation of dangerous offenders that had the greatest appeal.

Incapacitation in the form of mandatory sentencing, increased sentence lengths, indeterminate sentences, civil commitment and sexual predator statutes target violent and sexual offenders and are often based on the simple premise that incapacitation can attack the crime problem more effectively through restricting the ability of dangerous offenders to commit additional offences (Miles and Ludwig 2007, p. 23). The indeterminate nature of many of these penalties serve as a stark contrast to the overall shift towards the implementation of a more determinate sentencing and parole process in many jurisdictions (Cavadino and Dignan 2007; Travis and Lawrence 2002). The growth in use of such penalties also derives from a growing 'populist punitiveness' (Bottoms 1995) based on the sentiment that serious criminals should be harshly punished and that the public must be protected 'whatever the cost' (Garland 1990, p. 191; Simon 2007; Ashworth 2009). The United States may be the leaders in terms of selective incapacitation but such policies are not limited to this country with incapacitative and preventive measures being employed across many states, although the approach to such measures often depends on the legal culture of each jurisdiction (see for example: Australia; Canada: England and Wales; Germany; the Netherlands and New Zealand: Malsch and Duker 2016). In Ireland, there is some indication of the selective targeting of those perceived to be dangerous, with a growth in legislative measures targeting sex offenders (see, e.g., Sex Offenders Act 2001) and those involved in drug offences (see, e.g.,

Proceeds of Crime Act 1995; Criminal Justice Act 1999, 2006). O'Malley (2003, p. 134) notes that the measures adopted in Ireland have resulted in the 'selective intensification of punishment for certain offenders'. These legislative changes do not go as far as other jurisdictions and constitutional barriers prevent the implementation of penalties based on dangerousness alone (*People (Attorney General) v. O'Callaghan* 1966).

The indeterminacy of the life sentence can be used to serve the interests of public protection and the need for a conduit for expressive justice. It aligns with a 'shifting of the criminal justice system toward the detention of dangerous offenders' (Robinson 2001, p. 1432). But framing the parole process around the issue of dangerousness and incorporating risk assessments into the decision-making process also allows for the maintenance of discretion (and control) of those who have committed the most serious offences in the state, irrespective of the ability to demonstrate the risk of reoffending or dangerousness. Justifying the detention of a life sentence prisoner on the grounds of risk and public protection can belie the true purpose of detention: exclusion based on public disapprobation for the offence and the perception of dangerousness, rather than the reality presented in terms of likely recidivism (Simon 1998; Hood et al. 2002). This is particularly the case for those whose offence is a murder or an offence of a sexual nature. The widespread public assumption that these offenders are prone to repeat their crimes is not easily correlated with the available data on recidivism (Hood and Shute 2000; Hood et al. 2000; Sample and Bray 2006; O'Donnell et al. 2008; Friendship and Thornton 2001). Yet, from the public's perspective the risk of serious violence being committed upon release (irrespective of the empirical reality) does not allow for considerations of risk in the probabilistic sense and may result in decision-makers overriding risk information that may appear incompatible with wider perceptions as to dangerousness. What is required in such an instance is not risk taking, but certainty (Hebenton and Seddon 2009, p. 258). Given the informal nature of decision-making in Ireland it may be difficult in practice to resist a decision-making approach that feeds off public perceptions of dangerousness and the need to punish. As yet, it is unclear whether any of this is reflective of life imprisonment and parole in Ireland. But the following analyses the rationales other than risk and public protection in an attempt to explore the factors influencing time served and the purposes of parole as articulated by those central to the decision-making process.

The Intensification of Punishment

Members integrated their own conceptions of the purposes of punishment when considering individual decision-making. Their views on the purpose of parole, and the factors they deemed relevant outside of risk tended to be associated with traditional theories of punishment. Such an approach is not dissimilar to Irish sentencing practice which is characterised by its discretionary nature with few 'formal constraints on judicial sentencing powers' resulting in a lack of clarity as to the constituent elements of a sentence (although the Court of Criminal Appeal/Court of Appeal has shown some initiative in terms of sentencing guidelines in recent years) (O'Malley 2006, p. 53; 2016, pp. 15–18). The proportionality principle upon which Irish sentencing is based has been described as a 'necessary muddle' allowing for a wide degree of latitude that would not be acceptable in other jurisdictions (O'Donnell 2012, p. 259). Similar discretion is permitted in the parole process and while this may allow for a more personalised and compassionate approach to release, it can also facilitate severity in individual cases. Retribution and deterrence featured strongly in statements made by members when justifying the increase in time served by life sentence prisoners prior to release. In addition, members' views on appropriate terms of imprisonment connected with what might be described as the communicative role of punishment encapsulating elements of 'populist punitiveness' (Bottoms 1995). This feeds into the notion that members view their role as reaching beyond the individual and their likelihood of reoffending and into wider aspects of punishment and communication.

Decisions based on retribution are reflective rather than predictive, focusing on the act rather than the totality of the offender and the likelihood of future offending (Hawkins 1983b, p. 103). A retributive sentence is justified on the basis that the person deserves the punishment and that the person should suffer consequences in proportion to the offence committed (Von Hirsch et al. 1998). Retribution is incorporated through the proportionality principle in sentencing when assessing the circumstances of the offence and elements can also be identified across the legislative framework governing the release of life sentence prisoners (Criminal Justice (Temporary Release of Prisoners) Act 2003, s. 2(b) and (c)). The nature and the gravity of the offence was cited by members as important in the assessment of risk and it is likely that this was conflated with members views on retributivism. The Parole Board was granted permission to access the 'book of evidence' in 2003 with the then Minister stating that he hoped such provisions would halt the 'consistent diminution in the perceived value of life' (Lally 2004). It is evident from public statements by the Parole Board and former Ministers that retribution is a key element in the decision-making process.

> Where a person takes the life of another, then they have deprived their victim of the most fundamental of all human rights – the right to life. It is against this background that the Parole Board considers each and every individual murder case. (Parole Board 2008, p. 3)

> When a person commits a murder, often in cold-blooded fashion, he or she must be in no doubt of the consequences. He or she will serve a long prison sentence following conviction for such a heinous and despicable crime. (Minister Michael McDowell cited in: Lally 2006)

Retributive components in the decision-making of the Parole Board can be identified in members' responses on their approach to release. At a practical level, given the passage of a considerable amount of time since the commission of the offence and the subsequent legal proceedings, members are not well placed to consider the gravity of the offence, which in sentencing, includes an assessment of the culpability of the offender as well as the aggravating factors surrounding the offender's behaviour at the time of the commission of the offence. Given the lack of legal structure, the mandatory nature of the sentence for murder and the discretionary process of release, it is somewhat understandable that members engaged in assessments relating to offence seriousness. Murder can be committed in a wide range of circumstances and while the *mens rea* requires intention, the offence can at times be indistinguishable in terms of gravity from what may otherwise constitute manslaughter (O'Malley 2011, pp. 98–101). In addition, while it may be normal practice for a sentencing court to take into consideration retribution or other broader justifications for punishment, it would appear circumspect from a legal perspective to incorporate such elements into a release process governed by the executive and characterised by legal informality (see Chap. 6).

A number of members associated time served with satisfying the retributive element of the sentence. Former Ministers also placed considerable emphasis on retribution in the decision-making process.

> The likelihood of reoffending is one thing, but I mean if you've done something awful the public wants you to suffer for it, regardless if you suddenly become fallen off your horse on the road to Damascus and you want to enter the priesthood when you get out or whatever, it still doesn't matter. There is a requirement that the punishment fits the crime in the public mind. (MJ1)

> To me, the 10 years is the punitive element, it is then up to the prisoner to ensure that within that 10 years there is the rehabilitation aspect to it. (PB02)

> It has to be a significant length of time because it's a significant crime. If you've taken somebody's life, you know, you owe it to society to, you know, to… that's wrong but it is! If you don't have, what would you call it, I can't think of the word – retribution – if you don't have adequate retribution there, you know, it's going to make lives lesser. (PB01)

Members consistently referenced the communicative aspect of their work, emphasising the important role the Parole Board played in sending a message to both the offender and the public through the recommendation process. Statements by members can be linked to a deterrent theory of punishment. Deterrence is consequentialist in nature with an outlook that is prospective rather than reflective and may serve to address future behaviour and more particularly, prevent future crime (Von Hirsch and Ashworth 1998). Punishment can operate at an individual level (specific deterrence), deterring the actual offender from committing future crime through the imposition of punishment. It can also impact at a wider societal level (general deterrence), deterring others from committing future crimes through the publicity of the punishment. Thus, punishment based on deterrence aims at communicating to the offender and society the consequences of committing criminal offences, is based on notions of rationality and is reliant on the certainty rather than the severity of punishment.

The effectiveness of punishment as a deterrent in the case of mandatory penalties has been called into question by research across a range of penal systems (Tonry 1996, pp. 134–46). In Ireland, it is a legitimate consideration in sentencing within certain conditions (*People (DPP) v Larkin* 2008) but questions have been raised as to the effectiveness of imprisonment as a deterrent (Law Reform Commission 1993, p. 209; O'Malley 2016, pp. 103–105). Incorporating deterrence can present difficulties in sentencing as it is forward-looking in nature and is not readily compatible with the overarching principle of proportionality. It has remained a focus of public statements by the Parole Board and may provide a partial explanation as to the length of time a life sentence prisoner must serve prior to being considered eligible for release. Statements in the annual reports and by the participants in this study indicate that decision-making in parole is attempting to communicate a message of general deterrence in relation to homicide and violent crime. When considering individual cases, it appears that broader crime trends and the perception that there has been a rise in lethal violence in Ireland in recent decades is a factor in decision-making. There has been a significant increase in the number of homicides since the 1950s which has transformed Ireland from a 'policeman's paradise' (Brady 1974, p. 240; O'Donnell 2005) to a country with one of the higher rates of homicides in Europe (Tavares et al. 2012, p. 3). The annual average number of homicides increased from 10.3 from 1951 to 1960 to 61.6 from 2001 to 2010 (O'Donnell 2005, p. 103; Central Statistics Office 2013). The growth in the drugs trade has contributed to this trend in lethal violence (O'Donnell 2011; Campbell 2010) and this has been referenced in public statements on parole.

> Whilst each case must be carefully considered on its own merits nonetheless a message must go out to the public that persons who are convicted by a jury of the crime of murder will serve a very long sentence indeed. (Parole Board 2004, p. 5)

> People found guilty of murder involving aggravating factors such as use of firearms or gangland involvement should serve sentences of at least 15 to 20 years. I want to send that message out loud and clear. Respect for human life must be a cornerstone of our society. (Minister Michael McDowell cited in: Lally (2006) and *Breaking News* (2006))

The justification for the increase in time served was frequently associated with the need to 'send a message' of general deterrence to the public, and more particularly, those involved in 'gang' related activity.

> I mean you have the escalation in recent times, and we would have made note of it here at the Board a number of years ago about the increase of people carrying and using knives in the most, almost innocuous situations, and saying that 'hang on again, the message isn't out there that if you're seen to be doing this you will be treated severely and you'll be treated harshly'. So I suppose I do think that we have a kind of a general guide here at the moment of fifteen years. (PB12)

> Well it's a deterrent, you know, it's a deterrent. Murder has become very prevalent in society. Particularly in the capital, you turn on the radio or television and there's… and not alone in the capital but in the capital particularly it's becoming so prevalent, you know? And you must have some deterrent. And the criminals and the people who go out and who murder people, and gangs and all this, they must have some expectancy that if and when they're caught that they will serve a long sentence. (PB14)

There are a number of difficulties that arise as a result of incorporating general deterrence into the decision-making process surrounding the release of life sentence prisoners. It is questionable whether the Parole Board and the Minister have the ability to communicate beyond those directly concerned with the parole process. The sources of official information in the public domain are lacking in terms of data provision on life sentence prisoners and their release when compared with other jurisdictions (Griffin and O'Donnell 2012, p. 624). Requests for access to data on parole have been resisted (Griffin 2014). The information-rich website of the Parole Board of England and Wales highlights the importance that has been placed on communicating the Board's role to the public. In Ireland, there is little documentation available to the public or victims, and the leaflet provided to the life sentence prisoner is light in content (Parole Board 2013). The resistance to information provision fits within an overarching culture of secrecy evident in the practices of the executive and its agents in relation to criminal justice research and external evaluation (Department of Justice and Equality 2014; Heylin 2001). Ironically, the information on time served is only in the public domain due to the author requesting a politician to table parliamentary questions on the issue. The Parole Board does not release information on average time served in its annual reports. It seems contradictory then that those involved in decision-making associated their role with communicating a message of general deterrence given the lack of official data and the absence of media to facilitate this message.

The assumption that increasing the time served by life sentence prisoners will effect a reduction in the murder rate did not transpire. The Parole Board acknowledged this in 2006, yet members themselves were not deterred from justifying the length of time served by life sentence prisoners in individual cases on this basis.

> What has happened? The spate of murders continues unabated. Gangland killings, unheard of in Ireland some years ago, [have] risen to epidemic proportions. (Parole Board 2006, p. 4)

The inclusion of general deterrence as a factor to be considered has serious implications for those under review as the length of time served prior to release in their individual case may, to a certain extent, be dictated by an external factor which the prisoner cannot address, namely the increase in the murder rate or lethal violence connected with the drugs trade. Elements of specific deterrence can be identified in statements by members in relation to, for example, review process cycles and various factors relating to the risk of reoffending (see 'Previous Criminal History' and 'Nature and Gravity of the Offence' in Chap. 4). Specific deterrence is similar to general deterrence in the sense that it is based on the concept of rationality and the presumption that the individual offender will be deterred through the experience of punishment. Specific deterrence can easily be conflated with retribution and incapacitation and thus, can be difficult to extract as a strand in and of itself. It is difficult to analyse the deterrent effect of the practice of administering life sentences and time served on those that have subsequently been released. Reoffending and desistance can be related to a range of factors that may have little correlation to sentence length and its deterrent effect (Healy 2010).

While there was a clear emphasis on retribution and deterrence as a justification for the increase in time served and this evidences a more punitive approach to time served, members also placed considerable emphasis on rehabilitation. As is evident from the discussion in Chap. 4, decision-makers regarded engagement with services, educational attainment, addressing substance use, and the attitude and insight of the offender as key to any parole recommendation. Parole authorities' perceptions of these issues are often linked to the ability of the offender to demonstrate change and have proven to be influential factors in parole decision-making (Hawkins 1983b; Hood and Shute 2000; Padfield et al. 2000). Members' emphasised the rehabilitative impact that the review process had on incentivising engagement and good behaviour within the prison system as well as the positive impact of supervision upon release. The method by which the parole process affected change on the individual was referred to as the 'carrot and stick' approach. Members demonstrated belief in 'redeemability' (Maruna and King 2009) and viewed the manner by which the process operates as having the ability to provide a rehabilitative and transformative effect on an offender's behaviour.

> The carrot of the parole system forces these applicants to engage far greater with services that are available. I've seen many instances of people having no contact at all with the services within the prison until the Parole Board process kicks in. (PB11)

Thus, rehabilitative instincts operate alongside tendencies towards punitivism. As will be evident, public opinion and the perception that public opinion is overwhelmingly punitive also played a key factor in influencing decision-makers.

Incorporating Public Opinion

Members consistently referenced the incorporation of public opinion into decision-making when considering the appropriate point of release for life sentence prisoners. There was an assumption that public opinion was punitive in nature and against release at an early review. Discerning public opinion on crime and the criminal justice system is a complicated matter and lay assessments may lead to unfounded assumptions regarding public levels of punitiveness (Green 2005) and lack of understanding of the criminal justice system (Mitchell and Roberts 2011). An international study indicates the public remains 'deeply divided' on the issue of mandatory sentencing (Roberts 2003, p. 483). More specifically, when the public is presented with a general question on the appropriate punishment for murder, poll findings show strong support for a mandatory life sentence for those convicted, however when presented with a specific scenario support falls significantly (Roberts 2003, pp. 501–2). Research in England and Wales indicates that the public are misinformed about murder trends and have a tendency to underestimate the length of time served in custody prior to release, both of which can result in adopting a punitive approach to sentencing amongst the public (Mitchell and Roberts 2011).

Despite the rise in lethal violence, it appears that fear of crime remains relatively low in Ireland with 61 per cent of people stating they do not worry about becoming a victim of crime (Central Statistics Office 2016, p. 3). A study by the National Crime Council found that 63.5 per cent of respondents were 'not worried about crime', 21.5 per cent were 'concerned about crime' and 15 per cent were 'fearful of crime' (National Crime Council 2009). Almost three quarters (74 per cent) of people 'felt safe or very safe walking home alone in their neighbourhood after dark' with 92 per cent feeling 'safe or very safe alone in their homes after dark' (Central Statistics Office 2010, p. 1). While there are strong indications that the population feels safe in their community, 83 per cent of those surveyed by the Central Statistics Office (2010, p. 1) believed that crime was a serious or very serious problem. Such a disjoint may be indicative of a hardening in public attitudes towards crime and criminal justice driven by perceptions of crime rather than individual experiences of victimisation. It is possible the increased attention given to violent and organised crime in the media and at a political level has contributed to this, with O'Connell (1999) arguing that public perceptions of crime may be as a result of the distorted image of crime portrayed in the media.

The disconnect that exists in terms of the relationship between public perception and the reality of crime, the criminal justice system and sentencing is well documented (Roberts 1992; Pfeiffer et al. 2005) although data on this is limited in the Irish context (IPRT 2007). Nonetheless, a more politicised and punitive approach to criminal justice has developed in Ireland in recent decades and this may be partially based on an assumption that there exists a hardening of attitudes towards crime amongst the public (O'Donnell and O'Sullivan 2003; Kilcommins et al. 2004). Some evidence of this can be found in the European Crime Survey on Attitudes Towards Punishment (Kühnrich and Kania 2005, p. 15). Ireland was the second most punitive country (after the United Kingdom) when selecting an appropriate sentence for a recidivist burglar. Public opinion on issues such as murder, the mandatory life sentence or the process of release remains unknown. Nonetheless, clear assumptions exist amongst decision-makers in relation to the public's views on murder and sentencing for such an offence. The length of time served in custody prior to release was often correlated with addressing what was viewed as public dissatisfaction with lenient terms of imprisonment for life sentence prisoners. In particular, the perception that life sentence prisoners are released after seven years was the subject of consistent commentary by the Parole Board and its members. A concerted effort has been made to address this misperception.

> I think that when I did recalibrate the Parole Board's thinking, I think there was a general satisfaction with it. There was no more walking about, or people being out after seven years. (MJ1)

> Well when the Board was originally appointed there was a general public perception that those convicted of murder were released after seven or eight years. That perception should not have lasted very long. (Parole Board 2006, p. 3)

> Public opinion was against a shorter period of time. And of course public opinion would come along and say, probably the average was twelve, and people come along and say 'they're letting them out after seven or eight years'. Now that wasn't possibly true, maybe one exception or whatever, but the perceived view at that time was 'ah they're getting out too soon'. So we had to take account, you know, of public opinion. And the public have got to be protected and their views have got to be accepted. So yeah, that's why it was pushed up. (PB09)

> Well you see it's not my opinion because at the end of the day we work within a system, you know, we work within a democracy, so people are elected by the people and the people decide, in my view, what they want, and at the moment the people have spoken and have said that they feel that somebody going into prison for seven or ten years as a life sentence is too short and they want something done about that. (PB07)

Members were divided in relation to whether public opinion should be incorporated into the decision-making process however most acknowledged that the process did account for public opinion at some level.

> We would always be very conscious of public opinion. If public opinion thinks that life is being played down too much we would react. (PB04)

> There could be many people in society that would say that life should mean life and that no-one should get out, they should die in prison, and I don't know what percentage of people would have that view, and I think, you know, that we have to be conscious of what the public's attitude is to this, you know, to murder offences. (PB05)

In terms of the sources relied upon in identifying and incorporating public opinion, a number of members viewed themselves as good measures of public values and as representative of the community. Given that the appointment of members is political in nature and there is a trend of appointing former criminal justice agents to the Parole Board upon retirement, it is questionable whether this body can be described as representative of the community.

> The members of the Board are of this world, we are part of the public, we socialise, we work, we have a lot of areas in which we, you know, our antenna is alive to these things – in the pubs, the clubs, the family.... So we are part of that public. By-and-large the people on the Board, we weren't isolated, we weren't living in a cocoon, you know, we all live life and we're not ... the majority were well over their fifties, there was this one young lady on the Board, a young barrister, the rest were I would say over their fifties, so we had seen a bit of life, we were grey-haired (*laughing*) and bald. (PB09)

> Well I think we all represent the public, you know, if you look at the current make-up of the Board, people come from all areas of the country perhaps with different experiences, different expertise. (PB03)

A further source of public opinion identified by members was the media reporting of those reviewed by the Parole Board and crime reporting generally.

> Well I think you know of course at the end of the day you have to try and put it aside in the same way as you have to try and put the media, the *Star* or the *Sun* or the *Evening Herald* aside, and you have to try and see what you have and try and make the best decisions you have. But it does impact on you, you know, you have to just feel it because if you don't feel it, then it's just mechanical, and you see it's not a mechanical process, this is about human life, human feelings. (PB07)

> Do you mean genuine public opinion or some newspaper reporter who wants to sell papers? That's not public opinion but he can state public opinion demands X, Y and Z for argument's sake – it's their perception not the general public's perception. (PB01)

> Because, public opinion will tend to be guided by the heinousness of a particular crime rather than somebodies [sic] risk to it, and I don't think, no more than I don't think somebody should be tried in the court of public opinion, I don't think their sentence should be managed in that particular court either. (PB02)

While the media was frequently cited as a method of determining public opinion, there was also considerable concern with whether the reactive and sensationalist approach to the reporting of cases reviewed by the Parole Board was an appropriate assessment of the views of the public. This problem is particularly acute in the context of those that have a high public profile due to the nature of their crimes. Members frequently referenced the difficulties presented by the political nature of decision-making when reviewing a high profile offender for release. Public opinion was often mentioned in relation to high profile offenders or those whose offences were widely covered in the media. Such individuals were clearly identified as creating a conflict for members when addressing considerations of release given the potential for negative publicity for the Parole Board. The views presented here have implications for those subject to higher levels of media scrutiny and may result in an arbitrary intensification of punishment based on the external factor of the individual's media profile.

> Public opinion can generally be judged I think by the notoriety of the crime… Now if there is a, I won't call it a campaign but if there's a lot of media attention on a particular crime, which probably would indicate the feelings of the local community or the fears of the local community, it would probably be taken into account. It would probably be a factor, yeah. I mean we all read the papers, you wouldn't be able to ignore something like that. I could see somebody making the point, you know, that there's a lot of concern about this in the local community or in the media and we'd interpret that as reflecting the community, you know, so I think it would be fair to say, in my opinion, that it would be a factor, it would certainly have to be considered, yeah. I'm not saying what weight would be put on it but I think it would be a factor. (PB08)

> Oh there's no doubt that certain types of crime are vilified in the media. So for instance, people who commit, you know, multiple murders, child murderers, all those kinds of offences, there is definitely a pressure, there's no doubt about it, there's a pressure, there's a public opinion pressure that's usually communicated through the media. And there's no doubt about it that, now we're talking about a handful of cases, but there's no doubt about it that there is an influence, of course, because it reflects the people. (PB07)

> Let's be honest, we're human and if there's a particular case that comes in and you're reading it and, for example, you have particular memories of media coverage of a murder or whatever, you're inevitably going to think,

> 'ah Jesus, all hell is going to kick off here if this, you know, if it's an issue of early release or something', but it's not part of the decision-making process. Now I know there's a contradiction in saying that because if it comes into your mind you know it's difficult at a human level not to be, but it's not openly part of the decision-making process and I suppose I consciously would try and make sure it's not part of my thinking as well. (PB02)

Such views may serve to further reinforce an aversion to release in cases where the punitive sentiment amongst the public runs high in individual cases. The apparent perception being that a lenient approach to release would be viewed negatively in the public arena and that this would reflect badly on the Parole Board (and the Minister).

The role of the media was identified as influential in creating tensions between the Parole Board and Minister at times, and frustrating the process of release and reintegration of the offender.

> And I think particularly where [politics] could have an impact is if there is a high profile prisoner, and there have been examples, and they've been splashed all over the media. In the past there were high profile prisoners where there would have been recommendations for parole which weren't agreed with and I would believe that is exclusively on a political decision and I think that's wrong. (PB02)

> I can see cases where the media has responded in high profile cases in regard to what the Board has said, and I've had one particular case where, an extremely high profile case, where the Board was, you know, it got the tabloid treatment for its recommendation on a particular prisoner, and in that instance again it was kind of casting a very spurious kind of view of the Board and its recommendation, which ultimately was rejected by the Minister. (PB12)

Members identified a reluctance of the Minister to accept recommendations in high profile cases, which in turn impacted on a general reluctance to recommend release when similar cases arose for consideration by the Parole Board subsequently. Public opinion, although unknown in empirical reality, impacts on parole outcomes and often in a punitive manner.

The Role of Politics

The release of life sentence prisoners is an explicitly political decision and all stakeholders in the process are cognisant of this. The Parole Board recommendation process is constrained by the politics surrounding it. Members identified the impact of politics on their individual decision-making in a number of different ways. In terms of soliciting views on sentence length, responses were heavily influenced by the broader political approach to life sentence prisoners and the appropriate term of imprisonment. Members were questioned on the length of time they believed that a life sentence prisoner should serve where that prisoner had killed a person in a domestic context, had since shown remorse for his offending behaviour and was at a low risk of reoffending. Fifteen years was the most consistently cited figure by members in relation to the minimum term that a life sentence prisoner should serve prior to being recommended for release (12 years was the second most cited figure). The overall average (mean) was 13 years. Only one member stated that the offender should be released after 7 years and this was the lowest figure provided while the highest maximum term was 20 years. Members frequently referenced political constraints when providing a rationale for the length of time they viewed appropriate for a low-risk life sentence prisoner. A number of members expressed reluctance in considering a figure for release below what they perceived to be government policy. Others provided a figure below the threshold acknowledging the difficulty that would present in terms of the likelihood that such a recommendation would be accepted.

> Well you see we're stuck with that, and the Board is stuck with that, and the Board knows there is no point in making a recommendation at eight or ten years if government policy is that life is a minimum say of, it was twelve at one stage, it's now gone to fifteen. (PB08)

> So I suppose I do think that we have a kind of a general guide here at the moment of fifteen years, I think that's reasonable, you know, a life sentence is a life sentence but again I think it should always be continuously reviewed in the context of the climate you're in as well. (PB12)

> So whilst a recommendation from the Parole Board might go lower than the fifteen years I would still see the person, and remembering that the Parole Board is a recommending body not a decision-making body, I would think that a recommendation from the Parole Board which went outside the norms of what is now accepted as a life sentence, would be unlikely to be accepted, unless there were very, very, specific points in that particular case. (PB06)

In its first annual report, the Parole Board (2002, p. 2) indicated that the minimum term prior to release that they would consider for a murder conviction resulting in a life sentence was 12 years; however, this figure moved upwards to 15 within a number of years (Parole Board 2006, p. 7). In 2006, the then Minister indicated publicly that only in the most exceptional cases would he consider less than 15 years as the tariff for a life sentence prisoner (Lally 2006). The rationale for such an approach was not entirely clear, although the Parole Board annual reports (2003, p. 2; 2006, p. 7) appear to link it to an attempt to address the overall increase in the murder rate. The term the Minister may be willing to accept may change at any time, as is evident from an agreement between the Parole Board and former Minister Shatter (2011–2014) that a recommendation to release a life sentence prisoner could be accepted after 13 years (Parole Board 2012, p. 5). Nonetheless, it is clear from the statements of members that the Parole Board is unwilling to recommend a life sentence prisoner for release at a period below the term expressed by the Minister as the minimum term she is willing to accept at that particular time.

> The Minister's reaction has been to lay down general guidelines as to how long a person convicted of murder should, in this day and age, expect to serve. The Parole Board supports those guidelines and the Board agrees with the approach the Minister is taking. Certainly the present level of serious crime in this country is scarcely a time for increased leniency. (Parole Board 2006, p. 7)

Members made explicit reference to the different approaches adopted by various Ministers and the constraint this placed on the Parole Board as their recommendations had to account for the Minister at that particular time. This indicates that the length of time a life sentence prisoner can expect to serve prior to being recommended for release is somewhat dependent on the Minister in power at the point at which the life sentence prisoner is under review. There appears to be an interaction between the Parole Board and the Minister that is dictated implicitly by politics without being explicitly stated when making recommendations on individuals under review.

> I think up to now, you have to realise that within the political system various Ministers take different attitudes towards crime. Some are more lenient let's say than others. (PB01)

> One has to be honest that, depending on the Minister of the day and the kind of perspective they have on these issues, it can move it. I mean Minister McDowell would have been a Minister back in those days who would have had very strong views about life sentences, and I suppose the system here very much is dictated by that, you know? (PB12)

> There's an obvious link between a particular political perspective and the Parole Board recommendations. (PB02)

> At the moment the people have spoken and have said that they feel that somebody going into prison for seven or ten years as a life sentence is too short and they want something done about that. And that is a decision that's a political decision, that's not my decision. So, you know, I live in the real world. And if you look at some of the other political parties at the moment on the opposition they have indicated that they would make it longer. You know? (PB07)

> None of us have met the present Minister for Justice, but you do get a feedback that, you know, if for example you were making recommendations and you know there's no point in making a recommendation because it'll be shot down, well then, you don't make a recommendation. (PB01)

Decision-making appears to be sensitive to the views of the Minister in relation to life sentences generally and in individual cases. For example, one member stated that when dealing with a low-risk life sentence prisoner who could be released earlier than would ordinarily be accepted by the Minister, that in such an instance: 'you play your Minister' (PB04).

On occasion, members referred to explicit statements made by the Minister at that time. Others referred to the implicit approach of some Ministers in relation to the release of life sentence prisoners and unofficial feedback the Parole Board had received in terms of their recommendations. The tailoring of recommendations to account for politics and the perception as to the political approach might provide some explanation of the high rates of acceptance by the Minister of Parole Board recommendations (85.2 per cent acceptance rate) (Parole Board 2002–2015). There is a culture of cautiousness in operation here but in this instance it is not connected to the risk of reoffending. Rather, it is the potential political fallout from recommending a life sentence prisoner at a stage that is not politically acceptable that appears to be the driving force.

Malcolm Macarthur: Political Prisoner?

The exceptional case of Malcolm Macarthur illustrates the effect politics can have on time served for a high profile and notorious life sentence prisoner. Macarthur murdered a woman and a man in 1982 in what appeared to be random and brutal attacks. The incidents attracted widespread public attention at a time when murder was much less prevalent in society. This combined with his connections to the political and social elite (he was arrested at the home of the Attorney General) led to the then *Taoiseach* (Prime Minister) to famously describe the series of events surrounding the murders and his subsequent arrest as 'grotesque, unbelievable, bizarre and unprecedented' (Murtagh 1982). This phrase, popularised as 'GUBU', and Macarthur himself remained in the public consciousness through the close media attention paid to any matters relating to his detention and prospect of release. Macarthur was charged with both murders, however, at the beginning of his trial he entered a guilty plea to the murder of the woman and a mandatory life sentence was imposed (*Irish Times* 1983a). The Director of Public Prosecutions entered a *nolle prosequi* on the charge of the other murder without explanation causing further public controversy (*Irish Times* 1983b).

At the early stages of the review process by the Sentence Review Group Macarthur was viewed as unsuitable for release.

> He was the sort of fellow, amazing, very nice chap to talk to, you know, and the sort of chap you would gladly go through the national gallery with on an afternoon because he would be full of critical observations on paintings and so on. You had to pinch yourself and remind yourself that he has this mad logic. If he wants something he'd go through hell and murder to get it. (Interview with T.K. Whitaker, 8 October 2008)

This view changed over the passage of time. In 2004, 22 years after conviction, the Parole Board began to make a series of recommendations that Macarthur be placed on a structured programme for temporary release however these recommendations were rejected by various Ministers (Kelly 2004; O'Brien 2011). Decision-making became particularly complicated from 2002 to 2007 as the then Minister, Michael McDowell, had previously acted as junior counsel in Macarthur's defence (Donnellan 2002). McDowell delegated his statutory power to the Minister of State, Willie O'Dea, who decided not to accept the recommendations of the Parole Board to place Macarthur on a programme of temporary release (Williams 2003).

> I suppose you have the cases where you have very prolific lifers. I think for example like the Macarthur case would be one. So I think, now that was before I came on the Board, but I think probably the recommendation given by the Parole Board and that of the Minister differed. (PB07)
>
> That's why Mr McArthur [was] still there because [the Minister] didn't have the guts to release him because the tabloids would go, you know, the usual story. (SRG1)

There was no movement on release by subsequent Ministers until Alan Shatter accepted the Parole Board recommendations in 2011 (O'Brien 2011) and Macarthur was permitted 'full temporary release' in 2012, having served 30 years in prison (Kerrigan 2012). Statements are not ordinarily issued on individual cases but compelled by public interest, the Minister commented on the 'dreadful events of 1982 that shocked the nation so many years ago' (Alan Shatter cited in: O'Brien 2011).

An element of Macarthur's prolonged detention was no doubt related to the seriousness of his offence. It may also have been the case that the other murder for which he was charged but not convicted resulted in elongating his detention beyond the ordinary. But there was certainly an additional political element operating here, deriving from his public notoriety and the macabre celebrity he consistently attracted over the years. The potential for adverse publicity and the negative political consequences that might arise was likely to be more prevalent in the minds of deciding Ministers during this period rather than issues of risk or public protection. The former governor of the prison where Macarthur served a significant part of his sentence stated that the risk assessments indicated he was suitable for release but that this was 'held up by politics' (John Lonergan cited in: Baker and O'Keeffe 2012). A former Minister referenced Macarthur specifically in terms of Ministers acting in the interests of their own political preservation.

> I think he's now out, but it took an awful lot of time, and one of the reasons that he was kept in I think was that the politicians were just afraid of, you know that he would do something bizarre if he got out. I knew there was a zilch risk of reoffending. (MJ1)

While his temporary release did attract media attention there has been little by way of political consequence as a result of the decision to date.

The Macarthur case highlights how the political component of the decision-making process can serve to increase time served for offenders that, for whatever reason, capture the attention of the public, media and politicians. On Macarthur's committal in 1982, the average time of release for life sentence prisoners was 7.5 years. A significant portion of the additional years spent in prison can be attributed to the political preservation of decision-makers rather than the protection of the public. It is somewhat predictable that members would be attuned to the political dimension of their role given the nature of their appointment to the Parole Board. With the risk of damaging relations with the Minister operating on the deliberations of the Parole Board and the risk of public and political fallout for the Minister, it is also unsurprising that both have taken the cautious route through the incremental silting up of time served. If a life sentence prisoner reoffends on release, it is certainly easier to publicly and politically defend a decision on the basis that the time served in prison was longer than life sentence prisoners released under previous political regimes.

The Minister's Perspective

Given that members have indicated that they account for politics in their decision-making, an analysis of the perspectives of the deciding Ministers provides an important insight into the relationship between the Parole Board and the Minister. Views on the parole process differed considerably between one former Minister and the two others. One Minister, for instance, was an advocate for the reform of the process through the provision of a statutory framework, removing the political element from decision-making and empowering the Parole Board to make the final determination on release. This individual was of the opinion that the Minister's role should be limited to providing a non-binding opinion in serious cases where the Parole Board seeks her opinion. The Minister also stated that the rationale for removing the political element to decision-making related to the concern that risk aversion may arise where politicians, as publicly elected representatives, may be reluctant to release individuals due to concerns regarding adverse publicity and political criticism. This tacit acknowledgement that a culture of risk aversion exists at a Ministerial level is significant, given the conservative and cautious approach to risk already identified in the statements of members (see Chap. 4). Perhaps as a commentary on the flaws of the current process the Minister stated that an independent Parole Board should be impartial, objective, adhere to procedural fairness, operate with clear risk assessment criteria, and provide reasons for its decisions.

> The political role should be substantially reduced in order to avoid, among other things, excessive risk averseness. It is important to prevent a practice under which releases that should be granted are refused because of ministerial fear of adverse publicity and political criticism with possible personal electoral consequences. (MJ3)

> I believe that decisions on parole should be made by an independent statutory body. I believe that in serious cases the body should be required to obtain the opinion of the Minister for Justice and Equality on a proposed release but not be bound by the Minister's opinion. (MJ3)

This perspective was at odds with the views of the majority of members interviewed and other former Ministers who advocated for the maintenance of the *status quo*. Only four of fourteen members were of the view that the Parole Board should be empowered to make a decision rather than a recommendation to the executive. Both remaining former Ministers believed that political decision-making facilitated the incorporation of the perspectives of the community and was more accountable than an independent Parole Board, as Ministers were publicly elected representatives.

> I believe it should be the Minister for Justice and it should be somebody who is accountable, not an independent board who says 'we do it'. They are not answerable to the people, you know, the Parole Board can't be removed from office for getting it wrong. (MJ1)

> In a small country where everyone knows everyone, relatively speaking, it's hard to hide in Ireland, you know, if you're an offender, so it's probably a little bit better to have political involvement given our political system where the politician is generally close to the people, supposedly. (MJ2)

While the responses of the reforming Minister were future oriented, the views of the other former Ministers are more reflective of the process as it currently operates. These Ministers adopted a subjective approach to decision-making and their comments, perhaps inadvertently, highlight the need for reform. It has already been noted that the statutory criteria that the Minister is required to take into consideration when making a decision of this nature, are vague and allow for considerable discretion. They also appear to have limited application to decision-making given the responses of two former Ministers. One Minister stated that he primarily employed his 'intuition' while the other appeared to be concerned with bolstering public confidence in the rule of law. It is paradoxical that the rule of law is referenced with such fervour here given the absence of procedural fairness surrounding the parole process.

> I have to say, I didn't, to be honest, pay much attention to [the statutory criteria]. I have to say it was on my gut feeling. (MJ2)

Interviewee: Tell me about the statutory criteria again? I didn't apply them much because I didn't, I regarded allowing you out on licence really as a kind of remission or commutation of your sentence rather than a, maybe on paper, the Department regarded it as a temporary release but whether you regard it as allowing you out on licence or whatever, it was in my view a remission. What are the criteria?

Interviewer: *There is a list of criteria about…?*

Interviewee: The likelihood of reoffending and all this kind of thing?

Interviewer: *Threat to society….*

Interviewee: Yes, I do remember having to consider them, but I mean I think that they are important but I mean that fundamentally I think the overriding concern is public confidence in the rule of law. That is the overriding concern in my view. (MJ1)

The information presented in the review dossier appears to have been viewed with scepticism, particularly where what was being communicated indicated that an individual was suitable for release or a low risk of reoffending. This echoes what was expressed by a number of members in relation to their view of professional risk assessments. Thus, this 'common sense' approach to decision-making appears to be operating at both the Parole Board and Ministerial level and may militate against the release of a low-risk life sentence prisoner at both levels.

Interviewee: Again, it all goes back to gut instinct really, you know, and based on the recommendation of the Parole Board, by and large. I was somewhat a little dubious of someone, maybe the professionals, who would be saying that 'Diarmuid Griffin is a lovely fella and he is totally reformed and, you know, he's turned over a new leaf', I would always be very dubious to be honest.

Interviewer: *Why would you be dubious?*

Interviewer: I don't know, just, not maybe dubious but careful, to be honest you know. That might have been some of the reasons why I would have postponed [decisions] just to see how people would behave, even behave to the reaction of not getting parole on this occasion but you'd get it next time, you know? (MJ2)

> Because if you're dealing with the prison system stroke parole system which wants to see the back of a particular prisoner, they're a bit inclined to minimise, dress it up so that it is easier for the Minister to make the desired decision. You do sometimes have to say, 'well I have to look around corners and when a decision is made I'll have to defend it in public so just remind me again what was all this about'. (MJ1)

Ministers were asked specifically about risk as a factor in the decision-making process and while both Ministers indicated that the risk of reoffending was important, it featured within a myriad of other factors external to risk and risk assessment such that it appeared that risk was a secondary, or perhaps an additional factor to be considered once other factors were satisfied. A strong emphasis on retribution and general deterrence can be identified here, as well as the importance of public opinion and public satisfaction. However, the overarching theme that appeared to be operating on these Ministers related to political considerations. The political consequences deriving from their role in releasing life sentence prisoners and the conflict this presented as publicly elected representatives influenced their decision-making.

> Ultimately, I sort of based the whole thing on, as somebody who carried the can, you know, it's alright for a Board to be making a recommendation, but ultimately I would have to stand up if anything happened, so from that point of view that was my overriding, you know, objective. To make sure that I was happy that if something did happen, that at least I had completely examined the file and taken on board what the Parole Board said. (MJ2)

Perceptions of public opinion played a considerable role in decision-making and the publicity connected with this type of decision-making in the media had a considerable impact on Ministers and their decisions. While Ministers were critical of tabloid reporting on parole related issues and the release of life sentence prisoners, they also acknowledged the importance of gauging public opinion through the media and the requirement to make decisions that were publicly palatable. This appears to translate into lengthier sentences for life sentence prisoners to satisfy perceptions of public levels of punitiveness. A former Minister argued that increased levels of public scrutiny would render it even more difficult for the Parole Board to recommend the release of an individual at a point that did not match the punitive goals of the Minister.

> No, well I mean, I was suspicious of the tabloid media. I mean the only way you can gauge public opinion is as you hear it or as you feel it and you have to therefore, the media have a role in all of this because they are (a) the educators of public opinion under the Constitution and (b) they are the only way, or the only major ways whereby somebody in public office actually can judge the public mood. (MJ1)

> I had to put up during my time with all these horrific red top comments, you know. To be honest, I didn't pay a huge amount of attention to those, because you know, I'm not a politician for nothing. Obviously I had to be conscious of public opinion and how it would affect politically both me and then my government. You always have one eye on what the people think in making decisions. And that's the political process we live in. But you can't let it dictate, you know, what decisions you make, you know, but at the same time you're conscious. (MJ2)

> Perhaps if you want a check or safeguard on Ministerial cowardice you could have a system whereby the Parole Board's decisions became subject to public scrutiny. But I think the Parole Board wouldn't like that. I think if the Parole Board said 'let that man out' and I said 'no', I don't think they'd go running to the newspapers, if it were possible, saying 'we want him out and Minister [X] said no'. Minister [X] would win that battle every time. (MJ1)

Despite the risk of adverse publicity deriving from this type of decision-making, both Ministers were strongly of the view that decision-making should remain within the political domain. Ministers referenced other areas of government where political involvement had been removed from decision-making (such as the Department of Health and the Health Service Executive) and expressed dissatisfaction with this, which they viewed as removing the core work of politicians with little benefit to the public. They believed that the mandatory life sentence should continue to exist and did not believe that a minimum term imposed by the judiciary would be beneficial.

> I mean it's a small country and it's probably an easier country to have a system of political involvement. With decisions in a bigger country like the UK where you have 60 million people, you know having a politician making decisions, with the scale of things, there's bound to be cases where it will go wrong, whereas in a small country you know, where everyone knows everyone, relatively speaking, it's hard to hide in Ireland, you know if you're an offender, so you know, it's probably a little bit better to have political involvement given our political system where the politician is generally close to the people, supposedly. (MJ2)

> I think the present system, I don't believe that the trial judge should determine the length of time because I do believe that murder in particular and in the rare cases that life is imposed for non murder offences, those cases are of such public importance that an independent judge is not the right person to decide it, with the criteria I've been mentioning to you are much more publicly important and systemically important than you know, than getting a softie on the bench on the day, you know. (MJ1)

Political interest in parole tends to focus on individual decision-making rather than structural reform. Former Ministers were explicit that a decision to release a life sentence prisoner presented a political risk. Yet, the extent to which parole has been used as a tool in political discourse is minimal. John O'Donoghue (Minister from 1997 to 2002) capitalised on law and order during his time in and outside of office (O'Donnell 2001, 2004, 2005) and responded to public concern regarding the release of life sentence prisoners through the establishment of the 'Interim Parole Board' (Olden 2001; 528 *Dáil Debates* Col.311; John O'Donoghue 12/12/2000). However, political attention on parole is episodic and it does not only operate in the direction of severity. For example, Alan Shatter (Minister from 2011 to 2014) opted for leniency on the issue of minimum thresholds and time served (Parole Board 2012, p. 5). Thus, while there is evidence of a punitive approach this can easily be reversed depending on the approach adopted by the Minister of the day.

Conclusion

There is certainly evidence of a punitive shift when examining life imprisonment. The growth in the number of life sentence prisoners as well as the increase in time served is clearly consistent with increased punitiveness. An examination of rationales in decision-making indicates that the process has become susceptible to a form of populist punitiveness with the life sentence and time served being employed as a form of expressive justice and an attempt at addressing public discontent in relation to perceived leniency. Parole decision-makers appeared to be trying to provide meaning to the life sentence through their incorporation of various theories of punishment. Decision-makers were intent on expressing sentiments of retribution, denunciation and disapprobation through the mechanism of release and were cognisant of crime trends and social factors operating outside of the parole context. These views are supported at a broader level in the public statements of the Parole Board and former Ministers. Public statements on the term a life sentence prisoner can expect to serve have on occasion been reactionary and have been adopted in reference to external crime trends rather than a system failure of the parole process, such as adverse publicity arising from false negatives. This is interesting, as false negatives have occurred during the lifetime of the Parole Board although they have not received much public attention (see 'Release and Revocation', Chap. 3). How parole was perceived externally was important when making decisions and the overwhelming view was that the public viewed their decisions as lenient and decision-makers assumed public opinion to be punitive in relation to the release of life sentence prisoners.

Structurally, the parole process is vulnerable to politics and this impacts significantly on those subject to the process. Members' perceptions of the Minister, her views on the administration of life sentences and the length of time a life sentence prisoner should be required to serve are factors that may be contributing towards a more punitive direction in decision-making. Recommendations were being tailored based on members' perceptions of the Minister's approach to decision-making. From the political perspective, it seems that while one former Minister may be an advocate of reform, other Ministers perspectives were more closely aligned with members' views in relation to public opinion, politics and theories of punishment. Beneath the veneer of risk and public protection, lengthier periods of detention were often based on an attempt to send a message to the public as a means of sating the (perceived) punitive appetite of the public. Further detention of a life sentence prisoner may be based on perceptions of risk and dangerousness, rather than empirical reality. The process, in its informal and discretionary nature, renders decision-makers particularly susceptible to incorporating external factors meaning that the process is exposed to the prevailing mood of the public or politicians at any particular time, whether it be punitive or tolerant.

References

Adler, F. (1983). Nations not obsessed with crime (50). Littleton: FB Rothman.M

Ashworth, A. (2009). Criminal law, human rights and preventative justice. In B. McSherry, A. Norrie, & S. Bronitt (Eds.), *Regulating deviance: The redirection of criminlaisation and the futures of criminal law* (pp. 87–108). Oxford: Hart.

Baker, N., & O'Keeffe, C. (2012, September 20). Macarthur release was held up politics. *Irish Examiner*. Retrieved from http://www.irishexaminer.com

Behan, C., & O'Donnell, I. (2008). Prisoners, politics and the polls: Enfranchisement and the burden of responsibility. *British Journal of Criminology, 48*(3), 319–336.

Bottoms, A. (1995). The philosophy and politics of punishment and sentencing. In C. Clarkson & R. Morgan (Eds.), *The politics of sentencing reform* (pp. 17–49). Oxford: Clarendon Press.

Brady, C. (1974). *Guardians of the peace: Irish police*. Dublin: Gill and Macmillan.

Breaking News. (2006, March 24). McDowell: Gangland killers must spend 15 years minimum in jail. *Breaking News*. Retrieved from http://www.breakingnews.ie

Campbell, L. (2010). Responding to gun crime in Ireland. *British Journal of Criminology, 50*(3), 414–434.

Cavadino, M., & Dignan, J. (2006). Penal policy and political economy. *Criminology and Criminal Justice, 6*(4), 435–456.

Cavadino, M., & Dignan, J. (2007). *The penal system: An introduction*. London: Sage.

Central Statistics Office. (2010). *Crime and victimisation, quarterly national household survey*. Dublin: Central Statistics Office.

Central Statistics Office. (2013). *Homicide offences*. Central Statistics Office. Retrieved from http://www.cso.ie/Quicktables/GetQuickTables.aspx?FileName=cja01c1.asp&TableName=Homicide+Offences&StatisticalProduct=DB_CJ

Central Statistics Office. (2016). *Crime and victimisation, quarterly national household survey*. Dublin: Dublin Central Statistics Office.

Department of Justice and Equality. (2014). *Report of the independent review group on the Department of Justice and Equality*. Dublin: Department of Justice and Equality.

Donnellan, E. (2002, August 31). No decision yet on who may rule on Macarthur. *Irish Times*, p. 6.

Friendship, C., & Thornton, D. (2001). Sexual reconviction for sexual offenders discharged from prison in England and Wales: Implications for evaluating treatment. *British Journal of Criminology, 41*(2), 285–292.

Garland, D. (1990). *Punishment and modern society: A study in social theory*. Chicago: University of Chicago Press.

Garland, D. (2001). *The culture of control: Crime and social order in contemporary society*. Oxford: Oxford University Press.

Green, D. A. (2005). Public opinion versus public judgment about crime: Correcting the 'comedy of errors'. *British Journal of Criminology, 46*(1), 131–154.

Griffin, D. (2014). The politics of parole: Discretion and the life sentence prisoner. Unpublished PhD Thesis. University College Dublin.

Griffin, D., & O'Donnell, I. (2012). The life sentence and parole. *British Journal of Criminology, 52*(3), 611–629.

Hamilton, C. (2014). *Reconceptualising penality: A comparative perspective on punitiveness in Ireland, Scotland and New Zealand*. Oxon: Routledge.

Hawkins, K. (1983a). Thinking about legal decision-making. In J. Shapland (Ed.), *Decision-making in the legal system, Issues in criminological and legal psychology* (Vol. 5). Leicester: British Psychological Society for the Division of Criminological and Legal Psychology.

Hawkins, K. (1983b). Assessing evil: Decision, behaviour and Parole Board justice. *British Journal of Criminology, 23*(2), 101–127.

Healy, D. (2010). *The dynamics of desistance: Charting pathways through change*. Cullompton/Devon/Portland: Willan.

Hebenton, B., & Seddon, T. (2009). From dangerousness to precaution: Managing sexual and violent offenders in an insecure and uncertain age. *British Journal of Criminology, 49*(3), 343–362.

Heylin, G. (2001). Evaluating prisons, prisoners and others. *Studies in Public Policy* Retrieved from http://www.tara.tcd.ie/handle/2262/60511

Hood, R., & Shute, S. (2000). *Parole decision-making: Weighing the risk to the public*. London: Home Office.

Hood, R., Shute, S., & Wilcox, A. (2000). *The parole system at work: A study of risk based decision-making*. London: Home Office.

Hood, R., Shute, S., Feilzer, M., & Wilcox, A. (2002). Sex offenders emerging from long-term imprisonment. A study of their long-term reconviction rates and of parole board members' judgements of their risk. *British Journal of Criminology, 42*(2), 371–394.

Irish Penal Reform Trust. (2007). *Public attitudes to prison*. Dublin: Irish Penal Reform Trust.

Irish Times (1983a, January 13). Macarthur gets life for murder of nurse. *Irish Times*, p. 1.

Irish Times (1983b, July 23). No disclosure on rulings possible, DPP maintains. *Irish Times*, p. 5.

Kelly, O. (2004, July 13). Macarthur release discussed with families. *Irish Times*, p. 4.

Kerrigan, G. (2012, September 23). A sensational and startling case in a time of innocence. *Irish Independent*. Retrieved from http://www.independent.ie

Kilcommins, S., O'Donnell, I., O'Sullivan, E., & Vaughan, B. (2004). *Crime, punishment and the search for order in Ireland*. Dublin: Institute of Public Administration.

Kühnrich, B., & Kania, H. (2005). *Attitudes towards punishment in the European Union: Results from the 2005 European Crime Survey (ECSS) with focus on Germany*. Freiburg: Max Planck Institute for Foreign and International Criminal Law.

Lally, C. (2004, January 31). Parole board to get books of evidence access. *Irish Times*, p. 7.

Lally, C. (2006, March 9). McDowell defends length of murder sentences. *Irish Times*, p. 7.

Law Reform Commission. (1993). *Consultation paper on sentencing*. Dublin: Law Reform Commission.

Malsch, M., & Duker, M. (2016). *Incapacitation: Trends and new perspectives*. Oxon: Routledge.

Maruna, S., & King, A. (2009). Once a criminal, always a criminal? Redeemability and the psychology of punitive public attitudes. *European Journal on Criminal Policy and Research, 15*(1–2), 7–24.
Matthews, R. (2005). The myth of punitiveness. *Theoretical Criminology, 9*(2), 175–201.
Mauer, M., King, R. S., & Young, M. C. (2004). *The meaning of 'life': Long prison sentences in context*. Washington, DC: The Sentencing Project.
Miles, T. J., & Ludwig, J. (2007). The silence of the lambdas: Deterring incapacitation research. *Journal of Quantitative Criminology, 23*(4), 287–301.
Mitchell, B., & Roberts, J. V. (2011). Sentencing for murder: Exploring public knowledge and public opinion in England and Wales. *British Journal of Criminology, 52*(1), 141–158.
Murray, C. (2012). A perfect storm: Parliament and prisoner disenfranchisement. *Parliamentary Affairs, 66*(3), 511–539.
Murtagh, P. (1982, August 20). Taoiseach may face action over TV remark. *Irish Times*, p. 1.
Nash, M., & Williams, A. (2010). Introduction: Assessing and managing risk. In M. Nash & A. Williams (Eds.), *Handbook of public protection* (pp. 83–86). Oxon: Willan.
National Crime Council. (2009). *Worry about crime and its impact on quality of life*. Dublin: Department of Justice and Equality.
Nelken, D. (2009). Comparative criminal justice: Beyond ethnocentricism and relativism. *European Journal of Criminology, 6*(4), 291–311.
O'Brien, C. (2011, November 15). Temporary release programme sanctioned for killer Macarthur. *Irish Times*, p. 8.
O'Connell, M. (1999). Is Irish public opinion towards crime distorted by media bias? *European Journal of Communication, 14*(2), 191–212.
O'Donnell, I. (2001). Prison matters. *Irish Jurist, 36*(1), 153–173.
O'Donnell, I. (2004). Imprisonment and penal policy in Ireland. *Howard Journal of Crime and Justice, 43*(3), 253–266.
O'Donnell, I. (2005). Crime and justice in the Republic of Ireland. *European Journal of Criminology, 2*(1), 99–131.
O'Donnell, I. (2011). Crime and punishment in the Republic of Ireland: A country profile. *International Journal of Comparative and Applied Criminal Justice, 35*(1), 73–88.
O'Donnell, I. (2012, March 12). More scrutiny needed of life sentences. *Irish Times*, p. B6.

O'Donnell, I., & Jewkes, Y. (2011). Going home for Christmas: Prisoners, a taste of freedom and the press. *Howard Journal of Crime and Justice, 50*(1), 75–91.

O'Donnell, I., & O'Sullivan, E. (2001). *Crime control in Ireland: The politics of intolerance*. Cork: Cork University Press.

O'Donnell, I., & O'Sullivan, E. (2003). The politics of intolerance—Irish style. *British Journal of Criminology, 43*(1), 41–62.

O'Donnell, I., Baumer, E. P., & Hughes, N. (2008). Recidivism in the Republic of Ireland. *Criminology & Criminal Justice, 8*(2), 123–146.

O'Malley, T. (2003). Sentencing values and sentencing structures. *Judicial Studies Institute Journal, 3*(1), 130–155.

O'Malley, T. (2006). *Sentencing law and practice*. Dublin: Thomson Round Hall.

O'Malley, T. (2011). *Sentencing: Towards a coherent system*. Dublin: Round Hall.

O'Malley, T. (2016). *Sentencing law and practice*. Dublin: Thomson Round Hall.

Olden, J. (2001). *Report of Mr John Olden on the management of the sentences of Thomas Murray, life sentence prisoner*. Dublin: Department of Justice and Equality.

Padfield, N., Liebling, A., & Arnold, H. (2000). *An exploration of decision-making at discretionary lifer panels*. Home Office research report no. 213. London: Home Office Research, Development and Statistics Directorate.

Parole Board. (2002–2015). *Annual reports*. Dublin: Parole Board.

Pfeiffer, C., Windzio, M., & Kleimann, M. (2005). Media use and its impacts on crime perception, sentencing attitudes and crime policy. *European Journal of Criminology, 2*(3), 259–285.

Prison Service. (2014–2016). *Annual reports*. Dublin/Longford: Irish Prison Service.

Roberts, J. V. (1992). Public opinion, crime, and criminal justice. *Crime and Justice, 16*, 99–180.

Roberts, J. V. (2003). Public opinion and mandatory sentencing: A review of international findings. *Criminal Justice and Behavior, 30*(4), 483–508.

Robinson, P. H. (2001). Punishing dangerousness: Cloaking preventive detention as criminal justice. *Harvard Law Review, 114*(5), 1429–1456.

Rogan, M. (2015). The policy making process and penal change. In D. Healy, C. Hamilton, Y. Daly, & M. Butler (Eds.), *The Routledge handbook of Irish criminology* (pp. 434–449). London: Routledge.

Sample, L. L., & Bray, T. M. (2006). Are sex offenders different? An examination of re-arrest patterns. *Criminal Justice Policy Review, 17*(1), 83–102.
Simon, J. (1998). Managing the monstrous: Sex offenders and the new penology. *Psychology, Public Policy and Law, 4*(1–2), 452–467.
Simon, J. (2007). *Governing through crime: How the war on crime transformed American democracy and created a culture of fear*. New York: Oxford University Press.
Tavares, C., Thomas, G., & Bulut, F. (2012). *Crime and criminal justice, 2006–2009*. Brussels: Eurostat.
Tonry, M. (1996). *Sentencing matters*. New York: Oxford University Press.
Tonry, M. (2001). Symbol, substance, and severity in Western penal policies. *Punishment and Society, 3*(4), 517–536.
Tonry, M. (2007). Determinants of penal policies. *Crime and Justice, 36*(1), 1–48.
Travis, J., & Lawrence, S. (2002). *Beyond the prison gates: The state of parole in America*. Washington, DC: Urban Institute.
Von Hirsch, A., & Ashworth, A. (Eds.). (1998). *Principled sentencing: Readings on theory and policy*. Oxford: Hart Publishing.
Von Hirsch, A., Ashworth, A., & Roberts, J. V. (Eds.). (1998). *Principled sentencing: Readings on theory and policy*. Oxford: Hart.
Walmsley, R. (2016). *World prison population list*. Essex: International Centre for Prison Studies.
Williams, E. (2003, April 20). O'Dea vetoes Macarthur release. *Irish Independent*. Retrieved from http://www.independent.ie
Zimring, F., & Hawkins, G. (1995). *Incapacitation: Penal confinement and the restraint of crime*. New York: Oxford University Press.
Zimring, F. E., & Johnson, D. T. (2006). Public opinion and the governance of punishment in democratic political systems. *The Annals of the American Academy of Political and Social Science, 605*(1), 265–280.

Table of Legislation

Criminal Justice (Temporary Release of Prisoners) Act 2003.
Criminal Justice Act 1999.
Criminal Justice Act 2006.
Proceeds of Crime Act 1995.
Sex Offenders Act 2001.

Table of Cases

Ireland

People (Attorney General) v O'Callaghan [1966] IR 501.
People (DPP) v Larkin [2008] IECCA 138.

Table of Parliamentary Debates

528 *Dáil Debates* Col. 311: John O'Donoghue, 12 December 2000.

6

The Realities of the Situation

The applicant urged the Court to look beyond the legal situation and to have regard to the realities of the situation. The Court notes that that is, precisely, what the Supreme Court did in its examination of the case when it confirmed that it should not look simply at the formal provisions of the law but at the substance and effect of the law in practice concerning the sentence imposed on a convicted person.

European Court of Human Rights (Fifth Section)
Lynch and Whelan v Ireland
(2014, para. 34).

Introduction

Many European states, rather than foregrounding punitive goals, have focused attention on shaping the release process to provide protection to those subject to it, by adapting their release mechanisms to reflect human rights standards. These developments have been driven at a national level through the courts or the legislature, but reform has also been prompted by the instruments of Europe's institutions (Livingstone 2000). 'Europe' has greatly influenced issues of criminal justice through the Council of

D. Griffin, *Killing Time*, https://doi.org/10.1007/978-3-319-72667-0_6

Europe, the European Convention on Human Rights (ECHR) and European Court of Human Rights (ECtHR), the European Committee for the Prevention of Torture (CPT) and the European Union (EU). Since the 1990s, membership of the Council of Europe has required the ratification of the ECHR and CPT and acceptance of the complaint procedure of the ECtHR (Snacken 2010, pp. 285–7). The Council of Europe has adopted a number of recommendations on the management of life sentence and long-term prisoners, promoting the need for members to provide an appropriate legal framework governing their release (Council of Europe 1976, 2003). The CPT (2007, 2012, p. 26) is strongly committed to the release of life sentence prisoners and the jurisprudence of the ECtHR has impacted on release processes in a number of jurisdictions, particularly in the United Kingdom (*Vinter and Others v United Kingdom* 2013; *Weeks v United Kingdom* 1987; *Thynne, Wilson and Gunnell v United Kingdom* 1990; *Hirst v United Kingdom* 2001). Nonetheless, seeking a level of uniformity across the release process has proven difficult given the 'quirky and esoteric' nature of each country and the influence of local culture, history and politics on penal policy and practice (Cavadino and Dignan 2006: 452). In addition, any analysis of European countries is complicated by the lack of a clear collective sense of identity in the traditional ethno-cultural sense (Weiler 1995). Despite this, and unlike the United States, which now emphasises crime control over due process values, part of what can be identified as a 'European identity' is a sense of shared civic values and an allegiance to human rights protections (Snacken 2010; Nicolaïdis 2004; Rifkin 2004; van Zyl Smit 2006).

Common law countries and civil law European countries tend to differ according to the extent to which those subjected to the life sentence find themselves exposed to the politics of punitiveness or sheltered by a variety of human rights safeguards. The monist nature of civil legal systems rendered the ECHR directly effective at a national level, thus increasing its significance and impact. As a common law country, Ireland, like the United Kingdom, has a dualist legal system and the Irish constitutional framework requires international instruments to be made effective at a national level through legislation. This was done through the European Convention on Human Rights Act 2003, which gave further effect to the

ECHR at a sub-constitutional level. Fundamental rights protections already contained in the Irish Constitution and the 'constitutionalisation' of many criminal justice procedures indicates that Ireland has equivalent or stronger human rights protections when compared with the ECHR in some areas (Ní Raifeartaigh 2007). An area in which constitutional guarantees do not provide strong protection is the life sentence and its administration.

It would be logical to identify the judiciary as agents that could provide a counterpoint to the punitive tendencies of parole decision-makers (see Sweden for example: Lappi-Seppälä 2016) and act to provide the impetus for reform. But this has not transpired in the context of life imprisonment in Ireland. The Supreme Court declared the mandatory life sentence and its administration to be compatible with the provisions of the Irish Constitution and the ECHR (*Lynch and Whelan v Minister for Justice* 2012). A subsequent application to the ECtHR was found to be inadmissible on both substantive and procedural grounds (*Lynch and Whelan v Ireland* 2013, 2014). It may seem somewhat confusing that the Irish process, which has been described as 'stagnant' (Griffin 2015, p. 9) and 'arbitrary' (O'Malley 2011, p. 223) has been deemed to comply with fundamental right provisions. But for now, the issue of compliance has been settled.

Strengthening the procedural rights surrounding life imprisonment and parole could have the effect of providing certainty to those subject to the process and would bring Ireland in line with other European jurisdictions. Depending on the framework adopted, it could also operate to place constraint on decision-making requiring a more consistent approach to parole outcomes and time served. There exists a multitude of reasons that might result in the further detention of a life sentence prisoner, as has been identified in Chap. 5. Some of these were external factors poorly related to the risk of reoffending or the circumstances of the offender. Although the analysis identified general trends such as the rise in lethal violence and the hardening of public attitudes towards crime as influential on decision-makers, there are other, more practical factors that can operate to result in the further detention of a life sentence prisoner. Consider the situation that three life sentence prisoners found themselves in when being reviewed by the Parole Board in 2015. All three had served

17 years in prison (Parole Board 2015, p. 4). According to the Parole Board, two of the offenders had 'psychiatric problems' and one had an intellectual disability. Although the Parole Board were of the view that these life sentence prisoners should be recommended for temporary release the Parole Board found it was not possible to make such a recommendation as the necessary community supports were not available (Gallagher 2017). They were further detained on this basis. Similarly, life sentence prisoners on 'full temporary release' have been recalled to prison to serve additional periods in prison due to accommodation and medical issues (*Dáil Question* No. 205: Frances Fitzgerald, 02 May 2017). It scarcely seems appropriate that the release of life sentence prisoners be frustrated because the services are not in place in the community, particularly given the length of time available to put a plan in place from the point of the first review at seven years. But such outcomes are possible when legal safeguards are weak or absent altogether. A structured process that would require the Parole Board to comply with specific criteria and provide reasons for their decisions could operate to reduce or eliminate such unsatisfactory outcomes. With effective judicial oversight these outcomes could be reversed or eliminated altogether.

In *Lynch and Whelan*, both the Supreme Court (2012) and subsequently the ECtHR (2013, 2014) stated that, when examining whether the Irish life sentence was compliant with domestic law and the ECHR, the 'realities of the situation' were to be taken into consideration in assessing the applicants case. Adopting this approach, the ECtHR supported the interpretation of the Supreme Court, finding the life sentence to be 'wholly punitive' in nature. The Court affirmed that the executive was not involved in the sentencing process and that individuals subject to the process had recourse to the courts to review the legality of the sentence imposed or the exercise of the executive discretion of temporary release. But a dissonance exists between this interpretation and the actuality of life imprisonment and release. Given the data presented in the preceding chapters, it is difficult to reconcile the disjoint between the legal reality as interpreted by the courts, with the practical reality as articulated by parole decision-makers. This chapter attempts to make sense of the alternate legal and practical realities of life imprisonment.

The Legal Interpretation of the Life Sentence

Sentencing in Ireland is based primarily on judicially developed principles conferring considerable discretion on the trial judge. On the basis of the principle of proportionality the sentence must be proportionate to the gravity of the offence and the personal circumstances of the offender (*The People (Attorney General) v Poyning* 1972). In exercising sentencing discretion, the court must locate the case within the range of applicable penalties based on the offender's culpability, the harm caused and the offender's behaviour (Law Reform Commission 2013, pp. 17–32). Further, the court may take into consideration a wide range of aggravating and mitigating factors which can include: good character; behaviour while in custody; remorse; rehabilitation; and age (O'Malley 2016). Also relevant here is constitutional proportionality, which is distinct from sentencing proportionality and applies to all Acts of the *Oireachtas* (Irish parliament), the test for which permits the legislative overriding of a constitutionally protected right where the provision addresses 'concerns pressing and substantial in a free and democratic society' (*Heaney v Ireland* 1994). In such instances, the provision must: 'be rationally connected to the objective and not be arbitrary, unfair or based on irrational considerations; impair the rights as little as possible, and; be such that their effects on rights are proportional to the objective' (*Heaney v Ireland* 1994, p. 607). In addition, principles of justice dictate that 'like cases be treated alike and different cases treated differently' (O'Malley 2006, p. 50).

The vast majority of those serving life sentences in Ireland have been convicted of murder and have a life sentence mandatorily imposed at sentencing as a result of legislative provision (Criminal Justice Act 1990, s. 2). There is no statutory minimum term or tariff imposed by the sentencing judge and the role of the judge is limited to the imposition of the sentence. Aggravating and mitigating factors are not explored at sentencing. Those sentenced to life imprisonment may serve varying terms of imprisonment the length of which is decided on a case-by-case basis by the Minister for Justice (Minister), following the advice of the Parole Board. The constitutionality of the mandatory life sentence for murder was unsuccessfully challenged on several grounds in *Lynch and Whelan* (2012). Upholding the constitutional proportionality of section 2 of the Criminal Justice Act 1990, Chief Justice Murray indicated that a legislative provision may be unconstitutional where 'there was no rational relationship between the penalty and the requirements of justice with regard to the punishment of the offence specified' and that this was not the case for murder, which was 'unique in nature and was justifiable in treating all murders in a similar manner' (18 and 19; Law Reform Commission 2013, p. 17).

Mandatory sentences, which remain relatively rare in the Irish sentencing scheme, can appear to conflict with proportionality in sentencing as it restricts the court in the selection of the sentence, based on the individual case. However, mandatory or fixed sentences established by the legislature have been deemed to be constitutional (*Deaton v Attorney General and Revenue Commissioners* 1963; Law Reform Commission 1996, 2013). Life sentences can be distinguished from other mandatory penalties in that the sentence is also indeterminate with no certainty as to release. The appellants in *Lynch and Whelan* argued that the life sentence, due to its indeterminate nature, is not akin to a fixed penalty and therefore the principle that the legislature may prescribe a single fixed penalty for an offence as articulated by the Supreme Court in *Deaton* was not applicable to the indeterminate life sentence. Flowing from this, they argued that the executive, through the Minister and the provisions of the Criminal Justice (Temporary Release of Prisoners) Act 2003, actually determines the punishment of a life sentence prisoner through the release process thus violating the constitutional roles in sentencing of the branches of government (the judicial role is to select the sentence, the executive role is to administer that sentence and determine how much of the sentence will be served: *Deaton v Attorney General and Revenue Commissioners* 1963; O'Malley 2016, pp. 769–771). Murray C.J. rejected the arguments of the appellants deeming the life sentence to fall within the fixed penalty described in *Deaton*. Thus, based on the interpretation of the Supreme Court, while a judge must impose a proportionate sentence when exercising discretion this does not arise when the court is lawfully imposing a fixed penalty, as is the case with the mandatory life sentence for murder (p. 21). Of particular significance was the court's interpretation of the life sentence as 'wholly punitive'. 'Punitive' in the legal sense means punishment, rather than the more expansive meaning applied to the term in the criminological sphere. Interpreting the life sentence in this manner has had the effect of white-washing many of the practical realities of the life sentence and its administration that have been of concern for some time.

The '*wholly punitive*' Life Sentence

The Supreme Court characterised the life sentence as 'wholly punitive', designed to punish for the duration of the sentence:

> In the Court's view a life sentence … is a sentence of a wholly punitive nature and does not incorporate any element of preventative detention. It is a sentence that subsists for the entire life of the person convicted of murder. That person may, by virtue of a discretionary power vested in the executive, be temporarily released… but he or she always remains liable to imprisonment on foot of the life sentence should the period of temporary release be terminated for good and sufficient reason. (2012, p. 24)

Murray C.J. stated that there was a 'misconception that the punitive element of the life sentence terminates on temporary release' (p. 23) thus indicating that a life sentence prisoner continues to serve a punitive sentence while on 'full temporary release' in the community. The Court rejected the contentions that the system of release in place affected the punitive nature of the sentence in any manner, resulted in executive resentencing or an inconsistent approach in the sentencing of life sentence prisoners. Murray C.J. stated that the requirement that the Minister must consider matters such as the gravity of the offence or the threat posed to members of the community on release (Criminal Justice (Temporary Release of Prisoners) Act 2003, s. 1(2)) did not result in the exercising of judicial discretion.

> Such a consideration is incidental to the discretionary power and its purpose. It is not a decision on the sentence to be served. It cannot be seen in any sense as converting a subsisting punitive sentence into some form of preventative detention. (p. 26)

At the ECtHR the applicants challenged this interpretation arguing that in practice the life sentence was not 'wholly punitive' as the Minister had regard to preventive detention in deliberating on release. The executive power of 'full temporary release' routinely granted to life sentence prisoners by the Minister was tainted by uncertainty, indeterminacy and arbitrariness (2014, paras. 26–27). They argued that the executive, through the Minister and the provisions of the Criminal Justice (Temporary Release of Prisoners) Act 2003, actually determines the punishment of a life sentence prisoner through the release process, thereby violating the constitutional roles in sentencing of the branches of government. They also claimed that preventive detention formed a significant component of the life sentence, as both the Parole Board and Minister take the risk of reoffending into consideration in deliberating on the release of life sentence prisoners, *via* temporary release provisions. Given the practical reality, the applicants argued that the sentence was not simply punitive, but also incorporated a preventive component.

The ECtHR (2014, para. 35) accepted the assertion that the life sentence in Ireland was 'wholly punitive' noting that the granting of temporary release 'does not as a matter of domestic law terminate the sentence imposed upon him following [release]'. Both the Supreme Court and the ECtHR distinguished the practice in the United Kingdom whereby the punitive and public safety components were explicitly divided in the sentence stating that '…the discretionary power of the executive to grant temporary release to a life sentence prisoner is not inconsistent with the solely punitive character of a mandatory life sentence' (2014, para. 37). The Supreme Court in *Lynch and Whelan* (2012) cited *Kafkaris v Cyprus* (2008) with approval, noting that a 'wholly punitive' mandatory life sentence is permissible where there is a *de facto* and *de jure* prospect of release.

The interpretation of the life sentence as 'wholly punitive' fits poorly with the reality of the sentence. Length of time served by a life sentence prisoner is substantially dictated by considerations of public protection. This is the case irrespective of the legal interpretation of the life sentence as 'wholly punitive' and the view that the exercising of the discretionary power of temporary release by a Minister does not impact on the punitive nature of the sentence. It is evidenced through the statutory framework, public statements by the Parole Board and various Ministers and the inclusion of risk assessments by the Probation Service and the Prison Psychology Service. Further, the data presented in Chap. 4 indicates that decisions surrounding detention or release revolve around the risk of reoffending. Parole Board members (members) viewed the punitive element as expiring at a certain point during the term of imprisonment with considerations of risk then coming to the fore. On release, life sentence prisoners are supervised in the community for the remainder of their lives by the Probation Service. The role of the Probation Service in the context of life sentence prisoners is to provide welfare and risk management, rather than pursuing anything that might be thought of as a continuation of the punishment component. This part of the sentence is legally described as punitive on the basis that the life sentence prisoner is still serving a sentence, is on release at the discretion of the Minister and is subject to recall to prison at any point. However, such an interpretation is at odds with the permanent nature of full temporary release and the practical reality of 'time served' on release in the community. From a legal perspective, considerations of preventive detention are ancillary to the overarching punitive element. Of course, it is legitimate for considerations of public protection to form part of the quantum of punishment and the Minister, in the exercise of his or her discretionary power, is required to have regard to considerations of risk and reoffending. But the practice surrounding the release of life sentence prisoners reveals the extent to which the risk component is underplayed in the decisions of the Supreme Court and the ECtHR in their interpretation of the 'reality' of the life sentence and the process of release. When it comes to release, risk and dangerousness are at the forefront in the minds of decision-makers.

The Problem with Preventive Detention

Characterising the life sentence as 'wholly punitive' eliminates the constitutional difficulties that would most certainly arise if the courts acknowledged that there was a substantial preventive component to the life sentence. Constitutional barriers inhibit the implementation of penalties based on dangerousness alone. In the *People (Attorney General) v O'Callaghan* (1966) the Supreme Court rejected the likelihood of an accused person committing an offence while awaiting trial as a ground for refusing bail as it would constitute a form of preventive detention. This also applies to sentences of preventive detention (*People (DPP) v Carmody* 1988) as the incapacitative rationale conflicts with the proportionality principle in sentencing, the constitutional right to personal liberty and the presumption of innocence (*People (DPP) v K.(G.)* 2008, O'Malley 2016, pp. 41–43; Law Reform Commission 2013). The principle creates a difficulty in the sense that the courts cannot explicitly employ evidence of a risk of reoffending as an aggravating factor in increasing the sentence imposed (O'Malley 2016, p. 85). In *People (DPP) v McMahon* (2011) the defendant stabbed two members of staff at a hospital multiple times causing serious injuries to both parties. The defendant had previously been convicted of manslaughter and had been released prior to the incident. McMahon had a history of severely unstable and threatening behaviour. The Court of Criminal Appeal stated that it was concerning that a person so 'seriously disturbed' was nevertheless at liberty (para. 9). Given the need to protect society, the Director of Public Prosecutions (DPP) invited the sentencing judge to consider a life sentence so that the defendant could be monitored by the Parole Board (para. 10). A sentence of ten years was imposed for the offences of causing serious harm and assault causing harm. The DPP appealed contending that the sentence was unduly lenient (Criminal Justice Act 1993, s. 2). The Court of Criminal Appeal noted the issue as follows:

> [C]ourts are faced with offences committed by persons of whom it can be said with a high degree of assurance that they pose a real and serious threat to the public – whether by reason of fanatical commitment to a violent cause, or from simple and irredeemable evil (para. 15).

Can a court go beyond what is considered a normally appropriate sentence and impose a life sentence to ensure an offender who poses a threat to the public is prevented from carrying out that threat? In answering this question, the Court cited the principle articulated in *R v Veen (No.2)* (1988):

> It is one thing to say that the principle of proportionality precludes the imposition of a sentence extended beyond what is appropriate to the crime merely to protect society; it is another thing to say that the protection of society is not a material factor in fixing an appropriate sentence.

Thus, with a life sentence, considerations of dangerousness can form a component of the sentence but cannot be the primary sentencing rationale. In *People (DPP) v S.(M.)* (2000) Denham J. stated that a sentence may incorporate an element of preventive detention. But as noted in *People (DPP) v K.(G.)* (2008) there is a balance that must be struck between protecting the public and the states obligation to vindicate the rights of the individual, even if that individual is a recidivist or dangerous. An individual cannot be sentenced for past offences nor can he be sentenced for offences which he has not yet committed.

In the case of a mandatory life sentence for murder, issues of preventive detention arise at the back-end of the sentence (the release process) and the factors taken into consideration on release by the Minister. *Lynch and Whelan* (2012) were unsuccessful in seeking an interpretation that further detention during the parole process was a form of preventive detention. Issues of preventive detention arise in a more pronounced manner in the context of the imposition of a discretionary life sentence. It raises questions as to the rationale for the imposition of a life sentence rather than a lengthy determinate sentence and whether considerations of preventive detention are leading rather than forming a part of the deliberations on the imposition of sentence. In *People (DPP) v Ward* (2012) the Court of Criminal Appeal found an error in principle in the imposition of two current life sentences for the offences of assault causing serious harm and possession of a firearm. At sentencing the trial judge remarked: 'I am imposing this sentence … simply to ensure … that whenever he is released into the community in the future it will be at a point when the authorities are satisfied that he no longer represents [a] threat to others' (p. 4). Imposing a 20-year term in lieu of life imprisonment, the Court of Criminal Appeal found there had been a 'suggestion that what has been imposed on Mr. Ward is not just the sentence appropriate to the offences … but some form of preventative detention' (p. 5).

Although similar statements in relation to preventive detention were made by the trial judge in *People (DPP) v Daniels* (2014) the Supreme Court came to a different conclusion. The applicant challenged the discretionary life sentence imposed upon him for attempted murder, arguing that the rationale for its imposition was preventive in nature and therefore unconstitutional. The issue arose as a result of statements by Carney J. at sentencing, which appeared to focus on the need to impose a life sentence to manage the risk that he believed the offender would present if he was subjected to a determinate sentence and released prior to the reduction of that risk. Carney J. stated that his 'primary function' was to protect the community noting that he could not see how, given the evidence presented at the hearing, he could 'rule out [this type of crime] happening again' (The Nationalist 2003). Noting the harsh nature of the sentence, he stated that the Parole Board could monitor the offender 'to see when it is safe for society' to recommend release, adding the comment: 'I can't look into the future but the Parole Board can' (The Nationalist 2003). The Supreme Court acknowledged that the imposition of the life sentence had a preventive element, but this in effect was incidental and did 'not exceed what is required for purely penal purposes in so aggravated a case' (*People (DPP) v Daniels* 2014, para. 21). The argument of the Supreme Court was that, while the imposition of the life sentence is 'wholly punitive' in nature '…it also involves elements such as rehabilitation of the offender, deterrence and the protection of society' (para. 20). Despite the rationale presented by the Supreme Court in *Daniels*, it is clear that the imposition of a life sentence for any offence outside of murder can only occur in exceptional cases (*People (DPP) v McC* 2008; *People (DPP) v S.(P.)* 2009). There are just three people (including Daniels) currently serving sentences of life imprisonment for attempted murder, with only 5 per cent of the total life sentence prisoner population serving discretionary life sentences (*Dáil Question* No. 81: Frances Fitzgerald, 08 November 2016). The exceptional quality in this case clearly related to concerns around risk and this was more than a mere incidental consideration at sentencing. The decision of the Supreme Court certainly maintains the status of the 'wholly punitive' life sentence irrespective of whether it is at odds with the statements for the imposition of the sentence at the hearing in the first instance.

The Role of the Executive

The ECtHR has generated a wealth of jurisprudence on life sentences and the release of life sentence prisoners. These cases are primarily concerned with Article 3 (relating to inhuman and degrading treatment or punishment), Article 5(1) (relating to lawful detention) and Article 5(4) (relating to the right to take proceedings by which the lawfulness of the detention shall be decided speedily). The Court has continually emphasised that the life sentence itself is not incompatible with the Convention, however issues may arise in the context of the structures surrounding the decision to release or further detain a life sentence prisoner (van Zyl Smit et al. 2014). Prior to the decision of the ECtHR in *Lynch and Whelan* in 2014, the analysis of the Irish process of release and its compliance with the ECHR tended to centre on the jurisprudence of the ECtHR that relates to the release of life sentence prisoners in England and Wales (McCutcheon and Coffey 2006; Law Reform Commission 2013). But there are significant differences between the Irish process, which has no legal minimum term, and that of England and Wales, which operates a tariff-based system. A further distinguishing factor between England and Wales and many other European countries, including Ireland, is the criteria employed when determining the issue of release. In England and Wales there is a focus on risk and the danger posed to society when deliberating on the release of a life sentence prisoner post-tariff, whereas many other jurisdictions incorporate a much broader range of criteria. This limits the application of the jurisprudence of the ECtHR when looking at the review processes in countries outside of the UK. The ECtHR has, on several occasions, highlighted these distinctions when examining the processes employed in other jurisdictions (*Stafford v United Kingdom* 2002; *Kafkaris v Cyprus (no.2)* 2011; *Vinter and Others v. United Kingdom* 2013). The ECtHR ruled in *Stafford v United Kingdom* (2002) that setting a minimum term is a judicial function and that a subsequent decision to release had to also be made by an independent and impartial body. This was largely related to the requirement that the Parole Board focus on the risk of the individual and an acknowledgement that this was something that was dynamic in nature and thus required reassessment. Decisions in relation to release processes in other jurisdictions indicate that the Court is more willing to take a hands-off approach where risk features within a range of other factors or where a broad range of penological justifications are at play (*Streicher v Germany* 2009; *Meixner v Germany* 2009).

The question as to the type of review and whether it requires an independent court or court-like body is largely contingent on the process in place in each jurisdiction (*Stafford v United Kingdom* 2002). The ECtHR in *Vinter and Others v United Kingdom* (2013) stated clearly that although those serving life sentences may have committed abhorrent and egregious acts, they must retain the hope that, someday, they may have atoned for the wrongs which they have committed (para. 75). The issue then arises as to what type of review will be sufficient to satisfy the ECHR post *Vinter*. Perhaps disappointingly, it appears the threshold of what is required might be lower than anticipated. van Zyl Smit et al. (2014, p. 17) note that the Court's 'conclusion that different procedural standards are… to be applied when deciding whether to release persons from life imprisonment does not stand up to close scrutiny'.

The crux of the issue in Ireland is whether the review and release process requires a decision by a court or court-like body, or whether it is sufficient for this decision to remain within the remit of the executive. Neither the Supreme Court nor the ECtHR recognised that the executive, or more particularly the Minister, was involved in exercising a sentencing power when determining the issue of temporary release. This is primarily due to the interpretation of the life sentence as 'wholly punitive', preventing the reality of release from being truly scrutinised. The Irish life sentence is indivisible in the sense that there is no minimum term or tariff that represents the punitive and preventive component – legally it is entirely punitive. The Supreme Court has held that length of time served in prison is a matter that rests entirely with the executive (*Murray v Ireland* 1991). On the issue of executive resentencing, the Supreme Court in *Lynch and Whelan* (2012, p. 28) noted that '[t]he power of the executive, in this case the Minister, to release a prisoner… is a distinct executive function and does not constitute a determination of what punishment a person should undergo as a consequence of his crime'. The ECtHR found that the final determination of the applicant's sentence was the day his appeal against conviction was dismissed (2014, para. 50). The Court stated that the incorporation of considerations of risk and security by the Minister in the exercising of his powers of temporary release did 'not entitle the applicant to a judicial procedure to test the on-going legality of his current imprisonment' finding no approximation in practice between the tariff-based system of the United Kingdom and the practice of temporary release in Ireland (2014, para. 50). In any event, the ECtHR noted that domestic law afforded those subject to the life sentence the chance of appealing the sentence if it was preventive in nature (2014, para. 34) and that the executive's decision as to whether to grant temporary release could be subject to judicial review if legal issues arose in the exercising of that power (2014, para. 44).

When originally enacted, the executive power of temporary release was designed to permit release for a defined period. It was not envisaged as a mechanism for releasing life sentence prisoners to serve the remainder of their sentence in the community until their death. A distinct practice of release has developed that revolves around the decision-making of the Parole Board and Minister. From a practical perspective, it is counterintuitive to release a life sentence prisoner, ostensibly for the remainder of their life, subject to their compliance with the conditions of release, using a provision that is designed for short-term release. It may be appropriate to treat a decision to release an offender for a number of days at Christmas to spend time with his or her family as a privilege at the discretion of the executive. But is it appropriate to treat the process for releasing a life sentence prisoner on 'full temporary release', a period that may extend for several decades, in the same manner? In practice, the distinction between the Christmas leave situation and the permanent release of life sentence prisoners has long been acknowledged, but legally this continues to go unrecognised. The implication of this narrow interpretation has meant that life sentence prisoners applying for 'full temporary release' are in the unsatisfactory situation of being legally indistinguishable from those applying for short-term release notwithstanding the practical reality of the release process.

The Right to Review

The ECtHR in *Lynch and Whelan* noted that the exercise of the Ministerial power of release is safeguarded through the right to judicial review (para. 36). But such is the broad discretion afforded the Minister and the narrow grounds upon which the exercise of this power can be challenged, that, in practical terms, the right to judicial review has translated into little by way of substantive procedural benefit. In theory, questions surrounding the lack of structure, legal representation and oral hearing could prove to be fruitful grounds for judicial review. Yet, an analysis of the jurisprudence in this area of executive discretion would indicate that a successful application on these grounds is unlikely (O'Malley 2009; Morgan and Hogan 2007). The courts have been 'anxious to stress' that the granting of temporary release by the executive 'is not to be treated as an enforceable right' (O'Malley 2006, p. 436) as it is a function of sentence administration that rests 'entirely with the executive' (*Murray v Ireland* 1991). The granting of temporary release derives solely from the Criminal Justice Act 1960 and, at root, it permits the granting of release for a defined period of time (although, as noted, a distinct practice of 'full temporary release' has emerged for life sentence prisoners). Characterising temporary release as a privilege limits the legal protection and enforceable rights available to those subject to the process, including access to judicial supervision and review of decision-making (*Ryan v Governor of Limerick Prison* 1988). While decisions must observe the principles of natural justice and cannot be made in an arbitrary, capricious or unjust manner, the courts cannot intervene on the basis that they would have reached a different outcome (*Doherty v Governor of Portlaoise Prison* 2002; *Dowling v Minister for Justice* 2003). This standard, high in ordinary circumstances, is even more difficult for an applicant to reach given that the Parole Board simply fulfills an advisory role to the Minister and is not akin to a legal tribunal or decision-making body. O'Malley (2011, p. 221) argues that the characterisation of temporary release as a privilege rather than a right should not 'be a cause for judicial complacency' noting that while 'prisoners may not have a formal right to liberty before the legal expiry of their sentence… they have a strong interest in liberty which is too important to be left at the mercy of an arbitrary decision-making process'.

A number of judicial reviews by long-term and life sentence prisoners have been taken but with little success. In *Grogan v Parole Board* (2008, p. 8), an application for legal aid to be provided in order to prepare a legal submission to the Parole Board on the basis of fair procedure was refused with McMahon J stating that '[t]o acknowledge the need for fair procedures in such a situation would be to overstate the significance of the Board's powers and would detrimentally distort the nature of the process'.

The informal nature of the decision-making process and its legal status as interpreted by the courts is demonstrated in a statement by McMahon J. regarding whether an offender has a right to legal aid in making a submission to the Parole Board.

> The applicant herein, is a university graduate since 1998 and has, since his imprisonment, taken a law degree and a course in criminology. It cannot be said that he is not qualified or able to make an appropriate submission to the Parole Board in these circumstances. (*Grogan v Parole Board* 2008, p. 9)

The Parole Board's approach to the issue of legal representation is in keeping with the interpretation of the courts. The Chairman of the Parole Board has stated that independent legal advice would not change the policy of not permitting the release of an offender after the initial review at seven years and that legal representation 'would not add any value to the process' (John Costello, Sub-Committee on Penal Reform Debate, 24 October 2012).

A similar approach has been adopted by the courts when considering issues of delay in the consideration of life sentence prisoners by the Minister. The courts have adopted a restrictive approach when considering habeas corpus applications and have refrained from interfering with a process within the discretion of the executive based on the need to maintain the separation of powers (*Murray v Ireland* 1991; *People (DPP) v Tiernan* 1989). The principle of legal certainty dictates that 'a fundamental requirement for any authority to detain a person in custody is that the person detaining and the person detained should know precisely the duration of such detention' (*Carroll v Governor of Mountjoy Prison* 2005, p. 567; O'Malley 2009, pp. 1008–9). This might provide a ground for judicial review for a determinate sentence, but in Ireland the principle does not apply to life sentences or other orders of indefinite duration (O'Malley 2009, pp. 1008–9). Furthermore, as the Parole Board is simply an advisory body to the Minister, the courts have refused applications on the basis that fair procedures do not apply to such bodies to the same extent as a court or legal tribunal (*Grogan v Parole Board* 2008; *Barry v Sentence Review Group* 2001; *Corcoran v Minister for Social Welfare* 1991). Thus, while the ECtHR might have accepted that effective judicial oversight exists in Ireland, the narrow terms and high legal threshold required in judicial review proceedings has meant that this avenue has been ineffective in securing procedural rights for life sentence prisoners in real terms.

Conclusion

As it stands, the life sentence prisoner eligible for release has no more rights than a short-term offender requesting temporary release for work training or family visitation. Given the data presented in this research, it is difficult to reconcile the view that the life sentence is 'wholly punitive', that issues of public protection are incidental or that the Minister does not have a significant role in determining the punishment component. The courts' reluctance to acknowledge the distinct practice of 'full temporary release' has submerged issues of procedural fairness and legitimate expectation that apply specifically to life sentence prisoners as a unique category of offenders. There is no indication that the interpretation of these legal provisions, either domestically or at the level of the ECtHR, will change under the current system. The net effect is that life sentence prisoners are subject to the vagaries of politics whereby the length of time served is a moveable feast dictated by the political regime of the day.

References

Cavadino, M., & Dignan, J. (2006). Penal policy and political economy. *Criminology and Criminal Justice, 6*(4), 435–456.

Council of Europe. (1976). *Resolution 76/2 on the treatment of long-term prisoners.* Strasbourg: Council of Europe.

Council of Europe. (2003). *Recommendation 23 on management by prison administrations of life-sentence and other long-term prisoners.* Strasbourg: Council of Europe.

European Committee for the Prevention of Torture and Inhuman or Degrading Treatment or Punishment (CPT). (2007). *Actual/real life sentences.* Strasbourg: CPT.

European Committee for the Prevention of Torture and Inhuman or Degrading Treatment or Punishment (CPT). (2012) *Report on Switzerland.* Strasbourg: CPT.

Gallagher, C. (2017, 2 May). Parole head seeks priority housing for life term prisoners. *Irish Times*. Retrieved from https://www.irishtimes.com/news/crime-and-law/parole-head-seeks-priority-housing-for-life-term-prisoners-1.3067964

Griffin, D. (2015). The release and recall of life sentence prisoners: Policy, practice and politics. *Irish Jurist, 53*, 1–35.

Lappi-Seppälä, T. (2016). Life imprisonment and related institutions in the Nordic countries. In D. van Zyl Smit & C. Appleton (Eds.), *Life imprisonment and human rights* (pp. 461–505). Hart: Oxford.

Law Reform Commission. (1996). *Report on sentencing*. Dublin: Law Reform Commission.

Law Reform Commission. (2013). *Report on mandatory sentences*. Dublin: Law Reform Commission.

Livingstone, S. (2000). Prisoner's rights in the context of the European Convention on Human Rights. *Punishment and Society, 2*(3), 309–324.

McCutcheon, P. J., & Coffey, G. (2006). *Report into determination of life sentences*. Dublin: Irish Human Rights Commission.

Morgan, D. G., & Hogan, G. W. (2007). *Administrative law in Ireland*. Dublin: Round Hall Sweet and Maxwell.

Ní Raifeartaigh, Ú. (2007). The ECHR and the criminal justice system. *Judicial Studies Institute Journal, 7*(2), 18–49.

Nicolaïdis, K. (2004). The new constitution as European 'demoi-cracy'? *Critical Review of International Social and Political Philosophy, 7*(1), 76–93.

O'Malley, T. (2006). *Sentencing law and practice*. Dublin: Thomson Round Hall.

O'Malley, T. (2009). *The criminal process*. Dublin: Round Hall.

O'Malley, T. (2011). *Sentencing: Towards a coherent system*. Dublin: Round Hall.

O'Malley, T. (2016). *Sentencing law and practice*. Dublin: Thomson Round Hall.

Parole Board. (2015). *Annual report*. Dublin: Parole Board.

Rifkin, J. (2004). *The European dream: How Europe's vision of the future is quietly eclipsing the American dream*. Cambridge: Polity Press.

Snacken, S. (2010). Resisting punitiveness in Europe? *Theoretical Criminology, 14*(3), 273–292.

The Nationalist. (2003, September 25). Life for man who tried to murder girl. *The Nationalist*. Retrieved from http://www.carlow-nationalist.ie

van Zyl Smit, D. (2006). Life imprisonment: Recent issues in national and international law. *International Journal of Law and Psychiatry, 29*(5), 405–421.

van Zyl Smit, D., Weatherby, P., & Creighton, S. (2014). Whole life sentences and the tide of European human rights jurisprudence: What is to be done? *Human Rights Law Review, 14*(1), 59–84.

Weiler, J. H. H. (1995). Does Europe need a constitution? Demos, telos and the German Maastricht decision. *European Law Journal, 1*(3), 219–258.

Table of Legal Instruments

Criminal Justice Act 1960.
Criminal Justice Act 1990.
Criminal Justice Act 1993.
Criminal Justice (Temporary Release of Prisoners) Act 2003.
European Convention on Human Rights Act 2003.

Table of Cases

England and Wales

R v Veen (No.2) (1988) 164 C.L.R. 465.

European Court of Human Rights

Hirst v United Kingdom Application no 40787/98, 24 July 2001.
Kafkaris v Cyprus Application no 21906/04, 12 February 2008.
Kafkaris v Cyprus (No. 2) Application no 9644/09, Admissibility, 21 June 2011.
Lynch and Whelan v Ireland Application nos 70495/10 and 74565/10, 18 June 2013.
Lynch and Whelan v Ireland Application nos 70495/10 and 74565/10, 8 July 2014.
Meixner v. Germany Application no 26958/07, Admissibility, 3 November 2009.
Stafford v United Kingdom Application no 46295/99, 28 May 2002.
Streicher v Germany Application no 40384/04, Admissibility, 10 February 2009.
Thynne, Wilson and Gunnell v United Kingdom Application nos 11787/85, 11978/86 and 12009/86, 25 October 1990.
Vinter and Others v. United Kingdom Application nos 66069/09, 3896/10, 130/10, Merits, 9 July 2013.
Weeks v United Kingdom Application no 9787/82, 2 March 1987.

Ireland

Barry v Sentence Review Group [2001] 4 IR 167.
Carroll v Governor of Mountjoy Prison [2005] 3 IR 292.
Corcoran v Minister for Social Welfare [1991] 2 IR 175.
Deaton v Attorney General and Revenue Commissioners [1963] IR 170 ILTR 99.

Doherty v Governor of Portlaoise Prison [2002] 2 IR 252.
Dowling v Minister for Justice [2003] 2 IR 535.
Grogan v Parole Board [2008] IEHC 204.
Heaney v Ireland [1994] 3 IR 593.
Lynch and Whelan v Minister for Justice [2012] 1 IR 1.
Murray v Ireland [1991] ILRM 465.
People (Attorney General) v O'Callaghan [1966] IR 501.
People (Attorney General) v Poyning [1972] IR 402.
People (DPP) v Carmody [1988] ILRM 370.
People (DPP) v Daniels [2014] IESC 64.
People (DPP) v K.(G.) [2008] IECCA 110.
People (DPP) v McC [2008] 4 IR 92.
People (DPP) v McMahon [2011] IECCA 94.
People (DPP) v S.(M.) [2000] 2 IR 592.
People (DPP) v S.(P.) [2009] IECCA 1.
People (DPP) v Tiernan [1989] ILRM 149.
People (DPP) v Ward, unreported, Court of Criminal Appeal, 16 January 2012.
Ryan v Governor of Limerick Prison [1988] IR 198.

Table of Parliamentary Debates

Dáil Question No. 81: Frances Fitzgerald, 08 November 2016.
Dáil Question No. 205: Frances Fitzgerald, 02 May 2017.
Sub-Committee on Penal Reform Debate: John Costello, 24 October 2012.

7

Different Process, Same Outcome?

After being sentenced by a beak, a person will be back in front of another beak. The reason is that it is a quasi-judicial function. As a prisoner, I would prefer to take my chance with the Parole Board and someone who is used to weighing up matters than with individuals who have strong views on an issue.

Jim O'Callaghan TD
Joint Oireachtas Committee on Justice, Defence and Equality
Parole Bill 2016 Discussion.

Introduction

Up until the decisions of the Supreme Court (2012) and the European Court of Human Rights (ECtHR) (2013, 2014) in *Lynch and Whelan* many of the Irish reform proposals were underpinned by concerns in relation to the compatibility of the process with Ireland's European human rights obligations and the fundamental rights provisions deriving from the Irish Constitution. The Law Reform Commission recommended the establishment of an independent statutory Parole Board stating that it would address the questions as to the system's compliance with

D. Griffin, *Killing Time*, https://doi.org/10.1007/978-3-319-72667-0_7

the provisions of the European Convention on Human Rights (ECHR) as well as having the benefit of 'enhancing the consistency and transparency of sentencing outcomes in murder cases' (Law Reform Commission 2013, pp. 124–5). The Commission (2013, pp. 123–4) proposed that legislative reform should permit the sentencing court to recommend a minimum term where a mandatory sentence of life imprisonment is imposed. The minimum term would be a recommendation only and would therefore not interfere with the powers of the executive. The Irish Human Rights Commission concluded that the life sentence did not comply with the ECHR and its jurisprudence on the basis that the decision to release was executive in nature and that this matter should be determined by a court or court-like body (McCutcheon and Coffey 2006). Even the Supreme Court, despite its tendency not to scrutinise release processes due to separation of powers arguments, gave some indication that a statutory and independent parole board might be a preferable method of administering sentences (*People (DPP) v Finn* 2001, p. 46). In 2014, the Strategic Review of Penal Policy recommended that the release decision should be independent of the Minister for Justice (Minister) and should be vested in a parole authority. The European Committee for the Prevention of Torture (CPT) (2007) has emphasised the importance of planning the release of life sentence prisoners and establishing appropriate procedures for release. In the Irish context, it has recommended that attention be paid by the authorities to sentence planning for this category of offenders (2011, pp. 26 and 32).

In the absence of judicial intervention to date, the potential for reform rests largely with the legislature. There has been occasional political interest in reform since the recommendations of the Whitaker Committee (1985) on long-term and life sentence prisoners, but there has been a consistent lack of follow-through. In 2011, the Minister of the day announced his intention to reform the parole process but a bill never materialised (Department of Justice and Equality 2011). Reform of the parole process had been 'kept under review' by successive governments (632 *Dáil Debates* Col. 529: Michael McDowell, 22 February 2007; Department of Justice and Equality 2011, 2013). After a number of years in the political wilderness, reform of parole is back on the agenda. The Parole Bill 2016 (the Bill) proposes to establish a decision-making body independent of the Minister. The need for independence from politics has been a key issue agreed by most commentators. Nonetheless, it is important to examine the details of the Bill to determine its potential impact on parole outcomes.

The impact of social forces has often been the focus of criminologists when providing rationales for changing patterns in penal systems, particularly when explaining the causes of increased punitivism (Cavadino and Dignan 2006). But Garland (2013) notes that it is state and legal processes that require deeper consideration when explaining penal trends. Is a punitive turn the result of changes in social and economic conditions or more closely tied to the political and legal culture of the country (Nelken 2009, p. 294)? Legislative changes and the actions of decision-makers such as sentencing judges and parole boards have the potential to produce large variations in penal outcomes (Garland 2013, p. 484). Life sentences exist in most Western states as the ultimate penalty but legislative differences in relation to the mandatory or discretionary nature of the sentence for homicide and the range of offences for which a life sentence can be imposed has impacted greatly on the life sentence prisoner population in each jurisdiction. Similarly, the significant variety across different countries in terms of the release process and the discretion available to decision-makers affects the length of time a life sentence prisoner can expect to serve in prison. Nelken (2009) observes that examining criminal procedure allows us to make sense of the convergences and divergences across different systems. Although the transition towards punitivism is apparent in the analysis of life imprisonment and parole in Ireland, it is the national histories, institutional and legal structures as well as the cultural and political practices that have had the greatest influence. With this in mind, proposed legislative change has the potential to impact on the trajectory towards increased punitiveness or tolerance. Formalising the parole process through the creation of a statutory Parole Board independent of the Minister would certainly indicate a shift towards a more human rights-based framework and would bring us in line with other European jurisdictions. The findings in the preceding chapters indicated that the discretionary and political nature of the process rendered decision-making vulnerable to punitive tendencies. But, will bolstering the independence of the process result in a more consistent approach to parole outcomes and enhance the quality and consistency in decision-making? More specifically, what effect, if any, will these reforms have on the growth in the life sentence prisoner population and the creeping up in time served by life sentence prisoners witnessed in this jurisdiction over recent decades? As ever, it is in the details, rather than the statements of politicians, that the impact of these reform proposals can be gauged. In this concluding chapter, the various stages of the parole process as proposed in this Bill are examined in an attempt to determine its potential impact on process and outcomes in parole, while drawing on the data presented throughout this monograph.

The Parole Bill 2016

The Bill was introduced to the *Oireachtas* (Irish parliament) by *Fianna Fáil* as a private members' bill and is a significant step towards parole reform. *Fianna Fáil* is the main opposition party to the current minority government led by *Fine Gael*. There is a confidence and supply arrangement in existence whereby *Fianna Fáil* supply votes to *Fine Gael* as they do not have a majority, on the basis of agreed terms. Ordinarily, private members' bills do not progress through the *Oireachtas*, particularly when the bill has a financial cost, as is the case with this Bill. But the unique arrangement between the two main parties in Ireland has created more flexibility in this regard. Thus, the Bill has been supported by the government and has progressed beyond what might have been expected with a more conventional government. The Bill had passed Committee Stage in the *Dáil* (the lower house in Irish parliament) at the time of writing. It is primarily focused on creating an independent Parole Board, conferring powers on the Parole Board and providing procedural rights to those subject to the process. The Bill states that the Parole Board is to be independent in the performance of its functions, which primarily relate to directing that a person be released on parole (s. 6 and s. 7). The Parole Board rather than the Minister will determine issues of release and revocation and the intention is that the Parole Board will operate in a quasi-judicial capacity (Jim O'Callaghan, Select Committee on Justice and Equality, 24 May 2017).

The Minimum Term

Under the scheme, a life sentence prisoner will not be eligible for parole until a minimum of twelve years has been served in prison (an increase from the practice of seven years) (s. 20). Twelve years was adopted as it was believed a lower term would give a life sentence prisoner 'false hope' leading them to believe that they can be released at an earlier stage (Jim O'Callaghan, Select Committee on Justice and Equality, 24 May 2017). The seven-year minimum term has ceased to act as a meaningful base for release since the 1970s and is treated by decision-makers as the beginning of the review process rather than the point of release. Will this reform mean that the release of a life sentence prisoner having served the twelve-year minimum term is possible? Twelve years is still a decade short of the current average of twenty-two years but, as has been demonstrated, this is reflective of the drift into severity by decision-makers over the last number of decades. The interpretation of this provision by decision-makers is of critical importance in terms of its potential to place constraint on time served. The twelve-year term could operate as the default point of release for a life sentence prisoner unless the Parole Board can demonstrate that there are clear reasons for further detention, such as the risk of reoffending (see 'The Minimum Term', Chap. 3). Alternatively, the current practice of review process cycles may continue whereby the twelve-year threshold marks the starting point of a lengthy review process with multiple reviews and hearings being conducted prior to release. There is evidence that the latter may be the approach that is envisaged, as the Bill permits the Parole Board to make recommendations in relation to the sentence management of an offender (s. 7(2)(e)). It seems unlikely that the default position of releasing at twelve years would be palatable, publicly or politically, and thus the continuation of the review process cycles seems almost inevitable. As such, it is difficult to determine the impact of the increase in minimum term on actual time served.

Parole Board members (members) noted that sentence management for life sentence prisoners often only began at the seven-year point through the parole process: 'I've seen cases where they've only begun to engage when they start thinking about the parole process, so it can be an incentive in that way for them to engage' (PB09). Given the five-year increase, it is important that there is a shift in this practice and that sentence management begins earlier for life sentence prisoners and prior to reaching the minimum term of twelve years so as to prepare offenders for the parole process and release. Section 20(5) also provides that a judge at sentencing may impose a specified period during which a person shall not be eligible for parole. It is unclear as to whether this provision is applicable to life sentence prisoners, how this provision will operate with the twelve-year minimum term and whether it has implications in relation to the executive's power to remit and administer a sentence (Law Reform Commission 2013, p. 124).

The Decision-Makers

The Parole Board is to have 15 members including: a Chairperson (a judge, academic, barrister or solicitor); a psychiatrist; a psychologist; a representative of the Prison Service; a current or retired member of the *Gardaí* (Irish police); a Probation Officer; a representative nominated by the Irish Penal Reform Trust; four members selected through the public appointments process; and other persons deemed by the Minister as suitable for appointment (s. 8(2)). Those members appointed with professional backgrounds are to be nominated by their professional body. So, for example, a psychiatrist will be nominated by the College of Psychiatrists to the Minister (s. 8(3)). The proposal in relation to the make-up of this Parole Board is interesting as it maintains the policy of including officials of the Department of Justice (Department) in decision-making, albeit a representative of the Minister from within the Department will no longer be a member. One fifth of the members will be derived from the agencies of the Department (Probation Service, Prison Service and the *Gardaí*). While the Minister will no longer make the decision on release she retains some discretion in appointing members and Ministerial approval of the appointment of professional members is also required. The rationale for maintaining some Ministerial control related to the need to '… have some political involvement in it' so as to hold politicians to account at some level (Jim O'Callaghan, Select Committee on Justice and Equality, 24 May 2017). Out of this membership, parole panels will be formed to conduct reviews and hearings for the purpose of discharging its functions (s. 13). A parole panel is to consist of three or five members and is to be led by a panel convenor. A panel convenor must either be a District or Circuit Court judge or a barrister or solicitor of no less than nine years experience (s. 11). This requirement will mean that a significant portion of those appointed through the public appointments process or by the Minister will need to have a legal background as six of the fifteen members will not have these legal qualifications due to their backgrounds in other professions. Conceivably then, a parole panel of three members deliberating on a life sentence prisoner could be made up of a judge, a probation officer and a representative of the Prison Service. Alternatively, it could be made up of a judge, solicitor and barrister. The composition of the parole panel is central in generating balanced decision-making and the potential for bias can be checked through its make-up (Padfield et al. 2000). The creation of parole panels based on three or five members is more consistent with the practice of parole authorities in other jurisdictions but the mix of individuals that are required to be appointed as well as the combination of political appointments with appointments through a competitive process is somewhat confusing, of questionable benefit in terms of decision-making and could undermine the perceived independence of parole decision-making.

The Decision-Making Process

Although the Bill provides for reviews and hearings, it is envisaged that the parole panel will conduct a review in the majority of cases. It has the discretion to hold a hearing if deemed necessary (s. 14(2)). The parole panel may carry out interviews, receive evidence and commission reports on the parole candidate as it sees fit (s. 14). The process outlined in the Bill essentially mirrors the practice that currently exists in the pre-decision-making phase of parole. Risk assessments are to be provided to decision-makers alongside a range of other reports that may also include references to risk. A parole panel may interview an offender at their institution (s. 14(3)). The review is to be primarily paper based. If dissatisfied with the outcome of a review, a parole candidate is entitled to a hearing (s. 15(3)) and legal representation for the purpose of that hearing (s. 15). It is unclear if a new parole panel will be drawn from different members of the Parole Board or whether members of the review can deliberate for the same parole candidate at the hearing. A parole candidate is not entitled to a legal representative for the purposes of a review as it '...is an informal process where they just look at the papers' (Jim O'Callaghan, Select Committee on Justice and Equality, 24 May 2017). As reviews are the main mechanism of determining parole outcomes, parole candidates will continue to navigate this part of the process in the absence of legal representation.

Where a hearing is held, the parole panel will decide who attends and gives evidence and it will have considerable discretion in determining the nature of proceedings. It can limit what persons speak about at the hearing, may require a person to leave the hearing and will be empowered to administer an oath on persons giving evidence (s. 14(9)). A parole candidate is entitled to give evidence and make submissions to the parole panel (s. 16(3)). This provides a life sentence prisoner with greater input into the process than existing practice although this may be circumscribed by the parole panel as it can determine what a person giving evidence talks about (s. 14(9)(c)). The parole panel may receive written submissions from victims and, where a hearing is held and it is considered necessary, the victim may attend and make oral submissions to the parole panel (s. 14(13)). The victim may also be permitted legal representation for the purpose of the hearing. Curiously, the Bill does not refer to victim input from family members where the victim has died as a result of the offence. A decision by the parole panel following a review or hearing must include reasons and this shall be communicated to the parole candidate, the Commissioner of *an Garda Síochána*, the Prison Service and the Minister (s. 13(5)). Where a hearing is conducted, a parole candidate will be entitled to make a submission and attend while others make submissions (s. 16). If the victim is present, the candidate may not attend unless the victim, the candidate and the Parole Board agree. If parole is declined, the individual will be eligible to apply again in two years (s. 21(2)). The Bill is moot on appealing a decision of a hearing. Decisions will continue to be subject to judicial review but, as already noted, the scope of judicial review tends to be rather narrow and is concerned with process rather than outcomes.

The Criteria: Risk and the Rest

When deliberating on the outcome of a review or hearing the 'paramount consideration' for the Parole Board is 'the safety of the community' (s. 18(1)). Aside from the provision of risk assessments to the parole panel, the Bill does not provide much detail on the procedure to be followed in ensuring that decision-making is attuned primarily to public protection and the risk of reoffending. Jurisdictions that focus on risk often provide decision-makers with guidelines and frameworks to enhance the consistency and quality of decision-making (see for example: Serin 2011). The issues raised in relation to the limited understanding of risk terminology and assessments in Chap. 4 highlight the importance that those empowered to determine parole outcomes understand and apply risk information effectively and accurately. If decision-making is to become more representative of risk in the quantifiable and knowable sense rather than what has been presented in the empirical data of current practice, then professional expertise on the parole panel should be central. Examining the membership of the Mental Health Tribunals is worthwhile (Mental Health Commission 2009). The tribunal makes determinations on individuals involuntarily admitted to hospital as a result of a mental disorder (Mental Health Act 2001, s. 18). Given the nature of decision-making, the three-member tribunal requires a legal professional and a consultant psychiatrist to be a member of each tribunal. A parole panel requires a legal professional to act as panel convenor but does not require a professional with expertise in the field of risk assessment, despite its centrality in decision-making. Overall, the lack of detail in the Bill on the risk process is a matter of concern and gives the impression that, in line with current practice, risk may continue to be a surface-level sentiment without much thought as to how risk-based decision-making is to operate in practice.

Public protection is not the only factor at play as the Bill expressly permits decision-makers to take on board other considerations outside of risk. The Parole Board is to be guided by the following 'principles' in the discharge of its functions: the reasons and recommendations of the sentencing judge; the nature and gravity of the offence; the degree of responsibility of the person whose parole is being considered; the position of victims; and any relevant information from the trial or sentencing process (s. 18(2)). At Committee Stage the nature and gravity of the offence was viewed as critically important due to the different degrees of murder and the need to differentiate between '… somebody who is convicted of killing a group of children, as [o]pposed to somebody who is convicted of murder committed on the spur of the moment one night with drink taken' (Jim O'Callaghan, Select Committee on Justice and Equality, 24 May 2017). Again, this reflects the data presented on the factors outside of risk that Parole Board members viewed as important in deliberating on time served and release from prison. Although the courts have not interpreted the current process as equating to a form of resentencing, the research certainly raised concerns regarding the role of parole decision-makers and whether risk was really central to deliberations in individual cases. The Law Reform Commission (2013, p. 124) noted that formalising the parole process through statute should address the danger of the Parole Board taking into consideration factors ordinarily associated with sentencing such as the nature and gravity of the offence. In fact, this approach is being expressly sanctioned in the Bill. Of course, the nature of the offence is a static factor that is relevant to assessing an offender's level of risk but this is not what is being envisaged here. Matters of offence seriousness and culpability are principles that are presented as additional to considerations of risk and public protection. The Bill also provides for input from victims at the hearing and review and that the perspective of victims should be taken into consideration in the decision-making process. This could potentially impact to increase time served given that research indicates that victim input in parole is associated with parole denials and with systems that are punitive in nature (Morgan and Smith 2005; Polowek 2005; Zedner 1997; Padfield and Roberts 2010).

In addition to the principles, the Bill also sets out criteria to be applied by parole panels. They are, for the most part, a replication of the existing statutory criteria for temporary release that the Minister must have regard and the Parole Board have adopted as their framework (Criminal Justice (Temporary Release of Prisoners) Act 2003). The Bill is vague as to how these criteria are to operate with the overarching principles in a decision-making context. The inclusion of the criteria for temporary release in the Bill is troubling given the wide discretion they currently afford the Minister and the lack of constraint they appear to have placed on parole outcomes to date. Ultimately, this Bill will require parole panels to determine outcomes based on the safety of the community, while also balancing a whole range of other principles and criteria that may be unrelated to risk or public protection and may conflict with risk information in individual cases. If public protection is to be paramount in the deliberative process then it would be reasonable to think that a low-risk life sentence prisoner could be released at the twelve-year point. Parole Board members in this study identified numerous examples of low-risk offenders that they had reviewed in their work but indicated a reluctance to recommend release at the early stages of the review process as there were other factors that they considered relevant. This militated against early release despite the low risk of reoffending. How will a parole panel deal with a life sentence prisoner who has reached the twelve-year minimum term, is categorised as low risk by the relevant agencies, but has committed a serious crime that has had a significant impact on the victim or victims' family? It is difficult to envisage how decision-makers will reconcile the various principles and criteria in such a scenario. This is not merely a hypothetical matter. According to Parole Board members, low-risk life sentence prisoners that had committed 'once-off' offences were described as regularly appearing before the Parole Board.

Release and Revocation

This Bill proposes to confer a panoply of powers on the Parole Board including: the power to determine the release and recall of offenders; the monitoring of individuals granted parole; and the issuing of warrants.

The parole panel is empowered to make a parole order authorising the release of the offender from custody (s. 22). A parole order may contain a number of conditions including that the person: must reside at a specific location; not associate with individuals specified in the order; submit to supervision; not engage in specified employment; not attend specified locations; and not leave the jurisdiction (s. 22(2)). The Parole Board will have the power to monitor a person granted parole and can require a progress report to be provided and order a person on parole to attend a hearing (s. 23). The Parole Board may also vary an order of its own volition or on the application of the Minister, the *Gardaí* or the person subject to the order (s. 24). Similarly, it can revoke a parole order at its own behest or on the application of the Minister or the *Gardaí* (s. 25). The grounds for revocation are that the person poses an undue risk to society or has breached their conditions of release (s. 25(2)). If the order is revoked a life sentence prisoner will not be eligible to be considered for parole until two years have passed since the revocation (s. 25(9)(b)). The Parole Board or the Chairperson may issue a warrant authorising the *Gardaí* to apprehend a person released on parole and return them to prison if the Parole Board has 'reasonable cause' to suspect there are grounds for suspension or revocation (s. 26(1)). This power may be exercised without the holding of a review or hearing. A hearing must be scheduled 21 days after the person is returned to prison affording the prisoner the 'opportunity to be heard' (s. 26(4)). At Committee stage, the then Minister indicated that the issuing of warrants by the Parole Board was not appropriate and that amendments in this regard would be brought forward (Frances Fitzgerald, Select Committee on Justice and Equality, 24 May 2017). Overall, this Bill proposes to confer significant powers on the Parole Board that could seriously impact on the liberty interests of those subject to the process. While the Bill details the powers of the Parole Board, provisions on the exercise and oversight of these powers are lacking. The legal status of the Parole Board, as well as the proposed powers to be conferred upon it, require careful consideration by the *Oireachtas*.

Legal Implications

The procedure that the Bill aims to put in place for the release of long-term and life sentence prisoners is distinct from the temporary release provisions. As noted in Chap. 6, the informal nature of release for life sentence prisoners in some ways protected the process from adverse decisions in the courts, with a life sentence prisoner having no more rights than a prisoner requesting short-term release through the provisions of temporary release. Formalising the process for long-term and life sentence prisoners has the potential to expose the process to greater judicial oversight. The reality of the situation can be discerned from statute rather than trying to interpret the opaque practices of parole decision-makers. With a legal framework that proposes to impose a minimum term, prioritise public protection and references the need to take the trial, sentencing and culpability of the offender into consideration, there are certainly more concrete grounds for challenging the process than exist under the current system. Perhaps of most interest is the potential legal implications arising out of explicitly centralising matters of public protection in the parole process. The Supreme Court and ECtHR noted that the life sentence in Ireland is 'wholly punitive' with considerations of preventive detention by the Minister in the exercising of her power of temporary release as 'incidental' (*Lynch and Whelan* 2012, p. 26). The proposals in the Bill could serve to undermine the legal interpretation of the life sentence as 'wholly punitive' and thus raise issues of compatibility with the Irish Constitution on the grounds that the life sentence will now have a substantial preventive component. The proposals bring the Irish process closer to the practice in England and Wales where risk is key to parole decision-making and a decision by an independent and impartial body is required (*Stafford v United Kingdom* 2002). Further, the power of the sentencing judge to impose a period where a person will not be eligible for parole (s. 20(5)) appears to be similar to the tariff-based system operating in England and Wales. Such proximity in procedure requires meticulous scrutiny as to whether the provisions render the life sentence divisible in terms of a punitive and preventive component and the potential implications of this given the standards articulated in the jurisprudence on the process in England and Wales by the ECtHR and the provisions of the Irish Constitution.

Process Versus Outcome

This Bill proposes to provide certainty to the parole process through enhancing the rights of a life sentence prisoner as well as locating decision-making within a process that is no longer dependent on Ministerial discretion. Whilst enhanced procedural justice and due process are worthwhile and have long been identified as unsatisfactory, the key issues identified in this research relate to the sizable growth in the life sentence prisoner population and the increase in time served by life sentence prisoners over the last number of decades. Fairness of procedure is important as it brings certainty in terms of the rights of the offender and the parameters of the process. But ultimately, what matters most to stakeholders in the process and the public at large is the length of time a life sentence prisoner serves in prison. As the goal posts have consistently moved in terms of time served since the 1970s there exists real unpredictability when it comes to time served. Irrespective of the position taken in relation to the release of life sentence prisoners, it is difficult to justify the transition that has been witnessed in this jurisdiction over the last number of decades. Will a more formalised and apolitical framework result in greater consistency in parole outcomes? Or will the trajectory towards severity continue albeit through a framework that adheres to procedural justice? An analysis of the experience of life imprisonment and release in England and Wales should sound a cautionary note for the future of the Irish process.

The parole process in England and Wales has undergone significant reforms and been subject to intense scrutiny both in the domestic courts and by the ECtHR (*R v. Secretary for the Home Department ex parte Lillycrop* 1996; *R (on the applications of Wells) v Parole Board* 2009; *Hirst v United Kingdom* 2001; *Stafford v United Kingdom* 2002; *Vinter and Others v United Kingdom* 2013). These decisions have served to formalise the process transforming the Parole Board into a more independent and impartial decision-making body with it being required to comply with standards of due process. Yet, the increased human rights protections available to those subject to the process has not stopped the increase in time served over the last number of decades, from 9 years in

1979, 14 years in 1997 to 18 years and 5 months in 2015 (Appleton and van Zyl Smit 2016, p. 226). In Ireland, time served increased from 7.5 years (1975–1984), 14 years (1995–2004) to 19 years and 9 months more recently (2015–2016). The similarity in the trajectory in time served is provocative given the procedural change witnessed in England and Wales compared to the relative stagnation evident in Ireland. Enhanced procedural justice does not necessarily translate into greater consistency in parole outcomes. Appleton and van Zyl Smit (2016, pp. 235–236) note that the human rights weakness in the system in England and Wales lies not in the procedure but the 'the growing frequency with which life sentences are imposed and the increasing time that life prisoners have to serve before they are released'. There is an obvious benefit in improving procedural justice and providing greater certainty to those subject to the process but this should not be conflated with providing certainty and consistency in terms of time served. The only reference in the Bill in relation to time served is the provision on the minimum term and an analysis of the parliamentary debates indicates that process rather than outcome is the focus of the legislature, with little concern expressed in relation to the growth in the life sentence prisoner population or the increase in time served. As such, time served will remain within the discretion of parole decision-makers. Given the expansive set of principles and criteria that parole decision-makers are to take into consideration, it seems that discretion in terms of outcome will remain quite broad. It is difficult to predict whether the proposed structure is robust enough to operate constraint on parole decision-making such that there will be resistance to the external factors and broader social forces that have been influencing parole outcomes under the current process.

Conclusion

What is the meaning of the life sentence? As life does not ordinarily mean life in prison, it is sometimes argued that the ambiguity of the term is resolved through the possibility of life sentence prisoners being recalled to prison for the breach of conditions pertaining to their release and being subject to supervision while on release. But it is the length of time served in prison that captures the interest of most observers. If time served is taken as a measure of its meaning, then the life sentence means something different depending on the decade in which the offence was committed. In the 1970s, those subject to the mandatory sentence of penal servitude for life were released following a relatively short period in prison. At the time, the murder rate was comparatively low, prison sentences were generally much shorter, and there was little by way of public or political interest in crime. As a result, the informal and political system of release operated largely under the radar of public scrutiny. Much has changed in the intervening decades. Homicide and murder are much more prevalent in society, sentence lengths have grown considerably and the public and political interest in crime and disorder has increased. One in every nine sentenced offenders in prison is now serving a life sentence. Given the growth in the life sentence prisoner population, cumulatively and as a percentage of the overall prison population, it is no longer sustainable or acceptable for the release process to continue in its *ad hoc* form. The secrecy and lack of transparency surrounding decision-making does not serve life sentence prisoners, decision-makers, victims and victims' families, or the public.

The parole process itself has certainly been influenced by local factors and contingencies yet it has remained largely impervious to the weight of broader movements. This has made it difficult to map developments in Ireland onto trends and into the frameworks of other common law or European countries. When first embarking on this research, the focus was on examining the role of risk in the release of life sentence prisoners. The decision to concentrate on risk was based on the available information surrounding the release process, which indicated that risk was the central factor in parole decision-making. However, during the data analysis it became clear that while risk certainly played an important role, it was not always central. The analysis revealed an unusual and idiosyncratic approach to decision-making where risk featured alongside other, often competing factors. Decision-makers were particularly susceptible to external factors, such as the rise in lethal violence, when deliberating on individual cases. Principal amongst the local contingencies that have shaped the parole process is the discretion, informality and politics that characterises Irish criminal justice more generally. Decision-makers exert considerable influence over both the process and the outcome. Despite the broader resistance to punitivism in criminal justice, decision-makers have employed their discretion to move time served primarily in a punitive direction. This paints a bleak picture of parole with little indication amongst decision-makers or policy-makers of a desire to reverse or stabilise this trend. The mix of factors and the wide discretion afforded decision-makers renders it difficult to make sense of parole decision-making. Nonetheless, there is an odd coherence to the parole process if the analysis is based on numbers alone. Simply put, a life sentence prisoner committed to prison today can expect to serve a number of years more than his counterparts committed in the preceding years and substantially longer than those committed a decade ago.

Legislative reform is now on the horizon and this indicates a move in the right direction in terms of life imprisonment and parole in Ireland. There are three key issues identifiable in this research that require the focus of legislators and policy-makers: the growth in the life sentence prisoner population; the increase in time served; and the informal and political nature of the process. But what impact will the proposed reforms have on these issues? In relation to the life sentence prisoner population, a significant factor in its growth relates to the mandatory nature of the sentence for murder. If, at the time of adopting the mandatory sentence, the legislature opted instead for a discretionary life sentence, like most European countries, then the life sentence prisoner population would not have reached its current height. With offences where the maximum sentence available is life imprisonment the trial judge may only impose a life sentence in exceptional cases. Thus, if the legislature replaced the mandatory life sentence with a discretionary one, it would have a dramatic impact on the use of the ultimate penalty as a sanction. In such circumstances a judge could account for culpability and the different types of murders, something that was clearly impacting on decision-makers when deliberating on parole outcomes in this study. Mitigating factors, such as a guilty plea, could also be taken into consideration. The Law Reform Commission (2013, pp. 121–122) noted that as a discretionary life sentence is the maximum penalty for manslaughter adopting the same sentence for murder could blur the distinction between the two offences. However, such a reform could also reflect the reality that some murders are close to manslaughter in terms of culpability. A maximum rather than a mandatory life sentence for murder would not necessarily result in undue leniency in terms of sentence length where a life sentence is not imposed. The Court of Criminal Appeal has imposed lengthy determinate sentences in lieu of a discretionary life sentence for offences of a seriously violent or sexual nature, with terms ranging from 15 to 20 years (*People (DPP) v S.(P.)* 2009; *People (DPP) v K.(G.)* 2008; *People (DPP) v Ward* 2012). These sentence lengths are not vastly out of step with the average time served by life sentence prisoners over the last decade (ranging from 15.5 year in 2007 to 22 years in 2016: see *Table 1.1*), although remission also needs to be factored in here. Trusting the judiciary to impose the appropriate sentence for murder would mean that the life sentence would be imposed selectively rather than by default. If the aim is to stymie the continued growth in the life sentence prisoner population, reforming the mandatory nature of the life sentence would be the most efficient method of doing so.

In terms of release, the low number of life sentence prisoners being released annually and the general increase in time served has contributed to the rise of this population. As it stands, the legislature does not intend to reform the mandatory life sentence but it does propose to formalise the release procedure and create a Parole Board that will determine parole outcomes independent of the Minister. This certainly goes a significant way to expunging the practice of accounting for the political environs of the day and adapting outcomes to the (perceived) views of the public in individual cases. Of course, criminal justice systems are always susceptible to broader social forces and it is unlikely the macabre media and public interest in murders and life sentence prisoners is going anywhere for now, meaning that life sentence prisoners and parole decision-makers will continue to be subject to public scrutiny, media stories of alleged leniency and political pressure. The question is whether the structure of decision-making will be robust enough to resist such social forces. The Bill proposes to provide greater certainty in terms of procedure but its ability to enhance consistency in terms of time served by life sentence prisoners should not be assumed.

References

Appleton, C., & van Zyl Smit, D. (2016). The paradox of reform: Life imprisonment in England and Wales. In D. van Zyl Smit & C. Appleton (Eds.), *Life imprisonment and human rights* (pp. 217–240). Oxford: Hart.

Cavadino, M., & Dignan, J. (2006). Penal policy and political economy. *Criminology and Criminal Justice, 6*(4), 435–456.

Department of Justice and Equality. (2011). *Minister Shatter publishes the annual report of the Parole Board.* Retrieved from http://www.justice.ie/en/JELR/Pages/PR11000238

Department of Justice and Equality. (2013). *Parole Board Membership*. Retrieved from http://www.justice.ie/en/JELR/Pages/Parole_Board

European Committee for the Prevention of Torture and Inhuman or Degrading Treatment or Punishment (CPT). (2007). *Actual/real life sentences.* Strasbourg: CPT.

European Committee for the Prevention of Torture and Inhuman or Degrading Treatment or Punishment (CPT). (2011). *Report to the government of Ireland on the visit to Ireland carried out by the European Committee for the Prevention of Torture and Inhuman or Degrading Treatment or Punishment.* Strasbourg: CPT.

Garland, D. (2013). Penality and the penal state. *Criminology, 51*(3), 475–517.

Law Reform Commission. (2013). *Report on mandatory sentences.* Dublin: Law Reform Commission.

McCutcheon, P. J., & Coffey, G. (2006). *Report into determination of life sentences.* Dublin: Irish Human Rights Commission.

Mental Health Commission. (2009). *Your guide to the Mental Health Act 2001.* Dublin: Mental Health Commission.

Morgan, K. D., & Smith, B. (2005). Victims, punishment and parole: The effect of victim participation on parole hearings. *Criminology and Public Policy, 4*(2), 333–360.

Nelken, D. (2009). Comparative criminal justice: Beyond ethnocentricism and relativism. *European Journal of Criminology, 6*(4), 291–311.

Padfield, N., & Roberts, J. (2010). Victim input at parole: Probative and prejudicial? In A. Bottoms & J. Roberts (Eds.), *Hearing the victim: Adversarial justice, crime victims and the state* (pp. 255–285). Devon: Willan.

Padfield, N., Liebling, A., & Arnold, H. (2000). *An exploration of decision-making at discretionary lifer panels.* London: Home Office.

Polowek, K. (2005). *Victim participatory rights in parole: Their role and the dynamics of victim influence as seen by Board members.* Doctoral Thesis, Simon Fraser University.
Serin, R. (2011). *Parole Board Canada: Pre-reading material (ATRA and Decision Framework).* Parole Board Canada. Retrieved from http://www.ct.gov/bopp/lib/bopp/SDM.pdf
Strategic Review of Penal Policy. (2014). *Final report.* Dublin: Stationery Office.
Whitaker Committee (Committee of Inquiry into the Penal System). (1985). *Report.* Dublin: Stationery Office.
Zedner, L. (1997). Victims. In M. Maguire, R. Morgan, & R. Reiner (Eds.), *The Oxford handbook of criminology.* Oxford: Clarendon Press.

Table of Legal Instruments

Criminal Justice (Temporary Release of Prisoners) Act 2003.
Mental Health Act 2001.
Parole Bill 2016.

Table of Cases

England and Wales

R (on the applications of Wells) v. Parole Board [2009] UKHL 22.
R v. Secretary for the Home Department ex parte Lillycrop [1996] EWHC Admin 281.

European Court of Human Rights

Hirst v United Kingdom Application no 40787/98, 24 July 2001.
Lynch and Whelan v Ireland Application nos 70495/10 and 74565/10, 18 June 2013.
Lynch and Whelan v Ireland Application nos 70495/10 and 74565/10, 8 July 2014.
Stafford v United Kingdom Application no 46295/99, 28 May 2002.
Vinter and Others v. United Kingdom Application Nos 66069/09, 3896/10, 130/10, Merits, 9 July 2013.

Ireland

Lynch and Whelan v Minister for Justice [2012] 1 IR 1.
People (DPP) v Finn [2001] 2 IR 25.
People (DPP) v K.(G.) [2008] IECCA 110.
People (DPP) v S.(P.) [2009] IECCA 1.
People (DPP) v Ward, unreported, Court of Criminal Appeal, 16 January 2012.

Table of Parliamentary Debates

632 *Dáil Debates* Col. 529: Michael McDowell, 22 February 2007

Appendix

Collecting and Analysing the Qualitative Data

Following the initial phase of the research, which involved gathering and analysing a broad range of material, an interview schedule was drafted informed by the available sources and a number of interviews conducted with the Chair of parole authorities in neighbouring jurisdictions. The objective of the qualitative research was to examine the role of the participants in the decision-making process, their views on the factors influencing decision-making and their opinions on the reform of the process.

Negotiating Access

Given the lack of empirical data on parole or life sentence prisoners in Ireland, a scoping exercise was conducted that preceded the fieldwork. Interviews were conducted with a number of chairpersons of the parole authorities of Northern Ireland, Scotland and England and Wales. While these interviews did not form a key part of the analysis in this monograph they provided valuable information, which shaped the research and assisted in identifying key issues, which fed into the development of the

D. Griffin, *Killing Time*, https://doi.org/10.1007/978-3-319-72667-0

methodology. When arranging to interview chairpersons of the relevant parole authorities of Northern Ireland, Scotland and England and Wales, individuals were contacted directly in writing, responses were received directly and arrangements were made to organise a meeting in a relatively straightforward manner. By way of contrast, gaining permission and arranging interviews with current members of the Parole Board became a much more protracted and circuitous process. The official inertia or lack of interest in the project was not reflected amongst those who consented to being interviewed, who often expressed a genuine interest in the research.

Participants

Individuals that were members of the Parole Board from 2007 to 2012 were interviewed. Fourteen out of a total of seventeen members were interviewed (one further member died during this period). Three members did not consent to be interviewed. Members whose appointment ended prior to July 2007 or were appointed after June 2012 were not interviewed for the purpose of this research. A request to conduct interviews post-2012 was refused (communication with Chairman of Parole Board, July 2015). Requests were made to interview all Ministers for Justice (Ministers) since the establishment of the Parole Board. Three former Ministers agreed to be interviewed. There were four remaining former Ministers during this period: one stated that he did not make any parole decisions during his tenure; one refused to be interviewed; one did not respond to multiple requests for interview; and the remaining Minister was deceased. Due to the different roles of Ministers in the process and the time constraints given to conduct each interview, an adapted and abridged version of the Parole Board interview schedule was used for the three former Ministers. One Minister requested that a limited number of questions be submitted in writing to which a written response was provided.

The Interview

A semi-structured approach was used when conducting interviews in an attempt to elicit the participants' accounts and perspectives on their role in decision-making. The interview schedule employed a range of different techniques to produce rich information from the participant. The schedule contained a mixture of fact, opinion and example-based questions. Interviews are not professionally or politically neutral and the interviewer is a participant who is actively involved in the process rather than a passive collector of data (Chew-Graham et al. 2002). While a responsive or empathetic approach is often adopted in qualitative research allowing for the modification of questions and their sequencing (Kvale and Brinkman 2009; Fontana and Frey 2005), the sequence and wording of the interview schedule was followed in a relatively rigid manner throughout each interview. To facilitate flexibility, participants were asked an open-ended question at the end of the interview where they could comment on something that was not asked or elaborate on an issue already raised. Every attempt was made by the interviewer to minimise verbal and non-verbal responses throughout. Where the interviewee solicited views on particular issues, these were responded to in a natural manner. In certain instances, participants appeared to present the view of the Parole Board. Prior to the interview, it was emphasised that the purpose of the interview was to elicit their views and approaches in contributing to the decision-making of the Parole Board rather than the general views and approaches of the Parole Board as a collective. Conflating the individual perspective with that of the group became a theme of the interviews perhaps reflecting a cautious approach in engaging with the interviewer at the beginning of the interview. However, as the interview progressed the participants' views often began to replace their expression of the official view of the Parole Board with their own, shifting from 'we' to 'I'.

Consent and Ethics

Consent was obtained from participants in accordance with the guidelines provided by the UCD Research Ethics Committee (2010). Consent was voluntary, informed and based on full and open information. Prior to the commencement of the interview, participants were informed of the aims of the research and the purpose of the interview. All interviewees signed a consent form. This document informed participants of the purpose of the research, that the interview would be recorded digitally and that quotations would be used in the dissertation and future publications. The consent form permitted participants to remain anonymous and that all information provided by them would remain secure and confidential. This was viewed as important as the participants could be viewed as 'elite' interviewees (Richards 1996). Given the professional status of participants, issues surrounding the voluntariness of consent and whether consent was intentional and free of controlling influences did not arise to the same extent as other areas of criminological research (Nelson et al. 2011; Healy 2009).

Data Analysis

Data analysis can be described as 'a range of techniques for sorting, organizing and indexing' throughout and following data collection (Mason 1996, p. 7). Data collection and analysis is not neutral and can be shaped by the epistemological, ontological and theoretical assumptions of the researcher as well as the personal, interpersonal, emotional and institutional influences that may be at play (Alvesson and Skoldberg 2000; Mauthner and Doucet 2003). Thus, it was important to adopt a reflexive approach to data analysis (Denzin 1997) acknowledging the experiences and assumptions brought to the data analysis by the researcher whilst attempting to minimise their influence on the process and outcome. Despite the potential for researcher bias, one of the benefits of qualitative research is that it allows access to accounts that might otherwise remain hidden from view. There are limits to the degree of reflexivity that a researcher should identify and articulate as it may be impossible to fully access or portray this to the reader at the time of the data analysis (Mauthner and Doucet 2003). The techniques of data analysis employed for this research and outlined below were an attempt to produce high-quality data analysis whilst controlling and minimising the potential for bias.

Data analysis began in the field through the taking of fieldnotes detailing ideas, concepts and interpretations of the interviews and text. Interviews were digitally recorded and a verbatim transcription was created following each interview. Once the data collection was complete, the data analysis programme, QSR NVivo 10 was employed to facilitate the remainder of the analysis. While the use of this technology cannot create scientific objectivity on what is inherently an interpretative process (Mauthner and Doucet 2003) it did act as a mechanism in allowing concepts and categories to develop independently of the theoretical framework, research aims and the assumptions of the researcher. Thus, it was considered beneficial to use this programme to conduct a rigorous and comprehensive analysis. A number of cycles of analysis were conducted including coding, the managing of codes and data reduction (Bazeley 2007). Initially, open coding was conducted of the interviews. The purpose of this phase of coding was to deconstruct the data from the original chronology of interviews into a series of unrelated themes, which were broad in nature and encompassed a range of divergent views. Open coding allowed for themes and concepts to emerge that would not have been initially identified or did not fit easily within previously defined categories. It was important to adopt this approach in order to limit the potential for bias and to incorporate reflexivity (Jupp et al. 2000). 127 open codes were created through this process.

Following this initial phase of open coding, a process of reordering, renaming, merging, distilling and clustering related codes was conducted and resulted in the categorisation of codes and placing them into an overall framework. Many of the themes that emerged were easily identifiable through the questionnaire while other themes emerged through the coding process. This process of 'coding on', of scrutinising themes and subthemes in terms of divergent views on particular issues, allowed for a more in-depth understanding of the data. Following from this, and derived from the clusters of codes, summary statements were created to describe the codes, data reduction was conducted whilst referring to the research aims and theoretical framework, and the analysis which resulted in the formulation of each chapter began. The reliability, validity and authenticity of the data was tested through returning to the individual interviews to verify the findings made. This data was then synthesised into Chaps. 3, 4, and 5. The questionnaire focused on issues of process, risk, politics and reform and these themes are reflected throughout the monograph. While a substantial portion of the interview was dedicated to examining issues of risk, it emerged quite early on in the data analysis that there were other factors that appeared to be influencing parole outcomes. These factors, which related to theories of punishment, public opinion and politics, are analysed in Chap. 5.

Limitations

Unlike quantitative research and the quality criteria applicable to the same, a consensus surrounding quality criteria for qualitative research does not exist to a similar extent (Bryman et al. 2008). Despite these criticisms and the lack of consensus across social science disciplines, there has been a rise in the use of qualitative research over the last few decades and the discipline of criminology is no exception (for an Irish example see: Healy 2010). Thus, it was important that the research design should reflect a mixed methods approach whereby qualitative and quantitative data could gain benefit from the different methods across the spectra and allow these methods to be triangulated in order to address the weaknesses of both methods (David and Sutton 2004, p. 45; Bryman 2006). Ultimately, it was not possible to complete the quantitative aspect of the research thus limiting the research findings to the qualitative data (see 'A Note on Methodology' in Chap. 1). Limitations specific to the qualitative aspects of this research project related to the number of participants, arising out of the confined nature of the Parole Board. The reflexive approach to data analysis attempted to account for and address issues such as reliability, validity and credibility in the results generated.

References

Alvesson, M., & Skoldberg, K. (2000). *Towards a reflexive methodology*. London: Sage.

Bazeley, P. (2007). *Qualitative data analysis with NVivo*. London: Sage.

Bryman, A. (2006). Integrating quantitative and qualitative research: How is it done? *Qualitative Research, 6*(1), 97–113.

Bryman, A., Becker, S., & Sempik, J. (2008). Quality criteria for quantitative, qualitative and mixed methods research: A view from social policy. *International Journal of Social Research Methodology, 11*(4), 261–276.

Chew-Graham, C. A., May, C. R., & Perry, M. R. (2002). Qualitative research and the problem of judgement: Lessons from interviewing fellow professionals. *Family Practice, 19* (3), 285–289.

David, M., & Sutton, C. D. (2004). *Social research: The basics*. London: Sage.

Denzin, N. K. (1997). *Interpretive ethnography: Ethnographic practices for the 21st century*. London: Sage.

Fontana, A., & Frey, J. H. (2005). The interview: From neutral stance to political involvement. In N. K. Denzin & Y. S. Lincoln (Eds.), *The Sage handbook of qualitative research* (pp. 695–728). Thousand Oaks: Sage.

Healy, D. (2009). Ethics and criminological research: Charting a way forward. *Irish Probation Journal, 6*(1), 171–181.

Healy, D. (2010). *The dynamics of desistance: Charting pathways through change*. Cullompton/Devon/Portland: Willan Publishing.

Jupp, V., Davies, P., & Francis, P. (Eds.). (2000). *Doing criminological research*. London: Sage.

Kvale, S., & Brinkman, S. (2009). *Interviews*. London: Sage.

Mason, J. (1996). *Qualitative researching*. London: Sage.

Mauthner, N. S., & Doucet, A. (2003). Reflexive accounts and accounts of reflexivity in qualitative data analysis. *Sociology, 37*(3), 413–431.

Nelson, R. M., Beauchamp, T., Miller, V. A., Reynolds, W., Ittenbach, R. F., & Luce, M. F. (2011). The concept of voluntary consent. *The American Journal of Bioethics, 11*(8), 6–16.

Richards, D. (1996). Elite interviewing: Approaches and pitfalls. *Politics, 16*(3), 199–204.

University College Dublin Research Ethics Committee. (2010). UCD code of good practice in research. University College Dublin. Retrieved from https://www.ucd.ie/registry/academicsecretariat/docs/research_g.pdf

Index[1]

[1] Note: Page numbers followed by 'n' refer to notes.

D. Griffin, *Killing Time*, https://doi.org/10.1007/978-3-319-72667-0

L

The manufacturer's authorised representative in the EU is Springer Nature Customer Service Centre GmbH, Europaplatz 3, 69115 Heidelberg, Germany. If you have any concerns regarding our products, please contact ProductSafety@springernature.com

Printed and bound by CPI Group (UK) Ltd, Croydon, CR0 4YY
05/10/2026
02228140-0005